BEYOND THE GRAVEN IMAGE

Also by Lionel Kochan

ACTON ON HISTORY
JEWS, IDOLS AND MESSIAHS
POGROM, NOVEMBER 10, 1938
RUSSIA AND THE WEIMAR REPUBLIC
RUSSIA IN REVOLUTION, 1890–1918
THE JEW AND HIS HISTORY
THE JEWISH RENAISSANCE AND SOME OF ITS
    DISCONTENTS
THE JEWS IN SOVIET RUSSIA SINCE 1917 (*editor*)
THE MAKING OF MODERN RUSSIA
THE STRUGGLE FOR GERMANY, 1914–1945

Beyond the Graven Image

A Jewish View

Lionel Kochan

First published 1997 by
MACMILLAN PRESS LTD
Houndmills, Basingstoke, Hampshire RG21 6XS
and London
Companies and representatives
throughout the world

ISBN 0–333–62595–1 hardcover
ISBN 0–333–62596–X paperback

A catalogue record for this book is available
from the British Library.

This book is printed on paper suitable for recycling and
made from fully managed and sustained forest sources.

10 9   8   7   6   5   4   3   2   1
06 05 04 03 02 01 00 99 98 97

Printed and bound in Great Britain by
Antony Rowe Ltd, Chippenham, Wiltshire

Contents

Acknowledgements   vi

Introduction   1

Chapter 1   The Biblical Challenge   3

Chapter 2   To Limit the Holy   30

Chapter 3   Symbolism in Action   53

Chapter 4   The Mouth and the Monument   76

Chapter 5   Art in the Shade   93

Chapter 6   Man in His Image   112

Chapter 7   Time, Time and Time Again   136

Chapter 8   Reflections and Echoes   159

Notes   171

Glossary   208

Abbreviations   209

Index   211

Acknowledgements

This book enjoyed a flying-start when I was invited by Professor Menaḥem Friedman to the Institute for Advanced Study at the Hebrew University, Jerusalem (1991–1992) to participate in a seminar on the sociology of religion. My first acknowledgement must be to the facilities and amenities generously placed at my disposal by the Institute and by the National and University Library. This visit also brought me the friendship of Rabbi Dr Ze'ev Gotthold and Dr Almut Bruckstein from whose scrutiny of the text in its earlier stages and many subsequent discussions I have immeasurably benefited.

To Professor Bernard-Dov Hercenberg, Dr Harry Lesser, Mr Alan Montefiore and Professor Ḥayyim Soloveitchik I am also profoundly grateful for the care with which they read the text of the book at varying stages; they not only saved me from error and misapprehension, but also brought enlightenment to my understanding of the theme.

As ever, it is to my dear wife that my greatest thanks are due – for Miriam's forbearance, tenacity and unfailing good cheer.

L. K.

Introduction

The aim of this book is to expound the Biblical argument against idolatry, in the Bible's own terms, and also in those elaborated by later thinkers, rabbis and philosophers. This is not to suggest that idolatry is an idea that can be defined. It is rather an 'umbrella concept'. The book begins with graven images but to idolatry there is more than meets the eye, I hope to show. Biblical and later vocabulary has at its disposal a variety of terms, none of which makes explicit mention of idols: for example 'the worship of other gods', 'strange worship', 'the worship of the stars' or of 'the strange gods of the soil'. These expressions are all more or less synonymous – but only 'more or less' so, because each carries its own particular load of meaning which is certainly compatible each with the others but each of which also conveys a significantly individual emphasis. I hope to have conveyed something of the consequent ramifications by attempting to go 'beyond' the graven image. This latter can then be generalised and acquire even a symbolic character in such a way as to form part of a complex of ideas that encompasses such apparently disparate and unconnected matters as the feature of holiness, the art of memory, the respective functions of eye and ear in the process of learning, the role of symbolism in worship, varied modes in the manipulation of time, and so on. These and other topics take their place in a world-view, first formulated in the Bible but also open to the elaboration of later thinkers. Contact with the text is maintained. This procedure does make for a certain degree of repetition; I hope this will be justified through the continuity of outlook that is thereby shown to exist, or at least created. Past and present, no longer distinct, display their capacity to engage in an enduring exercise of mutual clarification and commentary.

This approach requires the treatment of idolatry as a phenomenon that, for all its indefinability, retains certain characteristics that are *sui generis*. But if this is so then it is also possible to treat the theme as though it had no history.

This is my preferred approach which also seems to me historically justifiable. The cadre and vocabulary of the idolater unquestionably vary but not the motivations or what has today been termed the 'psycho-sociological mechanisms'.[1] To R. David Kimche of Provence, the medieval Biblical commentator and grammarian, 'the idols' mentioned in Zechariah 13:2 are 'those that the gentiles serve today'. In truth, the contemporary reference is rarely absent – which does not mean that it is always the same 'idol' that is referred to.

For the most part, this book has a bias towards the theoretical and normative. But it includes also, as a means to clarify the theoretical, occasional mention of empirical practice; also of the disputes that accompany this or that particular practice.

The subject matter is inherently polemical because, to its iconoclastic Biblical enemies, 'strange worship' designates a whole class of impermissible activities and concepts. Only if the polemic meets with full justice can the gravity of the struggle be made at all comprehensible. But this demand must inevitably create tension with the demand for exposition. Between these contradictory and equivalent demands I have tried to hold the balance. I hope the value of this attempt will find its testimonial in the final analysis when the denunciation of the 'graven image' reveals itself as a call for the repeal of the existent, equating the overthrow of the idol, no longer a mere image, with the age of the messiah.

This book also gives me a chance to elaborate and, in some cases, to repudiate, views I no longer hold (see my *Jews, idols and messiahs*, Oxford, Blackwells, 1990, pp.129–191).

Biblical quotations have, except where the sense of the context required otherwise, been taken from TANAKH – The Holy Scriptures: The New JPS Translation, according to the traditional Hebrew text, The Jewish Publication Society of America, Philadelphia/New York, 5748/1988. Other quotations in translation are, except where otherwise indicated, my own work.

1 The Biblical Challenge

The God who brought the Israelites out of Egypt tolerates no other gods (Ex.20:1–3). The existence of the latter is not denied – merely that to the Israelites their service is disallowed.[1] This opposition is absolute in a way that excludes any possibility of accommodation, to such an extent that to reject the one is tantamount to the acceptance of the other, and vice versa: 'Whoever acknowledges idolatry is as one who repudiates the whole *Torah* and whoever repudiates idolatry is as one who acknowledges the whole *Torah*'.[2]

This confrontation is carried through into the Biblical text so as to form a major if not central theme. The Bible variously designates God as Israel's consort, doctor, lawgiver, master, judge, and political leader; to his god the idolater can look to perform the same diversity of roles. Idolatry, no matter how its understanding evolves and ramifies, always forms a sort of counter-system with values, social ideals, physical symbolism, political arrangements and so on that confront that system proclaimed by God and his spokesmen.

This struggle is authentic and calls on the *Torah* to fulfil the task of defeating idolatry – 'its whole aim', according to Maimonides.[3] For Rosenzweig, God has had to found 'his own religion (which is but an *anti*-religion) against the religionitis of man'.[4] As early as the patriarchal period in the history of Israel, the irreconcilability of the two systems is apparent. Long before the revelation and conclusion of the Covenant at Sinai, Jacob already understood that loyalty to his household gods and amulets (*teraphim*) was incompatible with the summons to erect to God an altar at Beth-El and must be put away.[5] When Jacob also proceeds to order his household to purify themselves and to change their garments, the medieval commentators understand this as a means to ensure that no traces of idolatry will remain in their possession: Jacob and all his household will now be cleansed in person, clothing and heart.[6] The mere presence of idols contaminates a household (Dt.7:26); the practice of idolatry contaminates a land (Jer.3:8–9).

3

This is no manichaean conflict between good and evil. Into the relationship between the adherents of the *Torah* and those of idolatry is introduced a certain complexity by reason of the fact that both inhabit the same world and are exposed to, and challenged by, the same temptations. Eroticism and submission to idolatry go hand in hand (Nu.25:1–2). On account of its pervasiveness and strength, the Talmud likens the lure of idolatry to sexual desire, 'which is still dancing around among us'. There is a state of tension here, between man and nature, which animates the entire Biblical message. But this same discussion also points out that without such desire 'the world would perish' (TB Yoma 69b; see also San.63b). The complex nature of idolatry derives not only from the ubiquity of its source but also from the necessity of that very source to human existence, no matter whether the existence be that of an idolater or not.

Now, at this point, it becomes possible to speak less imprecisely of the denotation 'nature'; in other words, of the mode whereby idolatry is manifest. Its use of imagery, for all the importance of the physical idol, is for the moment deferred. Rather, first to be appreciated is the fact that only through the teaching of the *Torah* does idolatry come into existence. It is, accordingly, the 'natural' state of man. The idolater is unaware of his status until he is forcefully confronted with his ignorance. This is by no means an 'unnatural' phenomenon – precisely the contrary – which makes its suppression all the more of a provocation to nature.

This unawareness applies no less to the Israelites because they share with the idolater his 'cleaving to matter'.[7] At issue is God's struggle to separate Israel from a world of immanence, autochthony, sexual licence, and the notion of an enchanted, animate nature. Early in the history of Israel the clash makes itself manifest in the sanguinary confrontation between Jacob's sons and the Canaanites of Shechem (Gen.34), 'the people of nature'.[8]

The struggle against nature encompasses a political dimension: when the elders of Israel petition Samuel for an earthly king, rejecting God as their king, they 'are forsaking Me and worshipping other gods', Samuel is wrathfully informed by God (1 Sam.8:4–8). No distinction is made between 'political treason' and 'religious treason'.[9] In the field of foreign policy, exemplified by the prophets in Israel's political treaties with the Assyrians and Egyptians, idolatry can also be found; the prophetic accusation is couched in the brutal terms of a nymphomaniac Israel lusting for sexual satisfaction with alien paramours (Ez.16:26 ff.).[10] This sort of politics is akin to the practice of witchcraft, divination, astrology, and so on. Between these occult practices and political idolatry there exists a positive affiliation: the prophet Samuel calls Saul's disobedience to God 'a rebellion [which] is like the sin of divination, a defiance like the wickedness of *teraphim* [household gods]' (1 Sam.15:23). Kimche, referring to this passage, castigates Saul, 'as though an idolater'. The same association between idol-worship and occult practice is made in the case of King Josiah, who is commended for his removal of 'the necromancers, mediums, idols and fetishes' in the land of Judah and Jerusalem (2 K.23); and since one version of the model relationship of God and Israel is conjugal, marital infidelity too is equated with idolatry (Is.1:21; Jer.5:7–8). No individual or generation is immune to its lure. The idol-worshipping King Menasseh is questioned in the Talmud by R. Ashi: 'if you were so wise', the rabbi asks the king, 'why did you worship idols?'. Menasseh answers: 'had you been there, you would have pulled up the skirt of your cloak and run after me' (TB San. 102b).

This world of earthly kings, peopled by occult powers accessible to necromancers, diviners and witches, of household gods and unchastity, is that world from which the *Torah* is to offer Israel the possibility of release.

To worship other gods has a special gravity: R. Judah Loew b. Bezalel points out, it is the only transgression that can be committed both in mind and body (ref. to Ez.14:3 ff.).[11] This uniqueness must affect the dimension of the prohibition and that is why the medieval commentator, Abraham ibn Ezra, explains that it is the only negative commandment to encompass 'both heart and mouth' (that is, act and verbal expression of intent): 'for if a man declares before witnesses that he is going out to murder or commit adultery, he will, if he performs no action, not be executed because of his speech. But [merely] if he says, let us go and serve other gods, Scripture commands that he shall surely be put to death' (Ibn Ezra to Ex.20:3 ff.).

There is more to idolatry than meets the eye; even so, the idol has a primordial importance in constituting, normally, a physical and visible image of some sort or a natural phenomenon, perceived by its worshippers, in every sense, as the seat of some immanent force or as a means to communicate with such a force. But a perception of this type epitomises the issue at stake in the divine challenge to nature and is tantamount to a crime against the creation. The Deuteronomist, when he reiterates the prohibition of imagery (Dt.4:16 ff.), explicitly harks back to the account of the creation in the first chapter of Genesis.

In what terms is it possible to categorise the particular offence and justify the abhorrence it provokes? The initial approach to an answer cannot be other than phenomenological. The Hebrew of the Biblical text is originally unvocalised and unpunctuated so that it is positively susceptible to a diversity of readings, an opportunity which rabbinic exegesis has taken full advantage of.[12] The very text also lends itself to a variety of renderings: the command to the Israelites – 'you shall not make gods of silver to be worshipped as well as Me, nor shall you make yourselves gods of gold' (Ex.20:20) in the version of the New English Bible,[13] can also be rendered 'You shall not make with Me . . .'; or 'You shall not make Me . . .'; or 'You shall not do with Me'.[14] Likewise, the crucial part of Aaron in the paradigmatic construction of the golden calf (Ex.32:4) can be variously rendered: 'that Aaron fashioned the gold (1) with a graving tool, or (2) a casting mold, (3) that he bound the gold in a cloak, or (4) a bag'.[15] Another example: *al panay*, meaning literally 'before My face' (or 'presence'), can also be rendered: 'before Me', 'beside Me', 'as long as I exist' (Rashi), 'over against Me', 'because of My presence'.[16]

There is also uncertainty in the internal division of the Decalogue both in the Exodus version (ch.20) and the Deuteronomic version (ch.5) – each of which must be a *locus classicus* in the context of any study of idolatry. However, it is the case that the first commandment – 'I am the Lord your God who brought you out of the land of Egypt, the house of bondage: you shall have no other gods besides Me'; and the second – 'you shall not make for yourselves a sculptured image . . .' do form a unit, in that the former gives authority to the latter (and of course to all the subsequent commandments).[17] This is the more especially so as the injunction – 'you shall not bow down to them' – in the second commandment, refers to the 'other gods' in the first.[18]

Uncertainties notwithstanding, these two commandments, expounded in the context (primarily) of the Pentateuch, do establish two obvious points: the compulsion to serve only that God who freed the Israelites from Egypt, and only in a way that he has decreed which absolutely excludes the use of images. The person who introduces into his worship an image may suppose that he is indeed engaged in an act of worship to God but this is self-delusion. The most solemn and threatening terms are used to warn the Israelites lest they 'forget the Covenant that the Lord your God concluded with you, and not to make for yourselves a sculptured image in any likeness, against which the Lord has enjoined you' (Dt.4:23). To include an image in an act of worship or even to associate an image with this act is in itself synonymous with disloyalty to the Covenant and degrades service to God into service to idolatry (see, for example, 2 Kings 17:27 ff.). It is sometimes likened to marital infidelity, as mentioned earlier. Gideon's construction of an ephod is said to make Israel play the harlot: that is, to betray God, her consort (Ju.8:22–28). An association has been made between the drink administered to the suspected adulteress (Nu.5:11–31) and the pulverised remnants of the golden calf that Moses forces its builders to swallow (Ex.32:20).[19]. In a remarkable figure of speech, Jeremiah combines the two concepts of infidelity and imagery: 'mutinous Israel . . . committed adultery with stone and with wood' (Jer.3:8–9).

What is the rationale that demands the exclusion of images in relation to the Covenant? There is both a general and a particular answer. The former must emphasise the priority given to ear over eye in their respective capacities as media of instruction, enlightenment and the construction of perception; conversely, as the media of deception, illusion and abuse. This dual theme is a recurrent and characteristic Biblical leitmotif.[20]

There are cultures in which the ear deceives: Ulysses and his crew waylaid by the sirens come to mind; so does the

success of the Lorelei in enticing to their doom the luck-
less seafarers of the Rhine. A Jewish equivalent, I suppose,
might well be the Talmudic dictum, 'the voice in a woman
is a lure' (TB Ber.24a). But in Israelite culture, the ear, on
the whole, is the seat and means of enlightenment and not
of self-destruction or self-deception, to such a degree that
in exceptional circumstances the ear can function as an eye
and apprehend with visual intensity: at Sinai, the sound of
words is heard, and the only shape perceived is that of 'voice'
(Dt.4:12). In the earlier version (Ex.20:19) the Israelites also
see that God spoke to them. The two senses complement
each other.[21] It is through narration – the father telling his
son – that tradition is secured (Ex.13:8), certainly not through
visual images and symbols. The prophets 'see' the words
they utter (Is.2:1; Amos 1:1); those who 'follow their own
counsels in the obstinacy of their evil heart are those who
do not hear and incline their ear' (Jer.7:24); those who do
listen are 'revived' (Is.55:3). Words, hearing and speech are
par excellence the prophetic mode of challenge and transmission; as they are that of God. Again and again, the author
of the Book of Proverbs emphasises that through the ear
attention to wisdom is aroused, the thoughts of the sages
communicated and wisdom attained.[22] When the Israelites
do 'see' God, it is through the medium of his actions (Dt.1:30;
4:3,9).

The interface between ear and eye is quasi-absolute.
Whereas, by way of the ear, wisdom can be inculcated, by
way of the eye danger is brought close and must be nullified by that reminder of the Covenant embodied in the fringes
(*tsitsit*): 'so that you do not follow your heart and eyes in
your lustful urge' (Nu.15:39). This is understood as an incitement to idolatry and exemplified in two cases: first, when
Samson seeks a Philistine wife, 'for she is pleasing to my
eyes' (Ju.14:3); second, when the Israelites 'go whoring after
the *baalim* of their neighbours' (ibid., 8:33).[23] The Talmud
cites a tradition: 'only over what a person's eyes see, does
the evil impulse bear sway' (TB Sotah 8a). This particular
dictum relates to unchastity but the range of temptation
open to vision is incited even when a voice is 'seen', as at
Mt.Horeb. The Deuteronomist recalls the occasion, to couple
with it a warning, *inter alia*, lest the Israelites 'act wickedly

and make . . . a sculptured image' (Dt.4:10 ff.). The same
danger is actuated in situations of lesser tension. Take, for
example, the altar where the priests slaughtered the sacrificial animals, in the performance of their designated role.
This must be made of earth or, if made of stone, the stone
must be unhewn (Ex.20:21–2).[24]

This is generally understood not so much as building instructions for an altar, but as a means to ensure that the
blood of the slaughtered animals – blood being considered
the repository of life (Lev.17:10 ff.; Dt.12:23; 15:23) – will
flow into the soil and not be made the object of manipulation.[25] The medieval commentators also direct attention to
the fact that any enhancement of the stone's appearance,
or any pattern of incisions, would tend to assimilate the
initially unshaped edifice to an attractive altar of gold and
give it the air of a mediator between man and God.[26] Visual
appeal engineered by the artist, sculptor or engraver, is tantamount in this context to a sort of profanation, an incitement to credulity. The greater the visual appeal, the greater
the danger.

There is already here the fear lest an appealing vision
distort perception and convert a utilitarian, man-made object into, perhaps, the semblance of a metaphysical power
by investing it with communicative attributes. Jeremiah re-
inforces his initial onslaught on the carved idol of wood
with the demand that it be not further beautified through
an overlay of gold from Uphaz or silver from Tarshish
(Jer.10:1–16). Ibn Ezra is concerned with the effect: this
visual enhancement will make it all the easier for the respect accorded to the image to enter the hearts of the masses
so that they will 'believe and worship'.[27] The imagined bearer
of the 'divine' effectively reveals itself to be deceptive in
contrast to the enlightenment enjoyed by those who have
learned to discount the image.

More than mere deception is involved: in the nineteenth
century Heinrich Graetz, the founder of modern Jewish
historiography, generalised the dichotomy between eye and
ear into a theory of idolatry. 'The pagan perceives the Divine in nature through the medium of the eye, and he becomes conscious of it as something to be looked at', Graetz
writes. 'On the other hand, to the Jew who conceives God

as being outside of nature and prior to it, the Divine manifests itself through the will and through the medium of the ear ... The pagan beholds his god; the Jew hears Him, that is, apprehends His will. From beholding to imitative representation is but one step, and the heathen cult of idolatry is a natural consequence of the pagan conception of God'.[28]

This message has as much a political as a religious ring and anticipates the theory of political aesthetics and imagery. But, for the moment, the immediate message relates to the eye through which the wayward imagination has been provided with material that will eventually generate an unwarranted idea of matter.

This general argument in favour of the privileged perception of the ear as against the greater accessibility of the eye – but also its greater susceptibility to abuse – determines the special negativity of the Biblical relationship to the image: more particularly the image that is associated with those 'other gods'.

This negativity is born of the conviction that those 'other gods' do indeed constitute a threat to the dominion demanded by the creator. It certainly cannot be concluded that to a pagan god there is no more than some carved image, say; no part of the Decalogue denies that those gods denominated 'other gods' exist, merely that to Israel the God who freed them from Egypt, and proclaims himself as such, is God.[29] For this reason, the danger offered by the gods of the Hittites, Canaanites and so on is clearly taken with the utmost gravity (see Dt.6:14–15; 7:1–5). In any case, the confrontation between Moses and Aaron, on the one hand, and the Egyptian priests (literally 'masters of hieroglyphs') on the other, manifests a rivalry that cannot be disregarded, in that the latter show themselves able to reproduce three of 'the signs and wonders' performed, through Moses, by the God of Israel. The Egyptians too can convert their rods into serpents, turn the Nile waters to blood and bring on a plague of frogs (Ex.7–8).[30]

But is it not unimportant whether or not 'other gods' exist? What solely matters is that they should be thought to exist, to enjoy a subjective existence in the consciousness of the Israelites; but this subjective existence, however illusory, will still be generated by the susceptibility of the eye to the image. There is a potent fear lest the beholder be so attracted by an image as to 'turn' to it and thereby, eventually, succumb, to the extent of engaging in some act of worship. This is the thrust of Rashi's understanding of Leviticus 19:4, 'turn not to idols and make not for yourselves molten gods: I am the Lord your God'. Rashi first explains that the word for 'idols' (*elilim*, singular *elil*) is connected etymologically with the word meaning 'not' (*al*) so that an 'elil' is a 'not-thing'. He next explains that the 'molten gods' of the second part of the verse have their beginning in these 'not-things' but, if these latter are 'turned to', they will end up by becoming gods.[31] The particular beholder has been incited to bring into play his imagination and, through visual stimulus, what was at the outset no more than a fetish has taken on the attributes of a god. This too is the thrust of the exposition given by Maimonides of the warning extended to the person who 'looks up to the sky and . . . sees the whole heavenly host [and] must not be lured into bowing down to them or serving them' (Dt.4:19). Maimonides understands this as a warning: 'lest you go astray with the eye of your heart' and attribute powers of governance to the stars, planets and so on.[32]

What largely gives to these gods, whether they exist or not, their power of attraction, is their physical imagery which is itself inseparable from their appeal to the eye. Obviously, in the case of the Egyptian 'masters of hieroglyphs', there is more to their power than the allurement of an image. But this does not detract from the generally attractive power of the image. Hence the reason for this preoccupation with the image *qua* image seems to be, literally to all appearance, because it is imagery that primarily distinguishes the one God from 'other gods'. If (virtual) invisibility is the criterion of the former, then the very visibility and impact on the eye of the latter is its distinguishing criterion. God does indeed have need of a voice in order to be able to communicate – but this is all. Beyond the fact that God, in the Biblical text, is necessarily treated in human terms, 'there is nothing', writes Hallo, 'to suggest what Yahweh would have looked like, how an ancient Israelite should have proceeded to make a "Yahweh-idol" or a modern archaeologist to identify one'.[33] The contrast is with the plethora of figurative imagery

in the contemporary world of ancient Egypt and Mesopotamia – sphinxes, pyramids, sacred groves, mummified kings,
amulets, scarabs, statuary, and so on – which the Pentateuch
rejects and which also brings out the radically new outlook
it is trying to enforce on the recalcitrant Israelites and their
descendants.

But if visual presence is the source of appeal, it is also
the source of vulnerability. Were there no imagery to signify their presence, these religions would not exist in any
meaningful and accessible manner. Without an image, idolatry
would be all but impossible. How could its message be transmitted? The very possibility seems excluded by reason of
the constant need of polytheism for some physical object in
its ceremony. This is certainly the Biblical view for which
polytheism and idolatry are identifiable by reference to their
resort to imagery.

If, therefore, the Israelites are to be prevailed on to conduct themselves as 'the chosen people', and forcefully alienated from allegiance to other gods, it is through the
imposition of the image-ban, for it is the image that gives
those other gods the power to convey their presence and
message and which provokes God's jealousy.

If this argument is correct it makes it easier to appreciate
a prime Biblical puzzlement: why does the Bible not engage in any debate with the theory of idolatry, as distinct
from its physical manifestation? This omission, if such it is,
characterises the Pentateuch as much as the works of the
prophets and the psalmist. Carroll writes: 'lacking any appreciation of the symbolic value of images, and without re-
alizing that the cult of images belonged to a belief in personal
gods, Israel entirely failed to come to grips with the essence
of polytheism'.[34] When Jeremiah seeks to deter the exiles
in Babylon from yielding to idolatry, his argument limits
itself to the perishability of those gods 'who did not make
heaven and earth' and thus to their spurious, fraudulent
character (Jer.10:11–15; see also Ps.96:5). The polemic, at
most, goes no further than what Cassirer calls Isaiah's attempt to 'inject into the mythical consciousness an alien
tension . . . in order to disintegrate and destroy it from
within'.[35]

In a celebrated article the late Yehezkel Kaufmann

maintained that the Bible simply gives no credence to the existence of 'other gods': 'while there are in the Bible some traces of the pagan deification of nature, there is no record of the vital attribute of polytheism: the belief in mythological deities ... a heathen belief in other living gods is beyond the scope of the Biblical narrators'.[36] It is also argued that 'the Biblical reduction of paganism to mere fetishism can be understood as an intentional misrepresentation for the sake of polemics'.[37] But if my argument is correct then that which holds that the Bible is virtually ignorant of the mythology of polytheism (Kaufmann) and also that which holds that it does not ignore but consciously misrepresents mythology (Halbertal-Margalit) are both questionable, the latter less so than the former. Rather, to challenge mythology as a system of belief would be no more than an exercise in supererogation for the polytheistic mythologist has already condemned himself by his need for an image.

If the Bible directs its animus overwhelmingly at the physical image the effect is to assimilate to that despised image whatever message it is thought to proclaim. At the very least it must blur the distinction between them.[38] If the message or force, or whatever, only exists, and only can exist, by virtue of some visual image, then it can truly be said that the message is subordinated to that image, and perishes with it. This being the case, why should the divine iconoclast direct his fire at the message when it is enough to destroy the enemy's icon and thereby dispose also of the message?

If through the operation of the image-ban, this imagery can be inhibited and suppressed, then, together with its proximate purveyor, what would otherwise have been delivered will be silenced.[39] Merely to prohibit the worship of the gods of the Amorites, Canaanites, and so on is inadequate; it is essential also that their altars, pillars, sacred posts, etc., be utterly destroyed (Ex.34:12–16).[40]

This demand is 'unnatural' but if the Covenant is to be fulfilled, 'nature' must be overcome which means, in its turn, that paganism must be overcome and this, finally, entails the destruction of the image as a signifying entity. Two incompatible worlds confront each other: 'you shall not make idols for yourselves carved images or pillars, or place figured stones in your land to worship upon for I the Lord am your God. My sabbaths you shall keep and My sanctuary you shall venerate. I am the Lord' (Lev.26:1–2; see also Dt.29:17).

Two interdependent consequences follow: first, that the image-ban is not imposed for its own sake but solely as a means to repress the worship of other gods. To Hume, the sceptic, this is as clear as to any rabbi.[41] From this it follows, second, that should an image bear no relationship to, and also be totally disconnected from, any form of worship it is allowable.[42] Only in the context of idolatrous worship does the Biblical prohibition of images apply.[43]

Obviously, in the Biblical context of Canaan, Mesopotamia, Egypt, and Babylon, the notion of an artifact devoid of some religio-social significance is unfamiliar. Nevertheless, in order to anticipate later discussion, let it be assumed that such an image is fabricated – the golden calf, say. Its mere fabrication is of no account at all.

In respect of any image however, condemnation takes the place of indifference so soon as it is introduced into the context of worship, that is, it is consecrated in one way or another. Thus two identical artifacts can be produced; to all appearance nothing will distinguish one from the other. But this is deceptive should one be regarded as an object of worship and the other not. To be an idolater is a state of mind, a subjective condition which is persuaded that through the performance of some ceremony of consecration an object can be considered to undergo or to have undergone a qualitative change in status. A ceremonial rite of passage must take place such as is exemplified in the Israelites' invocation to the golden calf, 'this is your god, O Israel' (Ex.32:4); or in the Assyrian ceremony ordained by King Nebuchadnezzar (Dan.3:2–3). Only the unconsecrated image is not an idol.[44] God's 'jealousy' extends paramountly to the 'other gods' established by a process of consecration.[45] The very process whereby the idolater intends to make his image appropriate and worthy of worship is precisely the process whereby it is rendered Biblically illegitimate and an abomination. The mere manufacture of the calf would be of no account at all.

There is an important corollary to this argument: since the object itself undergoes no change and the only sign of its consecrated nature derives from the regard in which it is held, it follows that if this regard changes so does *pari passu* the object's status. The same object may at one time be a consecrated idol and at another an innocent decoration, like a much discussed Aphrodite in the Roman baths at Acre, frequented by Rabban Gamaliel (page 95).

But to all this, where the image is that of a human being, an entirely different set of conditions do indeed apply (see Chapter 6).

The image-ban functions as a means to establish a qualitative differentiation between God and those other gods which are in one way or another associated with material imagery. This differentiation is reinforced by God's anonymity and this anonymity applies also to that emissary of God with whom Jacob wrestles (Gen.32:30). The answer to the request made by Moses of God – that God should reveal his name (Ex.3:13 ff.) – is couched in ambivalent terms. God's response: 'I am what I am', or 'I shall be what I shall be' or 'I shall cause to be what I shall cause to be', formulates disclosure and concealment in equal measure.[46] But when this ambivalent response is taken in conjunction with the absence of any physical representation of God, ambivalence disappears; it becomes clear that God has placed himself in a position such that he alone is able to determine the nature of his relationship with the Israelites and thus frustrate any attempt at manipulation through magic.[47] Knowledge of the name of the designated entity is crucial to acquiring power over the entity. This is the point made by Lévy-Bruhl: for primitive peoples, 'the name, an essential appurtenance, being the thing itself, homonymy is equivalent to identity'.[48] God is known through his actions and chosen historical role as the God of Abraham, Isaac and Jacob (Ex.3:15), as the God who brought the Israelites out of Egypt (Ex.20:2). This confinement to an activist designation makes it impossible to address God in any way other than by the prescribed offerings, social and political arrangements, and so on that God has himself demanded. The prohibition of the misuse of God's name in the third commandment is to be regarded as an additional barrier to any attempted magical manipulation.[49]

It seems to me that the effort to preserve the anonymity of God contributes, albeit indirectly, to the elucidation of a

familiar source of perplexity: why does the Bible permit itself to talk of God in terms of figurative language but firmly
repress any attempt to translate that language into physical
terms of a figurative shape? Why is, apparently, verbal imagery a matter of indifference to God whereas physical imagery is clearly of the utmost concern? The poets may well
be liars – a theme familiar from Plato to Nietzsche – but
the Bible views their 'lies' as immeasurably less noxious than
those of sculptors, painters, engravers, etc.

Two explanations are adduced: first, words alone do not
have the power to create a material image and can therefore not be responsible for that further step that would
eventuate in the constitution of a seat of fetishism or the
like.[50] This would explain why God may be heard but not
seen, even though the capacity to impinge on the ear would
presumably require some corporeal activity. So long, however, as the susceptible eye is shielded from temptation, then
whatever subjective image words may induce will be restricted
in its effect.

But for the medieval rationalists, primarily Maimonides,
this explanation is seriously defective because it would necessarily leave intact in the believer's mind the notion of an
anthropomorphic deity. Thus the vocabulary of presence led
Maimonides to stigmatise as 'heretics' – to whom he denied any share in the world to come – those who were persuaded to take *au pied de la lettre* those Biblical passages which
attribute to God body, shape and visibility even though those
'heretics' accepted the sovereignty of one God.[51]

Maimonides attributes this error to the failure to distinguish between the metaphorical and the literal. He understands the latter as a concession to, and *pis-aller* for, the
unlearned and unsophisticated masses. To those unable to
grasp the existence of an intellectual concept of God, such
discourse would make the concept, in comparatively harmless form, accessible and satisfying. It becomes a mode of
accommodation. The uninstructed, pending their enlightenment, would 'see' God in one form but those philosophi-
cally trained would be able to dissolve anthropomorphic
discourse into its true intellectualist connotation. The
views of Isaac Israeli, Judah Halevi, Baḥya ibn Pakuda, Isaac
Arama and Maimonides virtually coincide in this respect.[52]

Maimonides asks, for example, what meaning can be attached to the *Torah's* references to the hand, feet, fingers, eyes, ears of God?

> All these expressions are adapted to the mental capacity of the majority of mankind who have a clear perception of physical bodies only. The *Torah* speaks in the language of men. All these phrases are metaphorical, like the sentence 'If I whet my glittering sword' (Dt.32:41). Has God then a sword and does He slay with a sword? The term is used allegorically and all these phrases are to be understood in a similar sense. That this view is correct is proved by the fact that one prophet says that he had a vision of the Holy One, blessed be He, 'Whose garment was white as snow' (Dan.7:9), while another says that he saw Him 'with dyed garments from Bozrah' (Is.63:1). Moses our Teacher himself saw Him at the Red Sea as a mighty man waging war (Ex.15:3) and on Sinai, as a congregational reader wrapped in his *tallit* – all indicating that in reality He has no form or figure. These only appeared in a prophetic vision. But God's essence as it really is, the human mind does not understand and is incapable of grasping or investigating. And this is expressed in the scriptural text 'Can you, by searching, find out God? Can you find out the Almighty to perfection?' (Job 11:7).
>
> This being so, the expressions in the Pentateuch and books of the Prophets already mentioned, and others similar to these, are all of them metaphorical and rhetorical.[53]

This understanding of Biblical and rabbinic anthropomorphic discourse has been ascribed to the influence of Greek thought.[54] But even if, as Boyarin points out, it may therefore be necessary to revise the terms of the traditionally accepted Hebraic-Hellenic encounter,[58] it is still possible to suggest, on the lines adumbrated earlier, by way of a gloss to the 'metaphorical' explanation of figurative language given by Maimonides, that the very profusion of verbal imagery further accomplishes the function not only of concealment but also of denying to God the sort of physical depiction or representation essential to the existence and perception of 'other gods'. Not only is it the case that Biblical imagery of the divine is contradictory (compare 'the devouring fire' of Ex.24:17 with 'the rock, fortress, shield' of Ps.18:13) but also that this sort of variety will of itself inhibit any representation in material form; if rock, fire and human figure are all interchangeable with each other any unambiguous material representation is rendered impossible of execution. Put differently, the power of mimesis derives from its isomorphic relationship with what is imitated. But in this case the plethora of verbal imagery yields no unambiguous image, to say nothing of the fact that at Sinai nothing is seen save for the smoke, flames and cloud. (Dt.4:12; 15–19). No original for mimetic activity is provided. The only 'self-perception' made available by God to the Israelites is that of a special relationship, presented in a diversity of terminology, and this combination establishes a barrier such that any purported translation of words into things becomes impossible of transcendence; for the relationship of an image to what it signifies is not arbitrary or autonomous but dependent on an isomorphic factor which the varied verbal imagery in this case makes a nullity. The most even the Israelites were ever able to manage was a calf or a bull.

To the God of the Pentateuch, visible only in the most exceptional of exceptional circumstances, the other, the idol, is conceived in its visible physical capacity as the signifier of an alien, obscurantist force. This antithetical mode of idolatry confronts the God who dwells amongst his people (Ex.29:14; Lev.26:11–17; Nu.35:33), of whom his people is part (Dt.32:9), who can be consulted in the 'tent of meeting' (Lev.16:2 ff.) and who actively and personally involves himself in the course of their history; so much so that exile from the land is for David tantamount to the worship of 'other gods' (1 Sam.26: 19–20).

Change, in respect both of God and idol, sets in round about the beginning of the first millennium BCE, when the reign of David initiates a period of transition to a settled monarchy, with all such characteristic features as monumental buildings, erected with forced labour – the speciality of Solomon.[56] This period is further marked in the establishment of a bureaucracy, standing army, taxation system and royal harem.[57] This is also of course the period when the Temple at Jerusalem is erected.

These innovations are not welcome. Already with David, Solomon's father, God remonstrates. He has the prophet Nathan say: 'from the day that I brought the people of Israel out of Egypt to this day I have not dwelt in a house but have moved about in tent and tabernacle. As I moved about wherever the Israelites went, did I ever reproach any of the tribal leaders . . . why have you not built Me a house of cedar?' (2 Sam.7:4 ff.).

This notwithstanding, the response of Solomon is indeed to construct the Temple, and with this edifice is correlated a revised notion of God, enunciated in the presupposition of Solomon's rhetorical question: 'will God really dwell on earth? Even the heavens to their uttermost bounds cannot contain You. How much less this house that I have built' (1 K.27:8). The socio-political transition is part and parcel of the notional emergence of a God who is quasi-transcendent, universal and abstract. The notion of God dwelling in a sanctuary, 'in the midst' of the people (Ex.25:2), is lost and rationalised in terms of a God, only whose 'name' has an earthly habitation.[58]

The perception of idolatry from about the eighth century BCE corresponds to this altered emphasis in the perception of God, and to the idea of divine withdrawal from the material world in favour of a more abstract existence. The idolatrous image is thus no longer regarded so much as physical signifier of a rival, encroaching force, but rather as an essentially blasphemous and arrogantly human attempt to reduce God, now conceived as transcendental, to brute matter. 'I will not give My weight/glory/substance to another, nor My renown to idols', proclaims Isaiah, in the name of God (Is.42:8).

The prophetic mockery of a purported god produced from matter by a mere artisan characterises this transition and coincides with the beginning of what von Rad calls 'the transcendentalisation of Jahve'.[59] The god of the idolater is no more than a human artifact constituted of matter, to which the prophets normally apply the term 'wood and stone'.

The first Biblical mention of 'a man-made god' is no earlier than that of the Deuteronomist (27:15). Recent discussion of the redaction of Deuteronomy suggests that it belongs to the late seventh century BCE;[60] and this would then accord chronologically with a changed perception of idolatry sketched above, and correspond, negatively, to Solomon's earlier view of God whom 'even the heavens . . . cannot contain'. The antithesis to this conception of a transcendental God can obviously be no other than a god of matter.

There is no break with the Pentateuchal past in the condemnation of the image, but in the new, prophetic outlook, the emphasis is decidedly changed in that matter is now shown to lack any sentient or responsive capacity and be impervious to animation or possess any symbolic quality. There is also a change in tone – the image will be scornfully and derisively laughed to death. In fact, the mockery of other religions in the Bible is largely synonymous with the mockery of idols.[61]

The artifact must be distinctively sundered from any capacity to represent or transmit, and be shown indeed to consist of no more than 'wood and stone'. This is the burden of Hosea's scorn (eighth century BCE) for 'the calf of Samaria', the bull statue of God originally erected by King Jeroboam and placed in the sanctuary of Bethel. 'A god he is not', Hosea cries (8:5–6).[62] Isaiah (44:9–20) scorns the error that allows the idolater to locate any sort of divinity in a block of wood, serving indifferently to roast, bake or heat. Rashi (ad loc.) thrusts home the point: when the blacksmith falls thirsty, the idol he has himself fashioned is powerless to quench his maker's thirst – he must provide his own drink. Idolatry is the mistaken attribution to matter of vital power. In the derisory words of Jeremiah, the idolater says to wood, 'you are my father'; to stone, 'you did bear me' (2:27).

The aim of the prophets is totally to destroy any belief in the possibility of a living idol of matter.[63] The Psalmist, also, makes merry at the expense of the idolaters who imagine that for their idol to hear, eat, or walk all it needs are ears, mouth, legs, and so on (Ps.115:5–7).[64]

To enjoy the benefit of this perception you do not need to be an Israelite or even to be bound by the rejection of idolatry. Kimche appeals to a God-given reason, common alike to Jew and gentile, so that, although the latter were not explicitly commanded to refrain from idolatry, reason alone should teach them also to 'hold aloof from all abominations and from serving other gods of wood and stone . . . .'.[65]

The idol suffers not only from its very constitution as 'wood and stone' but also from its origin – people are making obeisance to 'that which their own fingers have made' (Is.2:8); and those fingers belong to artisans – joiners, carpenters, blacksmiths, goldsmiths and silversmiths (Hosea 8:6; Is. 44:9 ff.; Jer. 10:9 ff.). And, asks Jeremiah, can a man make gods for himself?' 'No-gods are they', he answers (Jer.16:20; see also Jer. 10:3,9). An attempt to efface consciousness of this human origin, against which the prophets are reacting, is found in the elaborate Mesopotamian ceremony consecrating an idol for worship. As part of this process, the hands of the fabricating goldsmith and carpenter are symbolically severed, and both craftsmen swear that they had no part in its manufacture: 'the meaning of what is here done is of course clear: the fact that the statue is the work of human hands is ritually denied and thus magically made non-existent, nullified'.[66]

The same phenomenon recurs in other religions: in classical Greece certain stone idols were regarded as 'things cast down by Zeus'; Cicero writes of an image of Ceres 'not made by human hand, but fallen from heaven'; in early Byzantium the term *a-cheiro-poièton* ('not made by hand') was used to designate certain paintings of the Virgin and icons of Christ. This view would obviate comparison with the 'gods made by human hands', denounced by Paul (Acts 19:26).[67]

But to the prophets any such ceremony or belief is hocus-pocus and the purported nullification or denial of human origin has no more than symbolic value, if that, and would partake of a confession of unease. The artifact is as man-made and as dumb after the ceremony as before. What is grave is the failure of the idolater to take this to heart. He, in effect, is no less dumb than the artifact, if, indeed the artifact does not conduce to his dumbness. The Psalmist and Isaiah both speak of inter-dependence between idol and worshipper (Ps.115:8; 135:18; Is.44:9). To the Psalmist's point that the idol has indeed a mouth but cannot speak Ibn Ezra gives particular emphasis: 'whereas the glory of man above all the creations of the lower world lies in his superior soul enjoying the power of speech' (to Ps.135:16). All the greater therefore is the self-degradation when the superior bows to the infinitely inferior, the articulate to the inarticulate. R. David Altschul (*Metzudat David* to Is.44:9) compares the 'unformed' artisan to his 'unformed' work. The images testify against themselves – 'they do not see and know nothing and how, then, can they be of benefit to others?'. Altschul (to Jer.10:14) condemns the image-worshipper who 'makes a fool of himself because there is knowledge in him' jointly with the image-maker who exposes himself to reproach, 'when he sees that the image he has cast is a sham'.

If the idolater is not worshipping God, then whom/what is he worshipping? Himself.

Rashi elucidates this other dimension to befuddlement, in his analysis of the 'other gods' of the first commandment ('you shall have no other gods before Me' – Ex.20:3). This cannot connote gods apart from God, Rashi comments; to subsume idols under the same category as God would be to commit an act of blasphemy. There is no relationship at all between the two.[68] To whom, then, are the 'other gods' other? They are in fact other even to their own makers and/or worshippers. 'Men call on them but they do not respond and it seems as though it (the idol) is something other for it never acknowledges the men who appeal'. To put it differently: the idol is man-made, as a repository and agent for man's hopes etc., but it remains unresponsive because it is no more than man addressing himself. It constitutes, in effect, a form of self-worship, in Hegelian-Marxist terms the idolater has alienated some part of himself in, and thereby projected himself on, 'the other', the idol.[69] This is a condition far graver than that of Pygmalion who, with his artifact did no more than fall in love. By contrast, to his artifact the idolater looks for guidance and instruction. This confused and mistaken communication of self with other – mistaken in the sense that communication with the non-other is assumed possible – is the second component of befuddlement. Not until Rashi's insight into self-worship is combined with Hosea's rejection of the 'god' in the bull of Jeroboam can the condition be overcome.

Advance in enlightenment does not end here: it leads further to the awareness that if the idol is a refractory entity, of wood and stone, the illusory projection of human self- sufficiency and subjectivity, then it clearly can not serve as symbol or mediator between man and God. Its reference is purely human: made by one man, a carpenter, say, and consecrated by another, a priest, say.

But mediation is not only not possible; it is also not necessary. What need of mediation have those to whom God speaks directly (Ex.20:19 ff.)? The commentators (Ibn Ezra, Nahmanides, Sforno) untiringly reiterate that, in order to apprehend or approach God, Israel has no need of any mediator or symbolic agency; God, in person, addresses them directly, as individuals and as a collective.[70] The same holds good in reverse. Armed with this insight, rabbinic thought will see little reason to differentiate among symbol, god and idol as obstacles to communication (see Chapter 3).

The differentiation between what is due to the creator and what is refused to any part of creation necessarily sets reason at odds with nature in its capacity as the other. This is the *sine qua non* to the onslaught on idolatry, and is frequently associated with what is considered to be an intellectually more perceptive form of cognition. The suspicion of imagery *per se* is part of cognition. Judah Halevi, the medieval poet and philosopher, contrasted the devouring fire on the top of the mount (Ex.24:17) seen by 'the common people' with the spiritual form 'visible only to the higher classes'.[71] Freud's enthusiasm for 'the triumph of intellectuality over sensuousness' is an echo.[72] When Cassirer removes from 'the sensuous image and the whole sensuous phenomenal world much of their symbolic meaning', he argues that 'this alone makes possible the new deepening of pure religious subjectivity which can no longer be expressed in any material image'.[73] Carroll can regard 'the aniconic cult . . . as an advance towards rationality in Israelite religion . . . the tendency to elevate the divine word in the Sinaitic tradition may belong to the incipient movement towards rationality that some would consider to be the heart of the Mosaic religious revolution'.[74]

The full implication of a cognition that dismisses the material and visual is realised in Maimonides's understanding of Biblical teaching: that is, 'the root of the commandments relating to idolatry is not to serve any one of all the created entities, not an angel, not a planet and not a star and not one of the four elements and not one of the things created from them, even though the worshipper knows that the Lord is God'.[75]

If these two standpoints are taken in conjunction the point is reached at which it becomes possible to regard Biblical iconoclasm in terms of an onslaught on nature, which takes the form of its disenchantment, as enunciated by a diversity of thinkers – atheists, sceptics, believers, agnostics alike. 'In the darkest times of the middle ages', writes Nietzsche, 'when the dense asiatic cloud had thickened over Europe, it was Jewish free-thinkers, scholars and doctors who under the hardest personal compulsion held fast to the banner of the Enlightenment and intellectual independence and defended Europe against Asia; it is not least thanks to their strivings that a more natural, reasonable and in any case unmythical explanation of the world, could at last again triumph. . .'.[76]

Obviously, this understanding of medieval Jewish scholarship, and medicine leaves much to be desired, for its idealising tendency. Who exactly are these Jewish free-thinkers? It is tempting to argue that Nietzsche is using Jews (and Greeks) as a stick wherewith to beat medieval Christendom. But the drift of his appreciation is clear enough and enjoys influential support. In the view of Horkheimer and Adorno, the Jews have 'robbed magic of its power'.[77] Heinrich Graetz exalted the part of prophet and psalmist in saving the Roman world from utter stagnation, in bringing a 'fresh current of air' into European history, as in the beginning of the sixteenth century 'when a general stagnation would have set in, had not, together with the renaissance of the classical world, "Hebrew truth" stirred up the Reformation':[78] Rosenzweig divests the created world of any purported symbolic meaning by his analysis of the first chapter of Genesis and its reference to plural entities, as distinct from the singular 'heaven' and the singular 'earth': 'even things which impose themselves on man as so specific in their type and positively offer themselves to individualisation as divine persons – such as sun and moon – here become "lights" and through this retrocession of their individuality to a plural category are mercilessly and without regard to person banished into the thing-world of the creation'.[79] For Henri Frankfort 'every finite reality shrivelled to nothingness before the absolute value which was God';[80] for Hans Jonas, 'much of prophetic energy had been expended on hammering home the truth that no part of the world was divine';[81] Lévinas: '[Judaism] has demystified the universe. It has disenchanted nature'.[82] Harvey Cox makes the account of creation in Genesis a lesson in 'a form of "atheistic propaganda"' ... designed to teach the Hebrews that the magical vision, by which nature is seen as a semi-divine force, has no basis in fact'. The Exodus 'symbolised the deliverance of man out of a sacral-political order and into history and social change'. The prohibition of idols in the Sinaitic Covenant relativises the gods and their value-systems. 'Iconoclasm is a form of deconsecration'.[83]

Max Weber is of course the classic exponent of Judaism, especially prophetic Judaism, as a prime source of the process of disenchantment. Iconoclasm, rationalism, 'Hebraic truth', the revival of the classical world, the Reformation – these key-terms from Graetz's presentation recur, in an incomparably more sociologically sophisticated form, in Weber's presentation, not, to the best of my knowledge, that Weber was familiar with Graetz's work.[84]

The apparent convergence between Graetz and Weber arises out of the latter's analysis of the Protestant ethic and the spirit of capitalism where he identifies rationalism with what is termed 'that great religio-historical process of the disenchantment of the world which began with the old-Jewish prophecy and, in union with Hellenic scientific thought, rejected all magical means of the search for salvation as superstition and blasphemy [and which] here found its fulfilment'.[85] The association between disenchantment and aniconism is made in terms of a twofold prophetic turn 'in an anti-aesthetic direction'. The first is determined by the rejection of orgiastics and magic: 'prophecy re-interprets spiritually the originally magically conditioned Jewish reserve at "image and likeness" from out of its absolutely supraworldly conception of God'. Second: in prophetic religion there is 'the tension' at 'the work of men's hands' which can offer no more than 'pseudo-salvation'.[86] 'At all times there has only been one means to break images and impose the rationalisation of life and conduct – great rational prophecies ... Prophecies have brought on the disenchantment of the world and thereby created also the foundation for our modern science, technique and capitalism'.[87] This disenchantment is equated by Weber with a world-view constituted of causality, calculability, 'the world dominion of unbrotherliness', the domain of individual autonomy and a science unaccountable for its instrumental exploitation of nature.[88]

But is this the disenchantment propounded by Graetz and *a fortiori*, the prophets? Absolutely not. The identity of terminology obscures two utterly different versions of disenchantment. In the case of Weber, there is confusion by reason of his incomplete appreciation of the prophetic conception of emancipation from idolatry.[89] Of prophetic iconoclasm, disenchantment, and so on Weber sees as a consequence no more than the transformation of the world into 'a causal mechanism'; it has ceased to be 'a divinely governed somehow ethically meaningfully orientated cosmos'.[90] For Weber it is indeed a paradox that emancipation should culminate in a world that is 'godless and prophetless'. Even more extreme is the position reached by Horkheimer and Adorno – 'the completely enlightened world is radiant in the sign of triumphant disaster'.[91] So far as Weber is concerned, the paradox is created by his standpoint in relation to immanence and the interpretation of life 'in its own terms'.[92] But once life, as the product of disenchantment, is understood in this way, it does indeed become impossible to entertain a theory of disenchantment that will put life itself to the question.[93]

This is however, the prophetic perspective overlooked by Weber and certain other sociologists of religion, for example Harvey Cox, to whom also 'secularization arises in large measure from the formative influence of biblical faith' (Cox, op. cit., p.21). But this is to confuse two different connotations of the sacred/secular dichotomy and to project, on to the Biblical, connotations originating elsewhere. In the former, as the following chapter attempts to demonstrate, the sacred connotes a differentiation in terms of purpose and instrumentality and is accordingly a transient attribute (should the purposefulness of the sacred be impaired or frustrated). In any case, great care is taken to avert the proliferation of the sacred. But this is to anticipate.

Noteworthy, for the moment, is the view that Biblical

disenchantment is in no way irreconcilable with an emancipation from idolatry and magic that, subject to its own terms, does accept nature as a meaningful cosmos which is not 'secularised' at all. There is tension indeed between the denial to 'wood and stone' of any animate qualities and the existential reality that it is the same 'wood' and 'stone' that sustains man and requires to be treated with the utmost respect, both in peace and war (Lev.25:2 ff.; Dt.20:19–20); eroticism, similarly, is a source of corruption that is also indispensable to the human future.

To develop the point further: on the one hand, nature is amoral through and through: an illicit sexual union can prove as fertile as a licit; a stolen grain of wheat grows as easily as a grain honestly acquired (TB AZ 54b; see also Guide, 3:43). But, on the other hand, matter is not inert or inanimate to the extent that it cannot become defiled by sexual malpractice, by bloodshed, by fetishistic pursuits (Lev.18:24 ff.; Ez.36:18).[94] In this respect matter is anything but inanimate or meaningless, so much so that breach of the governing rules entails the extreme sanction of dispossession and expulsion. If/when nature is abused, it hits back. It sets itself against secularisation into an inert, unfeeling mass.

The idea of divine transcendence, which is the source of disenchantment, must therefore not be confused with the absence of divine concern with matter. If the creator has organised his creation in such a way that only human adherence to certain rules can ensure its continued beneficience, then the creator does not entirely transcend his creation and remains to that extent identified with it; and at this point conventional disenchantment is disarmed, for cosmic meaninglessness is itself exposed as meaningless.

To take a simple and obvious example: where nature is disenchanted, Biblically speaking – as it undoubtedly is – it does not thereby degenerate into no more than a derelict dwelling whence Apollo, Wodan and their respective cohorts have been expelled. Its role changes. The Jew need shed no tear at the loss of 'that life-warm image of which only the shadow remains . . . a nature without the gods' (Schiller, Die Götter Griechenlands). On the contrary, nature remains as active as ever, but in a new capacity, as a means to the fulfilment of the *Torah*.

Soloveitchik's 'man of law' beholds nature as a repository of legal norms: has a fruit or tree or plant reached sufficient ripeness to meet the criteria for ritual use? Has the sun set and thereby signified the commencement of the Sabbath? Are there three stars in the sky to signal its conclusion?.[95] What is disenchanted as pantheistic or the dwelling of Apollo, the Bible sees as a means to its own purpose. 'The moon marks the seasons' (Ps.104:19) the stars, sun and planets are indeed 'lights', as Jeremiah said (Jer.31:35), utilitarian and purposeful, but they do more than illuminate in that they also have a part to take in the fulfilment of a religious duty.

Second: it is not possible to dissociate from a position that transcends nature the whole gamut of the weapons deployed against idolatry: the Biblical disengagement from matter, the demotion of the eye in favour of the ear, the demystification of nature, image-ban, and so on. The *point de départ* is precisely in a transcendent reality (that is not however so transcendent that it is unable to serve as a source from which the operation of disenchantment may be effected). God, ultimately, is in fact the agency of disenchantment, to the extent that were there no God, there would also be no disenchantment. Conversely, disenchantment that lacks acknowledgement of the *Torah* is no more than another form of enchantment. Otherwise the point is indeed reached when it would seem that the Bible repudiates idolatry only in order to make the world safe for the disenchanted world of modern capitalism, technology, and rationality.

The prophetic message encompasses a dual summons that is in fact one, to only part of which is Weber sensitive. Not two are here in action but a single indivisible process, in the sense that not until the *Torah* is accepted can the world be disenchanted. Isaiah makes this clear in his demand for the conquest of human self-worship, the exaltation of God alone and the utter elimination of the idol (Is.2:17–18). In the days of the messiah there will be no idols, Kimche comments (ad loc.). This again emphasises the precise equivalence between the twilight of the idols ('disenchantment') and enlightenment. To the extent that God's 'anti-religion' succeeds, man's 'religionitis' is destroyed (Rosenzweig, page 3 above).

What is then disclosed will be the promise of an anti-thesis to a reified world of nature whence all possibility has been expelled. Biblical enlightenment and an open future belong together. This struggle is waged on a multitude of fronts. In his comprehensive indictment of the enchanted world the prophet Micah brings together witchcraft, soothsaying, idol-worship, sacred pillars, man's obeisance to his own handiwork (Micah 5:11–12). To some of the elaboration and consequences of this teaching I now turn.

2 To Limit the Holy

In the confrontation of man with nature, the Biblical doctrine of idolatry precipitates *inter alia* three major teachings: that to conceive of matter – 'wood and stone' – as anything but inert, impervious to human animation and incapable of signifying the divine, save in the most exceptional of exceptional circumstances, is perhaps the greatest conceivable error of which man is capable; that direct access to God can be enjoyed by the individual; that to succumb to the employment of supposedly mediatory symbols is akin to a form of self-inflicted deception that also exposes its victim to political abuse (which must however, not be confused with a permissible political myth).[1] These three propositions are inter-dependent, form a unity and can be assembled in any sequence.

I could maintain for example that because matter is inert it is useless as mediator between man and God and hence that only direct communication is possible, if communication is at all possible; or that, because direct communication is possible, mediation is redundant, if not positively misleading and is in any case impossible because matter is inert; or it might be held that even if a mediatory symbol is a man-made artifact, constructed of wood and stone, it will arrogate to itself precisely that mode of direct communication which it falsely purports to facilitate by serving as a vehicle.

Common to these three arguments, however, is the need for a conception of matter in general as indifferent in terms of moral value, for only such a conception could hope to avert its (re)enchantment.

This danger follows from the possibility that brute matter might be considered, through a perversely mistaken notion of its refractory nature, the recipient or bearer or embodiment of a state of what is popularly known as holiness. But if matter is inert, how can any part of it be conceived of as distinguished in such a way as to be designated holy? If nature is desacralised, as much opinion has it, how can anything ever be holy? This state of desacralisation is all the more acceptable, given that holiness is not a self-subsistent attribute but only comes into existence when located in some spatial object or entity, space itself also having no independent existence but subsisting in the form of matter as the support of all being.[2]

Only myth contests the indifference of matter. Blumenberg writes of the manner whereby myth – here synonymous with idolatry – structures itself 'against the unbearableness of the indifference of space and time'. To destroy the intent of myth must therefore take the form of 'rendering spatial and temporal distinctions invalid . . .'.[3] No sooner is this achieved than the possibility of enchantment is diminished, for this will be dependent on discrimination as between one person and another or one locality and another or one object and another. But if matter is indifferent, any discrimination – in terms of holiness, say – will necessarily be extrinsic (and, moreover, exceptional, contingent and provisional).

The contrast here is with that ladder of 'hierophany' erected by Eliade; this extends 'from the most elementary hierophany – manifestation of the sacred in some ordinary object, a stone or a tree, for example – to the supreme hierophany (which, for a Christian, is the incarnation of God in Jesus Christ). . . .'.[4] Any such association would blur the distinction between an extrinsic (Jewish) notion of holiness and an intrinsic notion. Judaism, whilst reluctantly accepting the presence of holiness, even in matter, remains extremely sensitive to any fear lest holiness be confused with 'hierophany' and fetishism. For the same reason it is important to dissociate holiness, in the sense in which it will henceforth be used, from notions of 'the mysterium tremendum' popularised by Rudolf Otto, where holiness is invested with an *a priori*, self-sufficient, autonomous character.[5] With the dichotomous status of sacred and profane expounded by Durkheim in terms of rivalry, distinctiveness and the social versus the individual, there is a third contrast.[6]

In our case the horror evoked by idolatry is strong to the extent that it limits the proliferation of holiness, suspecting the omnipresence of the idol. To designate an object as holy is already to attribute to it certain qualities that normally also belong to an object designated as an idol. In both cases the potentiality for enchantment is created, because, although the purpose of the attribution is certainly different in each case, what is common in each case is the sheer fact of designation. To designate of itself creates the potentiality. Not to designate at all is the sole answer.

This situation, ultimately, is why Schneidau (op.cit., p.4) can be excused when he writes: 'no Hebrew institution can be sacred because if so it would become an idol'. This is certainly an exaggeration, as we shall see, but pardonable by virtue of the attention it directs to the intimate relationship of the reaction generated by the holy to that by the idol. This arises from a certain parallelism between enchantment, derived from, and based on, a differentiation introduced into matter, and the notion of holiness, also derived from the differentiation of matter: common to both is the denotation of certain specified features of the material world as supposed repositories of certain attributes or as the object of reverential care and treatment. Schneidau's assertion, precisely because it is unqualified, has the supremely important merit in that, further, it also directs attention away from the clash of confused concepts and towards the precautions that require to be taken in order to avert a clash of values.

There is ample justification in the Jewish world for this repression. Instances when parts of the world of matter are hallowed, in the sense that they are considered sentient and responsive, do abound. Kabbalists and mystics, such as Nahmanides, people the world of matter with animate forces. In his comments to Exodus 20:3 ('You shall have no other gods before me') and Deuteronomy 18:9 ('You shall not learn to imitate the abhorred practices') Nahmanides maintains that in fact sorcery can be effective. But it is precisely for this reason that it must be repressed, so that the world may remain 'in the simple nature as desired by its creator'. Nahmanides sees three types of beings in the sub-lunar world, each of which may lead to idolatry, and outlines three categories of such 'gods', each the object of a corresponding heretic. The first may indeed acknowledge the supreme power of the one God but he will direct his worshipful intent to one or another of the angels or 'separated intelligences', some of which govern the nations as their 'minister' (for example, of Greece or Persia) with power to affect the particular nation's fate for good or evil. The second will worship the sun, moon or stars, of which he will make images, hoping thereby to secure the sun's help in the fulfilment of his wishes. This type of heresy is also associated with the worship of powerful human beings. The third turns to the worship of demons (also considered to have power over a certain territory) and necromancy.

In related cases the mystic will even seek to animate and communicate with the spirit of a departed *Zaddiq* (sage and righteous man) via the process known as *Yiḥud* (roughly translatable as 'unification'): on a propitious day, which would exclude the Sabbath, new moon and festivals and preferably after midnight – 'if you perform the *Yiḥud* by actually stretching yourself out on the *zaddiq*'s grave (that is, in a prone position), you should contemplatively 'intend' that by virtue of your stretching out on top of him you also cause the *zaddiq* to stretch out his soul (*nefesh*), which will then spread out in his bones that are in the grave: (whereupon) he comes 'alive' and his bones become like a 'body' to the soul that is stretched and spread out within them'.[7] The mystic who engages in this exercise can now communicate with the soul of the departed *zaddiq*. Then there is the custom, practised by medieval pilgrims to Galilee, of worshipping at locations made holy by the presence of the sepulchres of holy men to which the local sub-culture attributed powers of instrumental magic in relation to birth, death, livelihood and the cycle of nature.[8] More recently, the eighteenth century *Tanya* of R. Shneur Zalman of Lyady, one of the founders of Ḥabad Ḥassidism, talks of divine illumination present even in inanimate stones and earth, ascending to the incomparable vitality imbuing animal and man ('the speaker').[9]

Such views might be considered a Jewish equivalent to 'the great chain of being'; and to *Yiḥud* a close parallel might well be found in the holiness attributed to the graves of Christian saints.[10]

The fear lest such a fate overtake Moses is no doubt why the Deuteronomist emphasises that 'to this day' the location of Moses's grave is unknown (Dt.34:6). Aaron is said to be buried in an unknown cave.[11]

Examples even of fetishism are to be found. A most distinguished rabbi of the eighteenth century, Jonathan Eibeschütz, maintained that the prescription of wearing fringes (*tsitzit*) and donning phylacteries (*tefillin*) 'saves and preserves from all evil and transgression'.[12] The Berkowitz family associate their survival during the Holocaust with the holding fast at all times to a 'holy book'.[13]

Extreme measures had at times to be taken in the interests of the struggle against idolatry and the cognate impulse to divinise/idolise. It is legally preferable to act in defiance of God rather than commit an idolatrous act; and this is reasonable because in the first case there is no challenge to God's existence whereas the second pre-supposes his displacement. The general concern to establish a distinction between what is due to the holy and what would become an attitude of idolatrous reverence for the holy, to avert confusing this category with the impermissible idolisation of matter, appears in the explanation given by the medieval rabbi, Elyakim b. Joseph, for the reasons that impelled King Hezekiah to break the staff originally prepared by God for Moses (2K.18:4): 'for by those days the children of Israel were burning incense to it . . . and although it has been established (AZ 44a) that although they were doing this it was not idolatry and it was not necessary to break the serpent. . . . but because Hezekiah saw that Israel was erring after it he arose and broke it so that they should not stumble. . .'.[14]

Perhaps however, the most daring statement on the impermissibility of confusing respect for the holy with an idolatrous attitude towards it belongs to R. Meir-Simḥa Cohen of Dvinsk: his context is the breaking by Moses of the Tablets of the Law. Meir-Simḥa argues that, when Moses saw the Israelites 'plunged in the abomination of the calf which they thought a god', he feared lest the Tablets succumb to the same fate and become deified: as though the people 'would replace the calf by the Tablets'. They had not come to accept 'the obligatory reality beyond concept and beyond depiction and therefore they erred with the calf'.[15] Better to destroy the holy than to idolise it.

To convey the notion of matter as non-sentient, non-responsive to human desire and undifferentiated, Hebrew uses the term *hol*. This has 'sand' as its literal meaning, thereby conveying the notion of neutral expanse, in the sense of denying any distinction to any part of matter. This 'neutralising' concept is used by Maimonides to refute the claims of the astrologer who would assert that 'one star is good and another evil, and that one part of the globe is aligned with this star and against that, although the whole globe is one body, the parts of which resemble each other, and in them there is no change and no mixture'.[16]

It is an outstanding characteristic of *Hol* – sand – the 'natural' state of the world – that its extent lacks all defining characteristics; it is therefore possible to conceive of frontiers, borders, and space in general as indeterminate, intermingled entities; certainly not as fixed and defined portions of territory. That the Talmudic term for kneading dough – *gebul* – is also used to designate the area usually referred to as 'frontier' points in the same sense.[17] Both in the one case and in the other the notion of mixing, obliterating distinctions, is paramount. Further, because in such a situation any physical distinction is purely notional, arbitrary and imposed, it is possible to 'play' with space, even in a serious context. 'Sand', lacking any determinate character of its own, can, within certain limits, be allocated a character and, for example, be designated as private or public space – following the dictates of religio-legal convenience. This is demonstrated in the measures taken by R. Nehemiah Nobel of Frankfurt on Main in 1914: he enlarged the bounds of private space so as to make it possible for the wartime influx of Jewish soldiers into the town not to have to transgress the Sabbath by the need to carry their equipment from private space to public space.[18] This certainly does not mean that the enlarged space became 'holy' but it does illustrate the malleability of space in general. The malleability of space is manifest even more strikingly in the varying boundaries attributed to the promise of the Land. There are at least three varying geographic entities, to say nothing of the territory delimited in Ezekiel's vision of the promise (Ezek.47:13 ff.).[19]

Hol is no simple, absolute entity – rather an inextricable, inseparable mixture of matter which defies any claim to purity. The problem this creates is discussed by the Talmud in relation to the prohibition against deriving any benefit from idolatry. How can this ideal be made possible? The offending idol can well be destroyed and ground to dust but will it not become manure of manure, or enter into a bridge, an oven, a vegetable garden . . . (TB AZ 48b ff.)? Certainly, means can be devised to circumvent or renounce or eliminate the grosser and more manifest modes of benefit but in the last resort, 'there is no redemption from an idol'; so compounded is the world of matter that into the most holy of objects or into the most saintly individual some element of blasphemy must enter. From such a mixture no absolute distinction between 'holy' and 'profane' – to use these terms in their usual connotation – can be derived. On a material or spatial reality that is neither 'holy' nor 'profane', remaining undifferentiated matter of no determinate status, such terms can simply exercise no purchase.

The refusal to countenance the notion of sentient matter is indispensable to the battle against idolatry and in its most extreme form will reject arguments for immanence and pantheism.[20] It is here that Lévinas notes the association of Judaism with the impulse to desacralisation, demystification: 'if the world preoccupies us, that is because it is insufficiently desacralised'.[21]

The antithesis to *hol*, the undifferentiated, is *kadosh*, the differentiated. This signifies designation for a particular purpose; as, for example, when God declares to the Israelites, 'I have set you apart from other peoples to be Mine' (Lev.20:26).

What is implied and entailed by entering into this state of *kadosh* (or *kedushah*) is postponed for the moment. At this stage, outstanding in importance is the state of tension created between the entity's original status and its new and enhanced status or, in our terms, between its undifferentiated and differentiated status. The instrumental functionalism generated by this change in status acts as a source of danger which is only to be overcome by a more or less concerted attempt to qualify the status of the differentiated.

The primary weapon must obviously be to refuse to matter the possibility of any lasting change in its nature as differentiated. The acknowledgement of spatial distinctions, derived from any such supposed change, will therefore be restricted to the minimum, and will also be distinguished from the respect due to the holy and what would degenerate into an attitude of idolatrous reverence for the holy: a comment to the Talmud takes as its text: 'it might be thought that a man should fear the sanctuary' and then continues: 'in regard to one's father there would be no need to speak thus for of course a man would not bow to him on account of his divinity but with regard to the sanctuary it was necessary [to speak thus] because it is in a state of *kedushah* . . .'.[22]

A glance at the conduct required at those sites of unquestionable note (for example, of God's manifestations), elucidates the import of this distinction: first, such sites are differentially evaluated; second, it is not so much that a location is singled out, not even the event associated with the location, but rather the action of God in bringing about the event associated with the location. The site at Mount Sinai of the divine manifestation calls for no blessing on the part of the beholder, for here, strictly speaking, no departure from the natural order took place. (In any case, the holiness of the site has a strictly limited duration – see also page 40 below).

Even there however, where such a departure is recorded, as a manifestation of divine power, the blessing to be pronounced must satisfy at least four criteria: first, the sign must have been performed for all Israel and not a part or even a majority; second, the precise location of the sign must be witnessed. Merely to behold the Sea of Reeds is not sufficient – that precise spot where the Israelites crossed during the Exodus must be seen. (This applies also to the crossing of the Jordan under Joshua); third, the miracle must involve the saving of life, which would perhaps exclude the sign performed for Elijah on Mount Carmel for it is debatable whether his life was threatened (1K.18:20 ff.); fourth, the blessing at the designated location must not be repeated at intervals of less than thirty days.[23]

Sinai is not blessed but the sun is, once every twenty-eight years when, according to rabbinic calculation, the sun returns to that point in the heavens where it was suspended at the creation.[24] But there is no contradiction here – because the point of the blessing is precisely not to single out this particular piece of matter in its own right but to emphasise its dependent status as part of divinely created nature.

It is blessed by virtue of its being part of God's handiwork, and thus in a state of subordination to God. At Lvov in 1869 when this rare ceremony took place, R. Joseph Saul Nathanson explained that the blessing was instituted 'in order to refute the opinions of those who worship it, thinking *that the sun is a deity*. But the very fact that the sun *returns* to the place of its inception demonstrates that it is not a divinity, for otherwise it would travel indefinitely, in accord with its own 'wishes'; who commanded it to return to its *place?* Evidently it must have a commander, whose bidding it does'. Thus, the blessing to God (' . . . Who does the work of creation'), Nathanson continued, shows that 'the *sun* is like all other created entities, and it is God who does the work of *creation*, the sun being bounded and of temporal nature, merely a servant to the King of Glory'.[25]

These instances make evident both the reluctance with which much Jewish thinking contemplates the notion that any part of matter might enjoy special status, further expressed in the delimitation of that status.

This delimitation is all the more required because the transition from profane, *hol*, to holy, *kadosh*, can encompass a very broad variety of entities and activities: oil (Ex.30:32), cattle (Lev.27:9), time (Ex.31:14, a particular day), a people (the Israelites), the priests (Ex.28:44 *cohanim*), war (Ex.13:3, 1 Sam.21:5-7; Micah 3:5), and so on. When this happens, the particular bearer of *kedushah* becomes separated from its 'fellows' so as to serve a particular purpose in a particular capacity. *Kedushah* normally has this character of instrumentality and emanates from God, directly or indirectly. This will normally in no way change the nature of the object or activity – merely incorporate a relationship to the divine.[26]

The transition from *hol* to *kadosh* involves no special problem and remains notional, but its consequence, as soon as the transition takes effect, is momentous. The transition from *hol* – 'sand', undifferentiatedness – to a state of *kedushah* – differentiatedness, separateness, designation for a particular purpose – has as result that the object, or person, denoted holy becomes subject to another set of requirements. The particular entity enters into a different legal category imposing a corresponding set of obligations. The Israelites, for example, are denominated a holy people in the Biblical formulation: 'You shall be set apart (*kadosh*) to Me, for I the Lord am set apart (*kadosh*) and I have separated you from other peoples to be Mine' (Lev. 20:26). This relationship both generates and is generated by the simultaneous imposition of a range of commandments: ' . . . who has set us apart by His commandments', in the traditional blessing.[27] The covenant sets the Israelites apart in their commitment to God in their religious and social life, as individuals and as collective, in the widest possible sense.[28] This separation applies also in respect of diet, which, it is said, 'represented the culmination of a progression in holiness, by which God had brought a people by steps to enjoy unprecedented proximity to himself'.[29]

Thus, although the act of setting apart is in itself a neutral act and can apply to all manner of entities and activities, it also of itself subjects the entity concerned to a set of obligations. In other words, if something or somebody is designated and set apart as holy, this is no static relationship between an entity and its predicate – still less does it change the nature of the entity – but it generates a set of obligations freshly applicable to the designated entity. The paraphrase offered by Rashi to the famous demand made on the Israelites by God – 'You shall be set apart for I the Lord your God am set apart' (Lev.19:2) – illustrates this *par excellence*: to Rashi the setting apart is synonymous with a set of prohibitions that forbids to the Israelites the acts of sexual license listed earlier in the chapter. He notes the frequent and close relationship of *kedushah* with abstention. from forbidden sexual acts. This exemplifies the dynamic relationship created by the act of sanctification.[30]

Conversely, where and when this commitment is flouted – for example, in the social oppression and immorality excoriated by Amos (Amos 2:7) – then *kedushah* degenerates into profanity, that is, reversion to a state of nature.

Kedushah has a strong and weak sense. The first is produced by the unmediated presence of God, when the consequent state has the strongest possible denotation, for, in the absence of the requisite precautions, such a case of direct emanation gives *kedushah* a lethal quality. It is exemplified in the circumstances of the death of Uz: his well-intentioned but unguarded approach to the Ark, when it is about to fall from the cart on which it is being carried, entails his death from an 'explosion' or 'outburst'.[31] Similarly, the *cohanim* – the priests, those charged with the preparation and slaughtering of the various offerings and through whose implementation of this procedure the deity is approached – must don special protective garments to avert the potentiality of disaster.[32] Not for nothing are the Israelites warned: ' . . . and you shall fear My sanctuary' (Lev.19:30).[33] This is potentially a lethal site.

In this strong sense the best example of *kedushah* is the effect associated with its presence at Sinai: this is powerful to the extent that it requires the evacuation of the Israelites and their sheep and cattle, for fear of some uncontrollable outburst attendant on God's presence at the site (Ex.19:12).[34]

R. Naḥman b. Isaac puts this in the context of his dictum; not the place honours the man but the man the place: he continues 'this is what we find regarding Mt. Sinai – so long as the *shekhinah* was present the *Torah* proclaimed "Neither let the flocks nor herds graze before that Mount" (Ex.34:3). But once the *shekhinah* had left, the *Torah* said "When the ram's horn sounds long, they shall come up to the Mount" (Ex.19:13)'. The same applied to the Tent of Meeting, Naḥman b. Isaac continued: 'so long as it remained pitched, the *Torah* ordered "the removal from the camp of every leper" (Nu.5:2); but once the Tent was struck, both those with a running sore and the lepers were allowed to enter'.[35]

Sinai reverts to its previous harmless, undifferentiated status so soon as God's presence departs; and, as shown above, this site of the revelation warrants not even a blessing. The location is severed from the divine *fons et origo* of its *kedushah*. This is no more than a transient state and thus the possibility is removed that the location might become worshipped, let alone idolised.

So much for *kedushah*, in its strong sense. The substance of the designated entity, through God's presence or activity, reportedly undergoes some change, with the holiness being limited to the duration of the presence. In the weak sense of *kedushah*, now to be examined, the factor of transience remains a characteristic.[36] In the present limited context, I cannot consider all the ramifications of this theme – no more, in fact, than project certain guide-lines but these, I hope, will still indicate the means to the importance of delimiting holiness in time and space as an operational concept.

One over-riding criterion in this delimitation is fitness for purpose, and this in its turn is normally conditioned by the integrity of the hallowed object. Should this be lost, then the object is no longer fit and able to fulfil its purpose and reverts to the status of *ḥol* – 'sand'. This would apply, for example, should an animal hallowed as an offering subsequently lose its physical integrity; likewise, a *cohen* – priest – who is physically damaged becomes ineligible for office and disqualified from fulfilling his functions;[37] and if a priest, whilst preparing the animal for offering, is not concentrating his intent wholly on the prescribed preparation and execution of the particular offering for which the animal is intended, then the preparation is invalid and must be discarded.[38] Integrity, as a pre-condition of sanctity, extends also to notional purposefulness.

Kedushah, even in its weak sense, does not need to forfeit its characteristic even should the object it qualifies lose its integrity and thereby its eligibility for use. It is possible to combine holiness with lack of wholeness and even unfitness.

The status of a *Sefer Torah* – Scroll of the Law – for example, is unconditionally one of holiness by virtue of its repository as the word of God. It is the object of meticulous preparation by a trained scribe, housed in a particular frame and dedicated to the purpose of reading and instruction so that only for this purpose may it be removed from its housing. As an educational medium this is its privileged status. To a lesser degree only does this status apply also to any decorative finials of silver or gold; they are considered 'instruments of sanctity' and may not be removed for an 'undifferentiated' purpose (unless it be to use them to acquire another Scroll or a Pentateuch).[39] However, should a Scroll be damaged through, for example, the erasure of a letter, or a tear, then it does not forfeit its sanctity but does become unfit for use and, if irreparable, that is, if its differentiatedness cannot in its entirety be restored, must be buried in the vicinity of a sage.

There is in fact inter-dependence between the presence

of God's 'name' or word, and the utilitarian notion of fitness for purpose in governing the status of holiness. Apart
from the dominance of the first, no fixed scale of values
exists. Articles such as phylacteries (*tefillin*) or *mezuzot*, both
of which must bear the word or name of God as an integral
part of their function, are *tashmishei kedushah* (instruments
of sanctity). Other articles, though also used in the exercise
of a religious function, such as a ram's horn (*shofar*) or a
palm branch (*lulav*) but which lack the name or word of
God are merely *tashmishei mitzvah* – instruments used in the
fulfilment of a commandment – and therefore lack *kedushah*.[40]

It follows therefore that where *kedushah* is dependent on
the presence of God's word, should this word fade or be
erased in some way, then the *kedushah* departs likewise and
the object becomes available for 'profane' use.[41]

The distinction between the two types of instruments is
not absolute and unchanging. Raba, a Talmudic sage, initially maintained that the curtain hanging before the Ark
(in which the Scroll was housed) was merely 'the instrument of an instrument' and therefore devoid of sanctity but
on seeing that the curtain when folded was used as a rest
for the Scroll, he concluded that it was in fact 'an instrument of sanctity' (TB Meg.26b). In the eighteenth century,
having regard to the changed function of the curtain, this
view was again revised. A responsum sent by R. Ezekiel
Katzenellenbogen (rabbi of Altona-Hamburg-Wandsbek, 1713–
1749), although essentially concerned only with the decorations on the Ark curtains, does make it clear that the curtain
had no instrumental function and was regarded solely in
terms of a decoration and could therefore make no claim
to holiness.[42]

Similarly, a synagogue *qua* building enjoys no lasting sanctity
but belongs to the category of 'instrument of a commandment', comparable in this respect to a *lulav* or a tabernacle.[43]
The holiness that all three attract applies for the duration
of the purpose they serve – to provide a festival dwelling
for seven days in the case of a tabernacle, for example – at
the expiry of which period they are no longer holy. In the
case of a synagogue, its building does not become holy until
its function as a meeting-place for prayer is actualised; that
is, it is only proper use that sanctifies the building, when it

is utilised for the purpose of prayer by the necessary quorum of adult males. Naḥmanides writes: 'the intent of houses of assembly and the merit of public prayer is that there should be for people a place where they can foregather and acknowledge God who created and established them, and they will make this known and they will say before Him: we are your creatures'.

Naḥmanides compares

> ... a synagogue to the instrument of a commandment such as a *lulav* or a tabernacle which in themselves, although they are discarded after the duration of the commandment, there is in them, during its duration, the sanctity of respect ... thus they said of the Ḥanukkah candle [towards which all disrespect is forbidden] that it is forbidden to count coins in its light ... and this [type of disrespect] applies also to the decorations of a tabernacle which must not be used as means to satisfaction the whole seven days [of the festival] for the decorations of the tabernacle are forbidden [to 'secular' use] for the duration of the commandment for the name of heaven rests on them ... they have been set aside for the commandment ... and although instruments of commandments ['*tashmishei mitzvah*'] they are discarded when the duration of the commandment has expired, during that duration they are treated as if they were holy. . . .

The notion of holiness in the case of a synagogue survives even its physical destruction so long as the notion of utility is affirmed in the wish of the townspeople to reconstruct the building. In such a case it will still be treated as holy, in the view of Naḥmanides: 'because the duration of its commandment has not yet expired and it is in order to restore and rebuild it, but if [the townspeople] have decided to sell it then the duration of its commandment has already expired, like a tabernacle after the seven days of the festival, and the holiness has departed from it'.[44]

Where purposefulness is the criterion of differentiatedness then it is all-demanding and monopolistic, both in relation to the purpose and the means to that purpose. Even if the latter be purely ceremonial, the *kedushah* will still limit the purpose of the particular object to that particular ceremony; the *Ḥanukkah* candles (that commemorate the re-dedication of the Hasmonean Temple – normally attributed to 164 BCE), must not be used for illumination, reading by, or for any other save their ceremonial purpose. Their status is determinate, exclusive and utilitarian. But here again the candles and oil used in a synagogue are not intrinsically holy or even *tashmishei kedushah*; only through their actual use do they become at all holy.[45]

Of the transience of sanctity no more likely epitome is to be found than in the case of those objects dedicated to the Temple (*kodshei bedek ha-bayit*) and/or the sacrificial offerings (*kodshei mizbeaḥ*). No object could command a greater degree of holiness yet in both cases this is removable and the object is susceptible to the forfeiture of its sanctified status in favour of a reversion to unsanctified status. The redemption procedure differs in that, broadly speaking, an object is redeemable on payment of its value plus a fifth; an animal however, consecrated as an offering, must first fulfil its purpose before it can be redeemed and become available for 'secular' use.[46]

To sum up briefly: an entity can be declared holy but only if it is unblemished (an animal for one of the offerings, for example) but if it loses this attribute, it simultaneously forfeits its sanctity; an entity can be holy for a limited period, following the expiry of which this is no longer the case (a tabernacle); an entity can be sanctified through use and, even if destroyed, its location will retain the same status if there is an intention to re-construct (a synagogue); a Scroll of the Law is permanently holy even if loss of integrity makes it unfit for use. No doubt there are other permutations on the themes of utility, integrity and time-span. But they will be unable to yield further evidence of the power of the struggle against idolatry in qualifying the differential status of any part of the material world.

HOLINESS OF THE LAND

The struggle against idolatry insists on the need to refuse differentiation in respect of space and matter. The criteria imposed by the process of *kedushah* testify to this process. Only for a limited time or in a strictly defined condition can a part of matter be differentiated in terms of purpose, and thus distinguished from *ḥol*. The fear is pervasive lest what is sanctified will also become idolised, so tempting is it to mistake the one for the other.

But if the required criteria are in fact satisfied and the impulse to sanctify frustrated, the sway of holiness is limited without loss to human autonomy. This is certainly not absolute; it is autonomy under the laws, but those very laws that govern the process of sanctification and offer release from subjection to space and matter are themselves subject to a variety of rabbinic modifications.

To the concept of territorial holiness the threat of divinisation applies no less than elsewhere: probably more so in fact, because here the legal category created by differentiation is impure, mingled as it is with considerations of *amour propre* in politics, history, demography and *raison d'état*. This is present from the very beginning of Israelite history. The pre-occupation with the Land – its promise, acquisition, treatment, loss, self-incrimination – is enormous to the extent that it is forcefully held: 'the whole biblical historiography revolves around the Land'.[47]

Nowadays the tourist trade is also involved: 'the idea is being insinuated', notes a recent observer, 'that any act or event acquires religious quality merely by being performed at a holy site ... Over the years, millions of pounds were spent on the promotion of the traditional burial sites in Galilee and the alleged mausoleum of King David in Jerusalem'. It is also suggested that Marian developments in the nineteenth and twentieth centuries have encouraged the cult of Rachel's tomb.[48]

To the tension generated by the struggle against idolatry, and any emergence of enchantment, the Land stands in a paradigmatic relationship. This generates controversy today as much as ever in the past. It often revolves around Durkheim's theory of religion as an enhancement of collective consciousness in the spirit of which Mordecai Kaplan assimilated Judaism to the religion of those civilisations where 'the collective consciousness was hypostasized or deified in a token, fetish or potentate. Each religion would elevate its heroes, historic events and places, holy texts and myths into *sancta* which enhanced the organic group spirit'.[49] But there is a danger where, following Durkheim, the social is made sacred and this, Edgar Wolff emphasised to a Franco-Jewish colloquium, 'has led to Maurassism and fascism'.[50]

Here I must forbear from entering into the whole complex *Problematik* of the relationship of the Land of Israel to the people of Israel but limit myself to an indication of the part taken by the theme of holiness in the formation of this relationship, including reference to the capacity of holiness to appear, disappear and re-appear. This in itself constitutes an inherent safeguard against idolisation and the invocation of *sancta*. The fact of itself that the holiness of the Land is no permanent status or designation, that it is relevant to varying circumstances of time and history – exactly like a synagogue, or a tabernacle, or a *lulav* – goes far to undermine territorial mystique. Obviously, the evaluation of these circumstances has differed from scholar to scholar – as is the case today – but this is immaterial to the central issue of a transient sanctity. It is complemented by others which combine to form an inhibitory mechanism of some complexity.

In the first place, which is in itself a source of enduring perplexity, the Israelites are not an autochthonous people but appear as a people subsequent to the territorial division of the world amongst other peoples. To the latter, their own relationship to their land is 'natural' in a way that stands in marked contrast to that of the Israelites who have received their land by virtue of a promise from the creator of all lands. This is the main thrust of the comment made by Rashi to Genesis 1:1, when he asks why the Bible should begin with 'in the beginning': 'because He has "revealed to His people His powerful deeds in giving them the heritage of nations" (Ps.111:6). When the gentiles say to Israel "You are thieves who have taken by force the land of the seven peoples", the Israelites can reply, "the whole world belongs to God which He has created and which He has given to whom He will"'. This is an answer that takes account both of historical developments and of divine decree, for even the latter had to be implemented by conquest.

This qualification – there are many others – needs also

to be accompanied by the distinction made between occupation of the land and its possession. The latter is reserved to God: the land 'must not be sold beyond reclaim, for the land is Mine: you are strangers and sojourners with Me' (Lev.25:23).[51]

This adds weight to the dimension of divine choice but it certainly introduces no change into the substance of what is chosen. The notion of 'a mystical geography' in certain medieval Jewish thinkers (such as Judah Halevi), as expounded by Shalom Rosenberg, which does indeed claim certain distinctive virtues for the Land of Israel, is ultimately derived from Greek theories of climatology.[52] The danger would otherwise emerge of a lapse from holiness into 'the divinisation of the people and the Land' which Isaiah Leibowitz finds exemplified in the work of the pupils of R. Abraham Isaac Kuk.[53]

Perhaps for this reason an early text takes pains to deny the possibility that the Land might be erroneously considered to possess intrinsic, inherent qualities distinctive from land elsewhere. Only the criterion of allocation is decisive: if it can be held that 'until the Land of Israel was chosen all lands were fitting for the (Ten) Commandments; after the Land of Israel was chosen, all lands fell away'[54] – then no more than the dimension of choice is added to an existing form of undifferentiatedness as between one land and another. Further, given Maimonides's ruling that produce grown from imported soil in a ship in contact with the Land of Israel is subject to the same religio-agricultural laws as produce grown from the soil of the Land,[55] it follows that the produce of the one is as holy as that of the other. Suppose, however, that produce of the holy Land is exported and, for example, made into dough: is the dough liable for separation as a priestly offering? The opposing views of R. Akiba and R. Eliezer seem to derive from their respective versions of sanctity; the former saw sanctity defined in territorial terms alone, separately from territorial produce and therefore, outside the sphere of holiness, no dough-offering is required; the latter however, finds that sanctity inheres in objects even when they depart from the delimitations of sacred space and therefore the offering is required.[56]

Although the choice of the Land is seemingly arbitrary – as arbitrary in fact as the choice of the Israelites themselves

(Dt.7:7–8) – it is still momentous in its consequences: both the Land and its Israelite inhabitants now attract to themselves the whole corpus of laws which differentiate both land and people sanctifying them at the same time as they also create a purpose. Holiness and purpose are inseparable and this combination can be expressed in terms of a specific mode of governance. The Land, in this respect, can be compared to a synagogue, or the Temple vessels or the *lulav*, all of which are hallowed through their use, that is by their relationship to the fulfilment of a certain task.[57]

That task, in reference to the Land, derives from the covenant concluded at Sinai. Whereas the divine promise to Abraham is only obliquely conditional, that to his descendants, at Sinai, is predicated on their undertaking to fulfil the conditions of the covenant.[58] These range from the cosmological to the social and are couched in mutually binding terms. In sum, they introduce into the relationship of the Israelites to their Land a differentiation which is evaluated and also validated in terms of a function;[59] and this function is best understood as an experiment, in the establishment of a purposive order of being. It is a 'utopian' experiment but for the fact that the 'utopia' is a more or less defined *topos*, sensitive and reactive to any breach of the conditions governing the success of the experiment. Into one comprehensive collective failure to heed the terms of the covenant, the Bible conflates sexual licentiousness, idolatry, injustice to the poor, neglect of the agricultural laws and abounds in the most solemn warnings lest the land thereby become defiled, and conduce to the collapse of the social order and, ultimately, exile and dispersion.[60] 'You eat with the blood, you raise your eyes to your fetishes, and you shed blood – yet you expect to possess the land! You have relied on your sword, you have committed abominations, you have all defiled other men's wives – yet you expect to possess the land!' (Ezek.33:25–6). The typology is that of a breach of covenant between the vassal, Israel, and its sovereign, the God of Israel.[61]

There is a congruence here between retribution and the incapacity of man and nature to tolerate abuses of the laws. In this respect, matter shows itself to be anything but inert – as distinct from the inertness of 'wood and stone'. In the former case, this makes it impossible to posit any meaningful separation between the way in which nature has been determined and the will of its creator. 'Divine' punishment is understandable in naturalistic terms. Matter reacts violently, should the condition of its enjoyment be flouted. The land can no longer fulfil its function, and will 'spew out' the Israelites as it had formerly done to the Canaanites (Lev.18:28).

Incidentally, the protracted nature of this process ensures that later generations will suffer from the errors of their forebears. The postulate of a vengeful God arises from the need to disavow a purely human responsibility for disaster.

The experiment, indicated above, takes place in a divinely designated area, which, by virtue of this very fact of designation, becomes that area where earth and heaven meet in the guise of a *tabur* – navel.[62] In this respect the Temple at Jerusalem might bear comparison with the Kaaba in Mecca or the temple of the Pythian oracle at Delphi. The Mishnah of the second-third century CE maps out a schematised area of sanctity, centred on the Temple compound at Jerusalem. This area extends in concentric circles of decreasing sanctity over Jerusalem, walled cities, the Land of Israel, until it finally reaches other lands which lack all sanctity.[63]

This spatial dimension differentiates the Jewish 'centre' from others in that it also constitutes a zone of settlement and is no mere extra-territorial ideal. To put it consequentially, as a location in the 'real' world it will necessarily partake of all the vicissitudes and uncertainties and general 'untidiness', historical and other, that are inherent in such a world. This fragmentation is a source of prolonged and complex rabbinic debate.

Historical events impinge in such a way as to give rise to two distinct legal issues: the sanctity of the Temple Mount in Jerusalem and that of the Land. That sanctity originally inhered in both is unquestioned; that of the Temple derives from the *Shekhinah* whereas that of the Land from a divine choice.

The Temple Mount, it is said, constitutes an example of static, institutional sanctity as compared with the functional sanctity of a synagogue, say, where the functionality lies *in personam* rather than *in rem*.[64] Can territorial sanctity however, survive the new historical situation created by the Babylonian conquest and destruction of the Temple under Nebuchadnezzar in 586 BCE and again under Vespasian and Titus in 70 BCE, followed by Roman occupation of the Land – and the exile of the Jews? Do these political changes also entail the forfeiture of *kedushah*? Are Temple and Land still holy? To this crucial question, rabbinic jurists give no unanimous answer, from Talmudic times and after. R. Johanan and R. José b. Halafta held that the consecration undertaken by Ezra was valid for the future also and not merely for its time (TB Yeb.82a–b). This is later supported by R. Abraham ibn Daud.[65] One of the leading Tosafists, R. Baruch b. Isaac, argued however, that following the second exile, the sanctity of the Land was annulled but that of the Temple Mount remained in force.[66] R. Shimon b. Zemah agreed here in respect of the Land.[67] Maimonides also made a distinction between the enduring sanctity inherent in Jerusalem and the Temple Mount, and the variable sanctity of the Land.[68]

The debates involve such considerations as the permanent (or time-bound) validity of Solomon's consecration of the Temple; the renewal (or perhaps only confirmation) of this consecration under Ezra and Nehemiah when the Temple was rebuilt by the returning exiles from Babylon; whether this renewal (or confirmation) was also time-bound or enduring. So far as the Land is concerned, similar indeterminacy prevails as to its continuing holiness, especially as the exiles from Babylon did not reoccupy all the territory originally conquered by the Israelites under Joshua and his successors, so that those areas now left unoccupied could not be hallowed. This applied to Ashkelon in the south and Acco (Acre) in the north, parts of which were holy and parts not, but they did not, for this reason, cease to form part of the Land of Israel. Does conquest provide a stronger title to the Land than the proclamation of Cyrus? Are tithing and the priestly separations of produce still required in conditions of foreign occupation? The Temple offerings in the absence of the Temple? These (and other) questions must all be resolved.[69]

But amidst the conflicting views there is none which altogether rejects the conceivable possibility that the holiness of Temple and/or Land might have been annulled and therewith the performance of the commandments dependent on the Land.[70] To determine the reality of the situation is the function of rabbinical debate. In this respect also, the attribution of holiness – as in the case of the 'differentiated people' – creates a set of corresponding obligations.

Subsequent demographic change introduced further complexity; for example, the creation in Babylon of a species of quasi-holy areas outside the Land which become the location of a dense Jewish population after the destruction of the first Temple in 586 BCE. In the third century CE R. Judah (relying on Jer.27:22) held it a religious transgression 'to leave Babylon for the holy Land', then under Roman occupation; similarly, to quit Babylon for other countries was also wrong, by reason of its status as a centre of learning.[71]

At the other extreme, if outside the Land of Israel there were areas enjoying (for particular historical reasons) a quasi-sanctity, then inside the Land there were also areas such as Ashkelon that were considered to lie outside the Land, in regard to their exemption from the obligations to which they would normally have been liable (such as the tithe and the sabbatical year) even though they remained in the Land and were not considered as part of the territory of idolaters.[72] In the third century CE Rabbi Judah Ha'Nasi ('Judah the patriarch") exempted Beth Shean, Caesarea and Beth Guvrin from these obligations because these cities had a gentile majority and he wished to encourage Jewish settlement by removing from Jews a burden from which their gentile rivals were *ab initio* free. These exemptions did not apply however, to Tiberias and Sepphoris (and probably Lod) where Jews were already in a majority.[73] In sum, there was interplay between demography and the patriarch's urbanising policy on the one hand and, on the other, the remission of obligations incumbent on agriculture practised in the very Land to which those obligations applied.

I hope that this short sketch of a crucial location of holiness has helped to show that, even in this highly sensitive area, it is still possible to introduce the necessary 'rationalisation of the life world'. It is true that legal categories do not entirely conceal political motives but they do at least contribute to the creation of a form of discourse that seeks to control or eliminate such motives. The degree of success is necessarily debatable. Less uncertain, however, seems to me the value derived from the conception of holiness as a transient attribute of matter, susceptible to loss and renewal. This makes it all the more difficult for the putative idolater to locate his god in matter, or for *kedushah*, even in the weak sense, to be confused with any form of pantheism. No identification is permissible between the divine and matter. Once this has been characterised, in the contest with idolatry, as 'wood and stone', then a barrier has been established that permits matter to be utilised in a manner convenient to man. 'The unbearable indifference' of matter (Blumenberg) gives way to an engagement with matter free from emotional attachment and investment.

In the particular case of land, this attachment is all the more vulnerable to sentiment: first, obviously, because without land there is no sustenance; second, because without land the Covenant loses much of its applicability and to that extent cannot be served as God requires.

In the case of an ordinary 'utopia', location, being by definition non-existent, is of no moment. The Biblical challenge knows no evasion of this type and confronts Israel with its collective 'utopian' task amidst an inescapable reality of territory and variable hostility. But because the necessity for land is exigent, it is more than ever essential to condition the necessity lest this become perverted through idolisation, or land regarded as other than a 'utopian' instrument. This precisely is what is achieved through the conditions attendant on its occupation which *eo ipso* recalls to the Israelites and their descendants a thoroughly unnatural relationship and serves as a barrier lest they succumb to its worship. The holiness of the land is in fact synonymous with its differentiated status as a territory subject to a system of safeguards for which its Israelite occupiers are responsible before God. Their fate in relationship to the land requires the maintenance of a balance between this system and their natural inclinations. Here too the struggle against idolatry demands disengagement from matter, from 'the alien gods of the soil' (Dt.31:16), for which purpose matter must itself be disenchanted in order that it may re-emerge in a guise adapted to a 'holy', differentiated purpose.

3 Symbolism in Action

'For there is one God, and also one mediator between God and men, Christ Jesus, himself man, who sacrificed himself to win freedom for all mankind' (first letter of Paul to Timothy, 2:5). In the Jewish Apocrypha, the concept of mediation before God is also present; in the Book of Tobit, Raphael, one of 'the seven holy angels' in Jewish angelology, is said to 'bear upwards the prayers of the saints and (to) have access to the glory of the Holy One' (Tobit, 12:15; see also 3:16–17; 12:12).[1] The liturgical poetry of Eleazar Kalir used midrashic themes to the same effect. But many sages condemned these works and, on the whole, Jewish thinking overwhelmingly rejects the desirability, let alone the possibility, of mediation or of any mediator between man and God. R. Jacob Anatoli, in his discussion of the second commandment, held that it was forbidden to entreat the angels of mercy – 'this custom is not healthy, and your actions will bring you close (to God) not angels and not others like them; it is needful to disdain them that you should not accept them as a god'.[2] If even the angels may not serve as mediators, how much less so a man. It is the struggle against idolatry that governs this rejection, I hope to prove.

Direct communication with God is the ideal and here the paradigmatic model is that of Moses. In his (successful) attempt to assuage God's anger at the 'calf', he exhorts God: 'remember your servants Abraham, Isaac and Israel, how you swore to them by your self . . .' (Ex.32:13; cf. also Dt.9:27). When Moses is confronted by the daughters of Zelophehad, concerned for the female right of inheritance to tribal land, and their marriage portion, he is able to consult God directly (Nu.27:1–11). Another example: the psalmist's unmediated plea to God: 'do not remember against us our former iniquities' (Ps.79:8).

This relationship is reciprocal; the case *par excellence* of direct communication is established at Sinai. Here, because the Israelites saw 'voices', and no shape or form, when God addressed them, the medieval commentators dismissed the need for any mediation between God and man.[3] 'Face to face', God spoke to the Israelites (Dt.5:4). The philosophers make the same point.[4] Midrashic sources maintain that an unmediated approach conveyed to the Israelites the very text of the Sinaitic revelation;[5] that not only were the living Israelites present at Sinai but also the unborn souls of the future; that, from Sinai the prophets and sages of the future received their prophecy and wisdom.[6] The future prophet and/or sage must first have been present at Sinai. Certain Talmudic sages, and Maimonides later, therefore argue that whoever later defected from the message of Sinai, 'his ancestors did not stand at the foot of Mount Sinai'.[7]

This does no more than gloss a paradigmatic mode of communication between God and man. The Covenant establishes a relationship of reciprocity inherent in which must be the reality of mutual communication. If God has no need of intermediary in addressing the Israelites, must not also the contrary apply? In the same way as Israel is exhorted, without mediation, to remember and remind itself of the obligations it has undertaken, so too can God be similarly addressed and his obligations brought to mind.

Why must mediator or intermediary be eliminated? The answer is simple indeed: at the very least any such attempt necessarily leads to the petrification of the idea by converting text into mediatory matter. Conceptually speaking, there is all the difference in the world when a verbal signifier, such as the 'hand' of God of the Biblical text, is taken literally and translated into the 'hand' depicted on certain headstones in, for example, the Sephardi cemetery in Hamburg.[8] When this happens an entity has come into existence which falsifies the intent of the text. The 'hand' of God has purportedly been reproduced in some inert material, the result of which is, so to speak, to reduce God to that same material. The fabrication presupposes that, between God and stone, say, there is at least enough similarity that the latter can reproduce the former. To the rabbis of the Hellenistic period, Lieberman points out, 'symbols are the same idols as mere fetishes. Although the Rabbis were not so naive as to think their heathen contemporaries to be mere fetishists, this distinction did not in their eyes lessen the idolatrous character of their worship'.[9]

Rabbi after rabbi teaches that the attempt to mediate between man and God by way of material symbol is the root cause of idolatry. It is brought under a twofold attack, which is in fact one. First, as Rosenzweig argued, God's revelation and covenant destroy man's self-created religion of 'projective' symbolism. This is one aspect of God's hostility to religion which has required the establishment of God's own 'anti-religion'.[10] Second, although the symbol claims to take the role of intermediary between man and God, it in fact serves to conceal the reality with which it purports to communicate. It becomes, in effect, a *terminus ad quem* while proclaiming itself a *terminus a quo*. It is still, after all, the work of man and made of wood and stone. In this regard the symbol as intermediary is most appropriately understood as a factor of disturbance taken to a destructive extreme. It extends the disturbance generated by, for example, an illuminated prayerbook (see below Chapter 5), to the point where all communication with the divine is conclusively arrested.

Obviously this view is not universal. Invoking this or that angel as an intercessory instrument has been mentioned already; and pilgrimages to invoke the spirits of departed sages share in the same aspiration. But against such activities stands a broad rabbinic consensus where spokesmen of varying schools of rabbinic thought find common ground. R. Moses Isserles (Cracow, sixteenth century) referring to Maimonides (whose arguments are discussed separately below) maintains that 'through a man's making of an intermediary between himself and God, the *Torah* will altogether collapse, for this is afterwards the occasion for disbelief in the Lord, (the man) saying that nothing is there but only the intermediary and through this idolatry proliferated in the world'.[11] R. Isserles's contemporary in Prague, R. Judah Loew b. Bezalel (the 'Maharal'), took his stand on Deuteronomy 4:12 ('You heard the sound of words but saw no form . . .') and argued on this basis that the maker of a form to God erred twice: first, the very making of the form, 'even if the maker intends to serve God alone, eventually becomes an intermediary between himself and God and anything that is an intermediary between man and Him whom he serves is absolute idolatry'; the second error is the attempt to make

a form 'to Him who has no form'.[12] In the calf 'which will
go before us' (Ex.32:1) R. Naḥman of Braslav (Ukraine,
eighteenth–nineteenth century) saw the quintessence of an
intermediary: the error of the Israelites was to make 'a cause
of an intermediary between themselves and God, i.e. they
believe in God but they believe also in the intermediary . . .
(but) God is the cause of all causes and the occasion of all
occasions and there is no call for (intermediary) cause'.[13]

What is the link between the attempt at a mediatory approach to God and the collapse into idolatry? Why, in other
words, can the supposedly mediatory entity never be or
become anything but an idol? Much of the answer is already
contained in the Biblical standpoint concerning the limited
nature of matter as no more than 'wood and stone' and
which is therefore inherently incapable of pointing beyond
itself (see Chapter 1). To suppose otherwise would be to
succumb to mythopoeic fantasy. This is the thrust of Rashi's
comment to Leviticus 19:4, now demanding a second look:
'do not you turn to idols and do not make for yourselves
molten gods; I am the Lord your God'. Rashi draws on the
distinction here between 'idol' and 'god': the first is a nothing,
a non-entity, but those who 'turn to them', meaning 'to
worship them', eventually look on those 'idols' as 'gods'. It
is not too remote to see in this comment a warning at the
capacity of the imagination to work on reality (and to transform it into a repository of purely self-centred, human aspirations). The same passage is understood by R. Hanin to
mean: 'do not turn to that which is conceived in your minds'
(TB Shab.149a).

The process whereby an intended mediatory entity between
man and God is created and then positively conduces to
idolatry is presented by Maimonides. His argument draws
on the mind's weakness in succumbing to the lure of imagery as a result of the malaise experienced in the absence
of imagery; thus the imagery of Biblical language depicting
an anthropomorphic God must not be taken *au pied de la
lettre* but as a form of accommodation and a concession to
'the understanding of mankind who can only know bodies
and the *Torah* speaks in the language of men'.[14] So far did
Maimonides go as to accuse of heresy those who conceived
of God as corporeal and with a shape.[15]

But what is permissible as a concession to the masses – even if only on condition that they are brought to appreciate that the language of the text is no more than metaphorical and symbolical – must be rejected without qualification so soon as symbolism takes the form of some material entity.

To become subject to this process it is not necessary to be an idolater *ab initio.* The argument is all the stronger for the manner in which even a monotheist can degenerate into an idolater and fall victim to alienation. Maimonides readily accepts that idolatry is not necessarily correlative with fetishism. 'The reason why idols are called images', he writes in the first chapter of the Guide, 'lies in the fact that what was sought in them was the notion that was deemed to subsist in them, and not their shape and configuration'. He enlarges on this later:

'Whoever performs idolatrous worship does not do it on the assumption that there is no deity except the idol. In fact no human being of the past has ever imagined on any day, and no human being of the future will ever imagine, that the form that he fashions either from cast metal or from stone and wood has created and governs the heavens and the earth. Rather is it worshipped in respect of its being an image of a thing that is an intermediary between ourselves and God'.[16]

Having regard to this concession to the idolater's belief in the possibility of 'an intermediary', Maimonides concentrates his analysis on the etiology of this belief and its consequence. His model situation is drawn from the manner whereby symbolisation in synecdochal relationship to God acts as a primary incitement to idolatry. The first men were not idolaters but in the days of Enosh their descendants succumbed: 'mankind made a great error ... and the sages of that generation said that because God had created these stars and planets to direct the world ... they are worthy to be praised and glorified and to be apportioned honour. And it is the will of God to magnify and honour those who magnify and honour Him. And when this came to their mind they began to build temples to the stars, their purpose being to obtain the favour of the Creator. This is the very

root of idolatry'. From this root grows a second stage towards absolute idolatry, as and when the temples came to
house figures of the stars and so on, constructed as objects
of worship, and the idea of God is lost sight of.[17] At this
point the temple and its figures have changed their relationship to the worshipper to the extent of obscuring the
superior reality in the mind of that worshipper, so that the
intent ideally directed at reality is now stultified by the man-
made objects. A division and distortion of intent has taken
place, wholly different from the mere disturbance of intent
occasioned by the presence of an image, and the image has
served to create an entirely new 'God', whom the worshipper mistakenly supposes he can serve through an image and
whom an image can mediate.

To the idolater obviously this is not the case. He is as
convinced as ever that the object of his worship remains
God. But this conviction is a delusion in that between himself and God this worshipper has effectively erected a barrier, which is tantamount to idolatry. This worshipper has
made himself guilty of the fifth type of heresy in the list
drawn up by Maimonides: if he is to serve God he also requires the presence of an intermediary between himself and
the creator.

No ill-will is involved, merely a conceptual error. *Per se,*
the construction of the temples in Maimonides's paradigm,
like that of the 'calf' later, incurs no intrinsic prohibition.
The error consists rather in seeing these artifacts as media
of communication and therefore as warranting worship, in
the illusion that this conforms to God's will. Maimonides
quotes Jeremiah (Jer.10:7–8) to make the point that 'the
wise men of the nations know that You alone are God: their
error and folly consists in supposing that this empty worship is Your desire'.[18]

It follows from this error – and indeed as Maimonides's
fivefold categorisation of heretics also makes clear – that
between a person who accepts the existence of God, but
who worships God through some intermediary and the person who is *tout court* an idolater, there is in substance no
difference.[19] The error equates the sincere worshipper of
God, who in the spirit of his sincerity erects, as in the model,
a temple to honour God, with the idolater who worships his

wooden idol for the sake of 'the notion that is deemed to subsist in it'. In both cases it is the presence of an intermediate object that is the precondition no less than the criterion of idolatrous worship. It is the intermediate entity that creates idolatry, not the reverse. Rabbinic thought in general and Maimonides in particular hold that it is impossible for the worshipper to distinguish between his intended worship of God and the entity that he looks on merely as a vehicle of his worship but which effectively becomes the object of his worship, even if it is not so at the outset.

In this conversion of what is initially an innocent object into an entity deserving of nothing but the utmost reprobation it is possible to see the working of the imagination. At one point in his Guide this is identified by Maimonides with 'the evil instinct'.[20] Its *modus operandi* is arbitrary and uncontrolled: the imagination

> ... apprehends only that which is individual and composite as a whole, as it is apprehended by the senses; or compounds things that in their existence are separate, combining one with another ... Thus, someone using his imagination imagines a human individual having a horse's head and wings and so on. This is what is called a thing invented and false, for nothing existent corresponds to it at all. In its apprehension, imagination is in no way able to hold aloof from matter, even if it turns a form into the extreme of abstraction. For this reason there can be no critical examination in the imagination.[21]

Now, if imagination can turn a form into 'the extreme of abstraction', it also enjoys the freedom to turn an abstraction into a form; and this is precisely what has happened in the days of Enosh, according to tradition. Whether or not the imagination has in effect operated as described by Maimonides is immaterial; the fact is that through its working an idea/abstraction has allegedly been given tangible form.

Folklore yields many cautionary examples of the unwelcome consequences to be expected when the imagination is led to locate spirit in a material object. No sooner has man acted in this way than his creation turns against him. Hence the Golem that runs wild, Frankenstein, Pygmalion, the refractory creation of Goethe's sorcerer's apprentice.

The intellectual tradition that separates the creations of the imagination from any notion of their relation to the real is seemingly maintained in the work of Hermann Cohen. This is the thrust of his argument, apparently directed against contemporary advocates of *Einfühlung*, such as Dilthey: 'we must neither direct our feeling into an object (*unser Gefühl auf einen Gegenstand . . . hineinfühlen*) whether of nature or of art, nor must the object in its dual significance transplant in us or even arouse in us a feeling'. *Einfühlung* of this sort must fail, Cohen asserts, because 'the animation of a dead material with human spirit and human soul does not use an already existing feeling; it is the primordial product of feeling'.[22] In other words, Cohen denies the existence of a capacity that would locate in matter any feeling; rather, the reverse holds good, in that matter itself can produce a feeling that is, however, illegitimate. Thus, if I have understood Cohen correctly, he shares with Maimonides a conviction of the danger inherent in the actions whether of imagination or *Einfühlung*, that seeks to communicate with matter or to receive from matter any communication. This would then be to strengthen the case against the intermediate entity.

The case is further strengthened by the fact that a figurative symbol, because it has a wider range of reference than a mimetic idol, is therefore more dangerous: the latter's range of reference is limited to its inherent confines whereas a symbol can 'show' the impossible, the invisible, the nonexistent.

Further: the presence of a symbol flouts a Jewish aversion to the attribute of holiness save for certain very limited situations (see Chapter 2). Consider the consequences when a piece of reality is used as a symbol for God. Tillich argues, reasonably enough, that 'the realm of reality from which it is taken, is, so to speak, elevated into the realm of the holy. It no longer is secular. It is theonomous'.[23] This means that the entity in question comes in some sense to partake of the divine, which would accordingly contribute to the proliferation of holiness and multiply enchantment and become liable to be confused with God.[24] But in this notion Jewish thinking will discern the lure of magic.[25]

In the last resort, if matter is regarded as inert, 'wood and stone', refractory to human interest, how can any communicative symbol-making activity at all be conceivable?

Obviously this does not inhibit symbolism conveyed by verbal means (properly understood, Maimonides would emphasise) but anything else is regarded with quasi-universal dismay. Hermann Cohen writes: 'monotheism makes no concessions to the plastic arts, for thereby the one God would be endangered, and no symbolism must threaten Him'.[26]

All these considerations militate against any manifestations of symbolism because, although a symbol may perform a large number of functions, primary amongst them is its supposed capacity to bring together two entities, one seen and one unseen. It serves as a means to relate the first to the second. As I try to show later, Jewish thought and practice do indeed allow for manifestations of symbolism but these have to take account of the rejection of the mediating concept and this applies to mediation through verbal no less than material means, and all the more so if symbolism, as is normally the case, inheres in the relationship of the profane with the holy or actually structures the holy.[27]

None of this must suggest that material and figurative symbols are not to be found present in Jewish public life. In his magisterial work on Jewish symbols in the Greco-roman period, Goodenough was able to identify in synagogues, catacombs, and so on certain major examples: *menorah* (lampstand), *lulav, etrog*, 'flask', ram's horn, representations of the *Torah* shrine – all of which had a part in the ritual of Temple and synagogue. Frequently, also, pagan symbols flanked the Jewish.[28] It may however be the case that later, in the seventh century, a movement challenging these types of imagery developed, leading to their erasure.[29] In the fifteenth/sixteenth century an entirely new symbol came to the fore – the two Tablets of the Law – decorating the doors of the Ark in the synagogues of Urbino, Livorno and Sermide, for example.[30] But it does not seem that these symbols claim any ontological significance – rather, the likelihood is that they are no more than adornments or perhaps means of identification, in the manner in which scalpels on the headstones of the graves of physicians from the Prague ghetto recall and identify the profession of the deceased. There is also the symbol as reminder, as in the custom of binding a hair from a calf (or cow, or ox) into the phylacteries as a warning to remember the sin of 'the calf'.[31]

The overwhelming contrast is with those examples of material symbolism in ritual which do indeed convey a message, for example: certain foods and fruits, a ram's horn, the flame of a candle, an overflowing beaker of wine.[32] Here no special problem arises; that an overflowing beaker of wine should stand for a sense of plenitude and wellbeing is a clear enough case of metaphor; that a man's first act, following the cessation of activity during the Sabbath, should be the kindling of a flame again calls for no special interpretation, all the less so as the ritual may only be performed at nightfall. Symbolic rituals limited to this range of activity are thoroughly in conformity with what has been termed an attitude towards symbols that 'has a distinctly positivistic air', rejects identity 'between the elements of theoretical constructs and their objects' and accepts 'relationships as the sole aim of such constructs'.[33]

But this permissiveness must be brought to a halt so soon as any material representation of God is sought; and this barrier would operate every whit as firmly in the case of those teachers who hold to an anthropomorphic God as in the case of those other teachers who utterly reject this notion.[34] Here, once again, the barrier between what is verbally acceptable and what is materially unacceptable must not be transgressed; and this prohibition would equally strongly apply to any Maimonidean attempt to re-interpret Biblical anthropomorphism into the discourse of metaphor and thus remove its power to befuddle the intellect, in the view of Maimonides.

Therefore, if any material entity is to symbolise God, it must be of such a nature as both to disguise and reveal this relationship. Stern quotes the case of the shank-bone on the *Seder* plate during the Passover celebration. At three combined levels – denotation, exemplification and expression – the shank-bone operates as a symbol. This entity functions symbolically as the might of God's 'outstretched arm' with which Israel is redeemed and the Egyptians punished (Dt.16:8). The verse mediates a material symbol creating 'a chain of reference (extending) here from the symbolic object to an exemplified feature, in turn to a scriptural use of the term for that feature, finally to the metaphorical denotation of the term in its scriptural context'; and at this point, a chicken's neck, now that the chain of reference has been established, can replace the shank-bone, and even be designated as such, Stern notes; so that the exemplifying object need no longer possess the feature it exemplifies, thereby further distancing the symbol from the symbolised.[35] No sooner is the attempt at literal resemblance invalidated, then there seems to be no discernible limit to the mode whereby God's 'outstretched arm' can be visually referred to. Goodman argues that resemblance is unnecessary to reference: 'almost anything may stand for almost anything else'. What is then achieved is denotation which is 'independent of resemblance'.[36] The consequence would in the present instance be all the more welcome in weakening the association between a literal reading of the text and representation by denotation.

This procedure, whereby the symbol is progressively dematerialised and alienated from the symbolised, lends itself as easily to the exposition of legal as of ritual concepts. Steinsalz gives by way of example the expression, 'the blow of a hammer'. This connotes, in Jewish legal discourse, the completion of a task, an activity that is normally forbidden on the Sabbath. But completion can take place in a variety of contexts which means that the same phrase, 'the blow of a hammer', can also connote 'sewing a collar on a garment'. This makes the 'hammer' into a 'needle' and eventually into an abstraction with a multitude of specific, concrete applications. It becomes an instrumental symbol with functionally equivalent applications.[37]

The same process of dematerialisation eventually ensures that the damage caused by a goring ox will be subsumed under the same heading of 'horn' as that caused by a bite from a dog. In effect, the symbol 'horn' becomes an umbrella-concept.

The same effect is achieved through reflection on the sounding of the *shofar* – normally a ram's horn – during, for example, the liturgy for the New Year. The horn can be dematerialised into an instrument having a multiplicity of realistic yet symbolic referents. It can be regarded, on this

Day of Judgement, as summoning up a relationship of judge and defendant between God and man; or as a reminder of the binding of Isaac and thus of Abraham, first of the patriarchs; or as a microcosmic reminder of the macrocosmic ram's horn sounded at Sinai, creating a people; or as the blast that will bring on the messianic era (Is.27:13). The ram's horn, throughout the whole of Jewish history, resounds not as a material symbol of that history but as a polysemic instrument of evocation which is also part of the very history it evokes; evocative perhaps of both beginning and end, for the horn of the ram caught in the thicket at Mount Moriah is said to be the same horn that will usher in the messiah.[38]

The symbol that is both material and immaterial attains its apogee in both respects when it is wholly annulled and at the same time brought to perfection. This state is synonymous with the human imitation of the divine – to be more specific, it is synonymous with man's performance of the commandments. But this is tantamount to the elimination of the symbol, for now nothing separates God from man in regard to their aspirations (not of course in other respects): this connotes a 'cleaving' to God (*devekut*, in the language of the Jewish mystics). This is dependent on understanding God's self-affirmation ('I am who I am', Ex.3:14) as an affirmation that God's existence precedes his essence and therefore, that although to talk of God's actions is 'equivocal' (in the Maimonidean sense), it is nevertheless meaningful to demand of man that he assimilate his actions to those of God in respect of loving-kindness, righteousness and judgement, in the terms formulated by Maimonides.[39]

But the absolute pre-condition for this assimilation of human action to the divine – this *imitatio dei* – is relief from intermediary, mediator or figurative symbol – no 'screen' (Rosenzweig) must obscure God from man. Cassirer writes:

> ... in the prophetic monotheistic religion, as religious thought and feeling are freed from the sphere of mere things, the reciprocal relationship between the I and God becomes purer and more energetic. Liberation from the image and its objectivity has no other aim than to place this relation in the sharpest relief ... the more the objective

world recedes, the less it appears a sufficient and adequate expression of the divine and the more clearly a new mode of formation comes to the fore, the formation of will and action'.[40]

But if, in the process of the unmediated cleaving to God, the symbol disappears, in the agent's performance of the actions dictated by God it reappears. This is consonant with man as the 'icon of God' and the only way in which God can legitimately be represented. In the *imitatio dei* man becomes his own symbol.

This theory of symbolism, elaborated not through signs, written or otherwise depicted, but through specified forms of action, characterises the outlook of three modern Jewish philosophers – Moses Mendelssohn, S. R. Hirsch and Hermann Cohen. Why we should have to wait so long for their theory to emerge and that it should then be confined to a limited Germanophone area is not easily understood (though it is clearly *in potentia* centuries earlier, for example in Jacob Anatoli's arguments that it is man's actions that bring him close to God – see page 53 above). To hazard an explanation: the theory may constitute some sort of response to contemporary politics, for it is in the unlikely context of a plea for the admission of Jews to the European polity through the grant of equal rights that Mendelssohn presents his argument. The link between the political claim and the linguistic presentation is formed from Mendelssohn's concern to understand Judaism as a religion free from dogma, articles of faith, and so on and therefore all the better fitted to enter the secular, religiously-uncommitted European state that Mendelssohn looked forward to.[41] But apart from the particular historical context it is also true that there is a connection with Mendelssohn's aesthetic where it is maintained that certain aspects of the sublime (power, genius, virtue) can only be brought to the senses (that is, symbolised) through their rendering in the language of poetry or verbal discourse.[42]

Mendelssohn identifies three means whereby the 'abstract ideas' of religion have been inculcated: first, through images and hieroglyphs; second, through alphabetic script; third, through the actions enjoined by the ceremonial law – by which he means the corpus of the *Torah*. Mendelssohn dismisses the first because, although convenient and an advance towards abstraction, the hieroglyphs also offered occasion for regression to fetishisation and the signs might be seen 'not as mere signs, but believed ... to be the things themselves'. Mendelssohn hazarded the hypothesis that 'the need for written characters might be the first cause of idolatry'. He dismisses also the second on the grounds that an alphabetical script confines ideas, laws, convictions, and so on to 'rigid forms' and thus distorts them; further, and particularly so, Mendelssohn argued, since the invention of the printing press, the script that is alphabetic has alienated men from each other. Writing has taken the place of contact between teacher and pupil, preacher and audience, man and nature: 'every thing is dead letter; the spirit of living conversation has vanished ... hence it has come to pass that man has almost lost his value for his fellow man'.[43] But in former times at least – and this is Mendelssohn's more important point in the present context – the human intercourse demanded of teacher and pupil had 'removed from all imagery' the enunciation of those truths necessary for 'the felicity of the nation' and connected them with 'actions and practices, and these were to serve them in place of signs, without which they (i.e. "the truths") cannot be preserved ... in everything a youth saw being done ... he found occasion ... to follow an older and wiser man and to seek the instruction which his master considered him capable of absorbing and prepared to receive'.[44]

To sum up: truths are conveyed through imageless 'actions and practices', in the context of teacher and pupil. Those truths denominated 'the ceremonial law', will lend themselves to decipherment as a symbolic system. The form of specified action serves as a sign that is identical with the teaching it inculcates, thereby removing any disjunction between action and teaching and leading to the elimination of the image as symbol in favour of action as symbol.[45]

'Rabbi Jacob said: he who is walking by the way and rehearses what he has learned and interrupts his rehearsing to say, how fine is that tree, how fine is that field, scripture regards such a man as if he were guilty against himself' (Pirkei Avot, III, 9). In his commentary to Psalm 72:16, Samson

Raphael Hirsch quotes this otherwise unknown 'Rabbi Jacob' and adds: 'Such a man shows how much he lacks in sense and understanding for the incomparably higher beauty which acquires shape in the human life constructed from the divine law'.[46] This passage from Hirsch's commentary manifests his commitment to a primary understanding of the *Torah* in practical, moral and human terms whereby the laws 'aim to impress the stamp of the morally good and beautiful on all human affairs'. Their content and concern is not 'the supra-worldly and the life beyond, far rather is it the whole of this-world's life in its rich diversity':[47] Hirsch eschewed speculation and theology in his deliberate emphasis not on belief but on action.[48] That man chastised by 'Rabbi Jacob', who interrupted his teaching in order to admire a tree, is precisely the man who is oblivious to the call to act.

Hirsch describes his own work as 'an attempt to translate into words the symbolical observances which you perform in obedience to the command of your God'.[49]

The Sabbath, for example, 'the first day on which God withdrew from active creation to invisible guidance of the universe and on which the earth was laid open for man's government, thus became the symbol of man's appointment by God; symbol of God's rule and man's destiny'. The offerings of two loaves and two lambs required on the Festival of Weeks (Shavuot/Pentecost) as part of the Temple service, are understood by Hirsch as 'symbolic of expressing the lesson that independence and happiness for Israel can ripen only on the tree of the Torah'; circumcision becomes 'a symbol of holiness', signifying that the body does not belong to the individual but to God to whose purposes it must be dedicated.[50]

This symbolic language makes no claim to communicate new truths, but it is empowered to yield 'a more profound and lasting impression of known, old truths'.[51] The advantage of a non-verbal symbol – and Hirsch mentions the Day of Atonement, the sanctification of the New Moon, the New Year – is that 'they all express ideas but not split up, like thoughts expressed in words; but in a unit like the thought itself, like the determination which it should beget; a unit therefore in its summons to the soul, through the symbolic act. Thereby also the expression of a totality permeated by

a *single* thought and inspired by a *single* resolve'.[52] Hirsch
follows Mendelssohn by virtue of the importance he also
attributes to 'the living word and the communal intercourse
of many fellow-students'.[53]

These few examples of Hirsch's symbolic understanding
of the *Torah* reconcile moral and rational demands with God's
purpose for man. What is crucially important is that the
symbolism, however fanciful at times, originates within the
ambit of prescribed actions. There is no difficulty in saying
that the symbols in question are actions as much as the
actions are symbols. It might be argued however, that in
that case, and since the symbols, as Hirsch admits, communicate no fresh truths, the whole symbolic apparatus is of no
importance at all, except as a means to enhance the understanding of action. But insofar as Hirsch introduces no division – which he certainly does not – between the
commandment and its symbolic understanding, then the
former remains intact as a mode of action. Even a symbolic
act remains an act.

Hermann Cohen's approach to the *Problematik* of the symbol
is best grasped, it seems to me, in terms of his attempt to
create an understanding of the symbol consistent with the
thoroughgoing denial that the knowledge of God is symbolic and that any symbolism can be mediated through matter.
'The Jew engages in no symbolism with his one God';[54] and,
'pantheism is symbolism'.[55] I recall, also, Cohen's dictum:
no symbolism must threaten Him' (page 61).

In contrast to many of his Biblical and rabbinic predecessors, God, as envisaged by Cohen, is an ideal construct, absolutely impervious to, and distinct from, any material
reference. Any purported symbolisation of God that would,
as it were, reduce God to one or other material manifestation of the world in general, is absolutely and on principle
rejected.

In this setting God is understood by Cohen as a 'model'
(*Urbild*) for the morality of man and as a source of laws
that have as their purpose 'the education and sanctification
of man' The laws are man-directed, concerned with man's
morality and not his felicity/blessedness (*Seligkeit*).[56] Further,
they are symbols whereby the 'model' mediates itself to man.
Here there is a type of symbolism that is not material and

therefore not threatening, as would necessarily be any plastic symbol.

Cohen could now operate with a conception of symbolism as a hermeneutical principle and in this light expound the bearing of certain key institutions and their defining laws. In his essay on 'the inner connections of Kantian philosophy to Judaism', Cohen sees in the institution of the Sabbath, for example, a symbol of Pentateuchal social legislation in two respects: first, that man constitutes a purpose in himself and is not 'a cog in the mechanism of culture'; second, the Sabbath symbolises the idea of human equality and, by the same token, of mutual love: for Cohen points out that the Pentateuchal text (Dt.5:14) uses the same term for 'as you' (*kmokha*) when it demands Sabbath rest, as it does when it elsewhere demands 'and you shall love your neighbour (because he is a man) as you' (again, *kmokha*).[57]

Cohen goes further in his symbolical understanding of the Sabbath when he makes it 'the symbol of the highest social morality', referring to Isaiah, 'who keeps the Sabbath and does not profane it, and keeps his hand from doing any evil' (Is.56:2) and the Sabbath, Cohen comments, is co-dependent with the whole corpus of the socio-agrarian Sabbath laws, culminating in the jubilee year.[58] In a similar frame of understanding, the New Year and the Day of Atonement become, respectively, symbols of divine judgement and of temporality.[59] Cohen also associated his thinking with what he sees as the prophets' symbolical understanding of the messiah whom Cohen presents as the ideal of the future· and its realisation of the ethical ideal.[60] In this one symbol Cohen has packed an individual, the pursuit of an ideal and an eventual historical, this-worldly resolution of the social problems besetting mankind, primarily those of poverty. The messiah as symbol becomes a powerful blend of idea and challenge.

At this point, it seems to me, Cohen must negotiate a very narrow path that separates the symbolism of action mediated through laws that aim to secure human wellbeing from the notion of God as an *Urbild* of moral teaching to which man must seek to approximate. Is there not mimesis here? This difficulty is compounded by Cohen's doctrine of the 'correlation' of God and man.[61] It could be argued,

moreover, that in both cases the very laws, even when interpreted in terms of action, themselves require a multitude
of material objects which would thereby frustrate the terms
of the immaterial-symbolic exposition. But this objection could
be met by reference to the 'Steinsalz hammer' or the polysemic ram's horn (see pages 63–4) which lose their refractory physical character when exposed to a multiplicity of
interpretations, applications and references. A hammer that
can become a needle is no ordinary hammer; a shank-bone
that can become a chicken's neck is no ordinary shank-bone,
is not, in fact, a shank-bone at all. Only as if it were a symbol of God's 'outstretched arm' does it exist; that is to say
it forfeits its material qualities and emerges as a dematerialised
symbol that is part of the very phenomenon that it symbolises. The ram's horn on the New Year, say, likewise rejoins
the Sabbath as a statement that is also part of the very proposition it asserts.

In his own particular way Cohen – far more elaborately
so than Mendelssohn – espouses an identification of action
with symbol. Action, in the performance of the laws, at least
as Cohen understands them, removes any threat of material
or mimetic symbolism and makes possible the correlation
of God and man through spirit, 'the mediating concept
between God and man'.[62] This certainly allows no room for
physical symbolism of any sort. The problem is whether Cohen
does not take his justified rejection of mimesis too far. Consider, for example, the respective interpretations by Cohen
and Maimonides of the verse: 'You shall be holy, for I am
holy, the Eternal, your God' (Lev.19:2). To the former this
manifests the God-man correlation 'and with that mythology and polytheism cease';[63] but to Maimonides this verse is
a summons to man to become like God, so far as he is able
to, 'which means that we should make our actions like unto
His'.[64] In practice perhaps, the difference may not be all
that great for Cohen also conceives of God as the 'ideal'
fount of moral teaching. To see the laws as symbols of that
teaching requires the same emphasis on the preservation of
their source from any mimetic or material intrusion and
hence on the unmediated nature of symbol as human action. For Cohen, as for Hirsch earlier, the symbol does not
take the place of the particular law but embodies the law;

and the action enjoined by the law is the symbolic performance of that law.

In recent decades, through the instrumentality of Zionism and the state of Israel, a new system of symbols has
materialised: a national flag, anthem, with attendant badges,
emblems, uniforms, monuments, and so on.[65] This is in
keeping with the perception of Herzl, the founder of political Zionism, that to 'think in images' was essential, people
being largely moved by 'imponderables . . . dreams, songs,
fantasies, black-red-gold ribbons'.[66] 'If we desire to lead many
men, we must raise a symbol above their heads', Herzl re-
marked, in reference to a proposed national flag.[67] This is
an encouragement to political aestheticisation. In the event,
the state of Israel has taken the Shield of David ('Magen
David') as a component of its flag, together with the seven-
branched lampstand/candelabrum (*Menorah*) of the Temple. The Zionist-socialist movement has also sometimes
adopted religious symbols of the past, subject to appropriate ideological adjustment.[68] Only in the presentation of war
memorials and memorial sites, the vast majority of which –
and there are about a thousand in Israel, approximately one
for every sixteen fallen soldiers – lack 'any kind of aggress-
iveness, glorification of the nation or hero- worship', is there
deviation from the standard model.[69]

But if these symbols are to be taken as commensurate
with those discussed earlier (for example, the Sabbath) they
must also be submitted to the same test. Can the Sabbath
or even a stylised depiction of the Decalogue be understood
as a symbol in the same sense as, say, a national flag?

There are in fact all sorts of reasons why any equivalence
is doubtfully possible. It is true of course that a Jewish form
of governance traditionally requires the co-operation of the
'three crowns', as recently expounded by Stuart Cohen:
the crown of the *Torah*, the crown of the priesthood and
the crown of the monarchy;[70] and each 'crown' has had its
own system of symbols, which do, at times, anticipate later
models e.g. 'the monumental architecture' erected during
the reigns of David and Solomon: the fortifications at
Megiddo, Hazor and Gezar, symbolising the grandeur of the
monarchy and conveying also a message of royal power, per-
manence and stability, to say nothing of the role of the

Solomonic temple at Jerusalem in 'the ideological justification of the State'.[71]

But the question remains and can be formulated in these
terms: can the present State of Israel claim a status such as
would validate its symbols in the terms indicated earlier?
Obviously, this question has provoked a multitude of diverse
responses, that cover every conceivable judgement. In practice, a *modus vivendi* amongst contending viewpoints has more
or less been reached – even though it may be uneasily in
need of continual adjustment – but precisely here at the
intellectual level judgements divide most radically. Does, for
example, the state connote 'the beginning of redemption'
– in the traditional phrase – or is its very existence a blasphemy? Both views, qualified by varying nuances, are held
by religious teachers.[72]

Into this contentious debate I have no intention of ven-
turing, but will limit myself to a qualified avowal of sympathy for the judgement of Isaiah Leibowitz who, on Israel
independence day, displays the national flag but by whom
an absolute distinction between Zionism and Judaism is
maintained; to whom the state exists instrumentally as 'a
framework for the national independence of the Jewish
people' (who are) 'fed up with being ruled by *goyim*' (Heb.,
other peoples).[73]

This particular judgement now makes it possible to differentiate, in terms of function, between those symbols the
reference-point of which is an institution that, whilst it may
be this-worldly and an agency of human society, yet intends
the betterment of that society, and those symbols the intent
of which is directed towards the status quo. The contrast is
between the Sabbath, say, as a symbol, the performance of
which inculcates certain values and the national flag as a
symbolic medium for, and paramount component of, the
inculcation of respect in the relationship of the national to
his nation-state.[74]

But this is no more than the consolidation of an existing
relationship or, at least, the initiation of a relationship to
the existent. It is certainly the case that a man who salutes
his flag or, in an extreme case, is prepared to be killed in
the defence of his flag, does not believe, as Durkheim puts
it, 'that he sacrifices himself for a bit of cloth'. He is doing

so because even a fragment of the flag and what it represents – the fatherland – are 'sacred in the same way and to the same degree'.[75] But this particular self-sacrifice is socially-bound and constructed and no more than an attribute of the social *status quo*.[76] The symbol in this case serves to perpetuate a situation, to comfort the believer and to reconcile him to a readiness to accept those deprivations of life, freedom and property, prophetically announced in the book of Samuel (1 Sam.8:11 ff). This distinctiveness of function differentiates the symbols of civil religion from such symbols as the Sabbath, the performance of which precisely intends to set man against nature and question the *status quo*.

In his exposition of Jewish symbolism, Finkelstein adumbrates the notion of an '"efficient" symbol, in that it not only connotes the idea, it also is capable of imbuing one with it'.[77] This presupposes that the 'idea' of the symbol is already known and now of course raises the question of motive or intention. It is not to denigrate the importance of intention to maintain however, that the executor of a symbolic action (for example, observing the Sabbath) is, irrespective of his intention, also participating in a procedure that, however alien it may perhaps be to his intention at the outset, comprises an intention of its own which will be manifest in the Sabbath observer's performative action. To that extent, even though the participant/executor is taking on an intention that is perhaps alien to his own, it is one to which he cannot be wholly insensitive;[78] and in such a case, the performer, however mutinously intentioned initially, will, rabbinic psychology maintains, in time succumb to the beneficent influence of his actions. The *Sefer Ha-Ḥinukh* (Book of Training) of the thirteenth century gives a representative statement of the argument:

.... know that man is affected in accordance with his actions, and his heart and all his thoughts always (follow) after the deeds with which he concerns himself whether for good or evil, and even a man of absolute evil in his heart, whose every instinct in his heart is all the day for evil, if his spirit is aroused and he exerts himself and concerns himself constantly with the *Torah* and the commandments – even though not for the sake of heaven –

he will at once incline towards good and by the force of his acts will kill his evil instinct, for hearts are drawn after acts.[79]

If this mode of behaviourist psychology is wholly to succeed in its pedagogic task, it is clearly preferable that the subject should be cognisant of the relevance of his actions to their origin and purpose, that is, that theory and practice should coincide. That is why, for example, R. Hanina could maintain: a person 'who is commanded and fulfils (the command) is greater than the person who fulfils it without having been commanded' (TB Kid.31a). It is not so much the case that moral autonomy is sacrificed to a heteronomous authority, as Kant would argue, but rather that the person who acts in obedience to the authority participates in a scheme of values that, whether or not he accepts those values, will inevitably force themselves on his consciousness, giving to his action a dimension that the autonomy of the individual moral will would be unable to furnish. A person can punctiliously and conscientiously fulfil, for example, all the prescriptions of Sabbath observance; but if it is only of his own volition that he does so, then he cannot in fact be performing a commandment at all. I do not think that this is a tautology because, outside a cosmic dimension that embraces the Sabbath, *inter alia*, as a recurrent recall of the creation, the commandment has no existence; not to mention the fact that to exclude God's participation in the formation and execution of human volition is to deprive the commandment of its *raison d'être*. The distinction made by R. Hanina presupposes a situation in which a decision made by man can be equated with one made by God. Since this is not possible the two acts are utterly different. But it does not follow – and R. Hanina does not say this – that the act of a man in response to his own volition is at all a nullity, simply because the act 'takes over' its performer.

If action in response to a command is to be considered symbolic – as the theories of Mendelssohn, Hirsch and Hermann Cohen require – the symbol, as a material entity, must disappear. Aniconism has direct relevance to the typology of Jewish symbolism, requiring that it be formulated in such a way as to become fitted to serve communicative purposes. This means that, having regard to the danger, actually or potentially present, in an intermediary or symbol, any figurative component must be attenuated, perhaps to the point of non-existence. The symbolic system must be such as will, on the one hand, negate any alienation from God through figurative representation or, on the other, comprise a system of signifiers that has its source elsewhere than in the divine. The material symbol, inert and dumb, barely distinguishable from an idol, must yield to a perception of the symbol as inseparable from, and identical with, the action it prescribes. Only in this way can the *Torah* exert an unmediated teaching.

4 The Mouth and the Monument

'To all action, forgetting belongs', Nietzsche maintains. 'Without forgetting it is utterly impossible to live at all'. Contrariwise, that man who would think 'only historically' is likened to a person forcibly deprived of sleep.[1] Renan is no less dramatic in his invocation of the need for forgetfulness, historical error, and indifference to origin if a nation is to come into existence. To oblivion the nascent body, if it is to flourish, must first consign discreditable episodes from its past.[2]

These views directly contradict a Jewish attitude *vis-à-vis* the past which is positively resistant to its repression; without the continuing recall of the past there would be no present, still less a future. In the minatory words uttered by the Deuteronomist the centrality of remembrance as guarantee of survival resounds: to remember God, to uphold the Covenant and to survive are equivalent and inter-dependent requirements; conversely, to forget God is tantamount to succumbing to idolatry, with death as the consequence: 'remember that it is the Lord your God who gave you the strength to exert yourself that you may uphold His covenant He swore to your fathers as it stands today. And it shall be if you do forget the Lord your God and go after other gods and/or bow to them I warn you today that you will certainly perish' (Dt.8:18–19).[3]

An agenda breaks down this general injunction into a demand for the daily recall of six salient events, warnings, transgressions and promises. To Nietzsche the Jews would clearly have been the arch-insomniacs. Certain episodes must be recalled in order to be remembered; others must be recalled in order to be dismissed from memory. Would it not be simpler not to recall at all such episodes? No, because the lesson of the otherwise repressed memory could not be learned unless it had first been recalled.[4] The usual list is as follows: the Exodus from Egypt (Ex.13:3); God's anger at the 'calf' (Dt.9:7)); the day the Israelites stood before God at Horeb (Dt.4:9–10); the attack from Amalek (Ex.17:14); Miriam's criticism of Moses (Nu. 12:1 ff.; Dt.24:9); and 'the Sabbath day to keep it holy' (Ex.20:8).[5]

Concern for the accurate recall of the past as a repository of teaching and edification extends with the same degree of emphasis also to the chain of rabbinic tradition. This is epitomised in the Talmudic dictum: 'he who repeats a teaching in the name of its teacher brings redemption to the world' (TB Meg.15a). Hence the Talmud's historical-mindedness and punctiliousness in determining who said what, in what circumstances, with what intent, in whose name.[6]

It must also not be forgotten that the injunction to remember establishes common ground between God and the Jew. The former can be enjoined to remember no less than the latter, which derives from the troubled contractual relationship established at Sinai.[7] Hardly has the Covenant been concluded, than Moses must remind God not to denounce it (in his wrath at the construction of the calf) and to remember his undertaking to the Patriarchs: 'I will make your offspring as numerous as the stars of heaven and I will give to your offspring this whole land of which I spoke, to possess forever' (Ex.32:13; cf. also Ezek.16:60).[8]

Clear enough is the content of memory – a compound of historical experience, a divine promise and a corpus of teaching. The greatest care is taken to suppress any notion of a golden past so that the retrieval of an illusion should not impair the indeterminacy of the future.

The important question asks: how is recall achieved? The answer is crucial to the struggle against the image, but for the moment I limit myself to a rhetorical question and an oblique response: if an idol is dumb and inert, can a physical memorial to the past or present be any less so? The answer is certainly 'no' and in this negation is revealed the extended influence of the fight against matter in determining both the *modus operandi* of memory and its function, and also how these actually modify the past and re-create it.

The threat from the image derived from its power to be constitutive of reality. In so far as this is the case, what is the nature of the reality that is thus constituted? Illusory. It certainly meets the desire for the re-presentation of the absent but only at the price of limiting the absent to the dimensions of an image. The result is a form of make-believe.

Memory, however fortified in this way, remains circumscribed. The absent remains absent while only the present subsists. The memory preserved or 'revivified' will be conditioned by the mummified corpse, statue, effigy, and so on, and can achieve no more than 'the reification of that which was once alive ... as much a revolt against death as a nature-bound magical practice' (Adorno); or art's creation is of 'a pseudo-life, over graves, as it were ... but at least for moments the old feeling stirs once more and the heart beats to an otherwise forgotten measure' (Nietzsche).[9] Fashions change: at one time the memorial artifact will be an embalmed mummy; at another, Titian's portrait of Charles V. But at work in each instance is the wish to recall the original, 'snatch him from the flow of time, bind him to life'.[10]

If, however, the awareness of substitution is not experienced then there develops a fixation on the image of the past. The image itself, that is, a finite object in space, becomes the focus and locus of memory. This however, is inherently unable to fulfil its designated purpose so that a form of stultification is created, limiting the capacity of memory to expand beyond the confines of the finite. It may be, to hazard a psychological explanation, that the frustration experienced at, and engendered by, the materially finite actually generates Ruskin's 'pathetic fallacy', evident in miracle-working icons, statues of the Virgin that move their eyes or weep or turn away from distressing scenes in their vicinity.[11] Be that as it may, the artifact, essentially, is all but inarticulate, its range of expression limited to a very simple message indeed. It fails to re-animate past life, for which it can do no more than offer a more or less successful make-believe substitute.

In the perception of the masses, statues and monuments do have a defined and recognised political role in the formation of memory; otherwise each new régime, political or religious, would not normally take the effort to remove the images of its predecessor: the Place Louis-le-Grand in Paris successively sported statues of Louis XIV, Napoleon, Henri IV, and Napoleon III , until the whole edifice succumbed to the *communards* of 1871.

While it is in existence the monument will certainly provide a fount of memory in the conventional sense and arouse
associations, after the fashion of the Brandenburg Gate or
the Arc de Triomphe or the statue of Peter the Great in
St. Petersburg. These can 'speak' for, and of, martial glory
and conquest but the range of articulation available to such
images is strictly limited.

Even if it be accepted, in the words of an apologist for
lieux de mémoire that these do in fact have a 'capacity for
metamorphoses, an endless recycling of their meaning and
an unpredictable proliferation of their ramifications',[12] these
will still remain bounded by their original denotation.

There is another point: the monument requires to be
decoded before it can speak at all. It is so dumb that the
spectator must himself bring to the monument its message.
A person who, for example, lacks absolutely all knowledge
of the French revolution would by the same token lack any
ability to grasp the message conveyed by the Bastille. This
edifice speaks only when it is, so to speak, addressed by an
already informed spectator; or, perhaps, it may need to bear
a label that proclaims its connotation. In either case, it virtually lacks a voice of its own which only some extraneous
source can supply.

In the last resort, a monument to the past or present, as
a bearer of memory, remote or recent, contradicts itself.
On the one hand, it presents itself as the epitome of per-
manence, endurance and strength – and must in fact do no
less if it is not to forfeit its very *raison d'être*. On the other
hand, it shares in the vicissitudes of matter. The statue of
Ozymandias, 'king of kings', is now reduced to 'two vast
and trunkless legs of stone . . . Round the decay of that colossal
wreck, boundless and bare, The lone and level sands stretch
far away'.

But in Jewish thinking and behaviour, rare indeed are
places of pilgrimage, memorials and monuments. The 'image' theory of idolatry shows its power in refusing to grant
to a material artifact any but the most limited capacity to
maintain in being the past or the absent as a reality that
speaks to the present. It is true that this position was only
reached over a period of centuries; for example, in the case
of funerary memorials, the embalming of Jacob and Joseph

and arrangements for their respective burials are explicitly mentioned (Gen.50:1 ff; 50:25). But later, in the case of Moses, care is taken to specify that 'no-one knows his burial place to this day' (Dt.34:6). Even there however, where a memorial is erected, it amounts to no more than a heap of stones, such as the structure erected to mark the spot, 'as a memorial for all time', where the Israelites under Joshua's leadership crossed the river Jordan (Josh.4:3 ff). Stones also mark the site of Jacob's encounters with God, at Beth-El and elsewhere (Gen.28:18; 31:45). At Peniel, there is not even a stone, only a name (Gen.32:31). In any case, the stones do not so much designate a location but rather attest to God's appearance at the location.[13]

The very anonymity, at least in terms of imagery, that marks and confirms these appearances/occasions, acknowledges the requirement that only an abstraction can, as it were, encourage and receive the manifold variety of messages projected on to it by any particular observer, whereas a realistic and figurative monument will limit the polysemic message.

At the other extreme stands the monument to the past that is nothing but names, or virtually so, the name being in any case the predominant characteristic. This feature marks the Hall of Names at the Yad Va'Shem memorial in Jerusalem, and the 'monument-museum' erected at Fossoli, site of a German deportation camp in North Italy. The entire wall surface of one room is engraved with the names of Italian deportees murdered in the death camps; 'most striking in all this is the massive emphasis on writing', writes the historian of the camp. 'One has the impression that the team assembled by architect Belgiojoso (who had been interned at Fossoli) has deliberately foregone the expressive potential proper to architecture, feeling it incumbent to entrust the remembrance of such tremendous historical events to a means of communication which is more immediate, or at any rate more explicatory'.[14]

To either extreme – the monument that is anonymous and shapeless, or that where names alone predominate – the counter-example, flouting both, is Nathan Rapoport's Warsaw Ghetto Memorial (1948). This has been derided as 'so blatantly derivative that it undermines its own pretence. 'We too have heroes!' is what it is really saying'.[15] The ghetto hero Mordecai Anielewicz becomes a 'Liberty leading the People', and the young woman to his rear belongs rather to Delacroix, 'with the Tricolore in one hand, a rifle in the other'.[16]

Even less effective does the physical memorial become when set alongside the exemplary and traditional form of memorial, the 'Memorial Books' (*Yizkorbikher*), composed as a means to recall the communities murdered during the Holocaust, in preference to their commemoration in stone. Admittedly, these would not offer the same occasion for dignitaries to genuflect, but their eloquence is their sanction. In his introduction to precisely that Memorial Book devoted to Warsaw, the author writes: 'all that remains for us is to narrate and record for the generations its happenings and history, its life and its suffering, its joy and its sorrow and the days of the terrible destruction of the great metropolis ("mother and city") in Israel'.[17] Only a verbal medium lends itself to the transmission of this history – far more readily and effectively so than a memorial that will decay with its material bearer, losing all ability to convey even its modest message to later generations. It was in part for this reason that Ben Gurion rejected 'commemoration with trees and stones' (of those Jews killed in the Israeli war of independence, 1948/9); he chose 'a literary commemoration' – a collection of the literary and artistic works of the fallen soldiers themselves.[18]

The monument is the obstacle to memory, which it may even betray: 'As a likeness necessarily vitrifies its otherwise dynamic referent, a monument turns pliant memory to stone', writes James Young.[19]

The counter-weapon here is a form of memory adapted to the retention of words rather than things, for the latter disturb the former, not to mention that only words can be the vehicle of the Word. Rabbinic psychology here has two points to make: first (in contrast, for example, to Plato's teaching in Meno) that the mind is a blank so that the person who learns as a child is compared to 'ink written on clean paper';[20] second, this psychology requires a manifest disjunction between the capacity to recollect the words of the *Torah* and any aspect of its materialisation, in such terms as to favour the verbal medium. R. Naḥman of Braslav presents this argument in his comment on the verse: 'let not this

Book of the Teaching cease from your lips' (Josh.1:8). It is
precisely because the Torah is a spiritual entity, lacking any
spatial attribute, that it can be absorbed. R. Naḥman dis-
cerns an inner *rapport* and congruence between the spirituality of the *Torah* and the capacity of the human mind, 'so
that man can grasp the *Torah* in its entirety, and he will
forget nothing. For a spiritual entity does not take up space,
and the *Torah* can spread and dwell in his mind. But he
who materializes words of *Torah* and makes a substance of
it, then it acquires size and extension to the limit that a
man can contain in his mind and not more and if he should
wish to grasp more then he will expel what has already entered
his mind, as is the way of every material entity . . . and from
this comes forgetting'.[21]

This is not to suppose that physical monuments, memorial stones, and so on have not been called into play. Less
than a century ago the publication of a book of photographs
of some of the most distinguished Hungarian rabbis was
justified by reference to Isaiah (30:20) 'and your eyes shall
behold your teacher'.[22] Even so, suspicion of the image has
also here helped to structure an art and practice of memory
to which material aids were largely dispensable – as in the
case of the Huguenot Peter Ramus (Pierre de la Ramée).[23]
When the *Torah* provides material reminders of salient events,
it does so in a normative context to which the material is
secondary and in which the reference turns back on itself
so that nothing extraneous intrudes. Such material reminders include circumcision (of the covenant between God and
the descendants of Abraham), the donning of the phylacteries (of the Exodus), the offering of the first-fruits (of
Exodus and the Land).[24] From the stipulated blue colour
of the threads of the 'fringes' (*tsitsit*, Nu.15:39–40) a normative chain of association is created; thus from the fact
that blue and white must be distinguishable in the light of
dawn before the morning prayer ('Hear, O Israel . . .') can
be uttered, the act of so doing recalls the duty so to pray
(TB Men. 43b).

Judah Messer Leon, the fifteenth century author of a work
on rhetoric, quotes other Biblical commandments as springs
of memory and of teaching. The commandments regarding
tabernacle, ark, candlesticks, altars, tables, all the vessels,

the temple and the service; 'cause remembrance of great truths of divine revelation, although they may also symbolize products of human reason and other wonders. These marvellously constituted examples and likenesses are infinitely more effective than are backgrounds and images for the matters of which they serve as likenesses'. Messer Leon sees the fringes as resembling 'in function . . . the images of words'.[25]

The mnemonic role of the Temple candlesticks, the ark, the altar, and so on is to some extent generalised by R. Judah of Modena, in his treatise specifically devoted to the art of memory – *Lev Aryeh*. It has a somewhat apologetic air, for R. Judah, whilst reiterating the importance of remembering, also deplores the weakening of this faculty through the development of writing. He is defending a cause in the process of being lost, which is also the position of the Erasmian humanist.[26] Modena writes, for example: 'experience proves that he who trusts to his pen weakens his memory and when a thing is written it is detached from memory'.[27] As a means to avert this decline and positively strengthen memory, Modena counsels recourse to what he calls 'retentive signs', referring to Christian practice. These signs are essentially material and comprehend a broad variety of entities, constituting what Modena calls 'a spatial memory'. Thus ideas are assigned to images – 'artifice will help nature', and here Modena refers back to Messer Leon's espousal of the capacity of the Temple's appurtenances to convey what Modena calls 'matters from the world of spirit'. Modena himself adds to these entities of 'spatial memory' the example of a text, of which the letters, lines, arrangement of page and column will facilitate remembrance of the text (see Yates, op.cit., p.233 for the precedents of Quintilian and Ramus); the oral teaching of a fellow scholar can be recalled through its association with his diction, gestures, movement of passers-by, the location;[28] Modena compares a physical location (house, courtyard, room, urban quarter, and so on) to writing-paper on which the would-be remembrancer writes, 'as though with his pen and ink', depicting some such image as an eagle descending to the ground or a lofty cedar tree keeling over to teach, for example, that haughtiness brings a man low. But how to show what the eyes have not seen and cannot see, Modena asks? This is a problem to arise not only in the case of God 'Who has no bodily shape and has no body' but also in the case of the angels, Satan, evil spirits, the soul, the spirit, the Garden of Eden, Gehinnom (hell):

> ... to what shall we liken these and how shall we depict them? I looked very deeply into this matter for to us, the children of Israel, to whom is prohibited all statue and picture, this will be very strange (or unwelcome). I therefore said that you can imagine in your mind the Lord, Blessed be He, in the consuming fire (ref. to Ex.24:17) at the top of the drawing in the place determined and what you want to register you will register in that drawing and this will become what pleases you, for the sake of the Lord, Blessed be He, as though by way of likeness, in your desire to recall.

This aniconistic metamorphosis enforced by the Second Commandment does not apply to the depiction of the angels, for example, who could be shown in the guise of handsome young men with wings, the angel of death bearing a knife or scythe; or to the soul, depictable as a slender young maiden clothed in snow-white garment.[29]

This is one way to reconcile an aid to memory with pictorial designation. But even the deliberate designation of God as no more than 'a devouring fire' is surpassed by Rabbi Joseph Rosen (1858–1936, 'the Rogatchever') who presents the relationship between memory and the visual in the framework of their mutual exclusion: 'memory is not appropriate save in respect to a matter that is not present before us'; and this is supported by reference to Talmudic statements concerning the location of the altar in the Temple, seen in a vision, and the ashes of the ram offered in the place of Isaac (TB Ber.62b; Zev.62a). In both cases the recall is subsumed in the vision but the *Torah* falls into a different category and the 'Rogatchever' concludes, by way of generalisation: 'since the recall of the *Torah* is a matter that endures and acts without pause, therefore the category of memory does not belong here'.[30] In effect, the life-world takes the place of remembrance which is thereby subsumed in the former.

In these circumstances the duty to remember is performed not by the monument, preferably not by inscription or imagery but by the individual's own trained capacity for recollection, with the mouth as the vehicle of transmission. Repetition is the favoured means whereby not only is the memory trained but also replenished with the teachings of the past. Without repetition 'a man can forget in two years what he had learned in ten. Twelve months without repetition and he will pronounce pure what is impure and impure what is pure; if he fails to repeat his Mishnah for twelve months, he will muddle up the sages; for eighteen months and he will forget the chapter-headings; for twenty-four months and he will lose the headings to the tractates, eventually he will sit in silence'.[31]

Maimonides compiled his Code (Mishneh Torah – Repetition of the Law) in such a way as to facilitate its memorisation: this compendium is organised 'in groups of the laws according to their subject matter', he writes in the introduction. Then the groups are divided into chapters according to their subject matter: 'Each chapter is sub-divided into smaller sections so that they may be memorised in sequence'. The whole work follows a topical sequence, Maimonides emphasises, and not the number of commandments.[32]

The Talmud makes occasional use of acronyms and mnemonics as an aid to recall;[33] and of chanting the text of Scripture or Mishnah.[34] Later scholars, e.g. Isaac Abrabanel and Johanan Allemanno, also favoured this practice.[35]

To hear the word is considered compatible with its rendering in either audible or written form. The Talmudic sage, Raba, makes the point that what is to be 'remembered' of the days of Esther (ref. to Esther 9:28) is to be inscribed in a book in the same way as the explicit mention of an inscribed remembrance of God's promise to exterminate the memory of Amalek (ref. to Ex.17:14). This brings together the two aspects of memory: 'not to forget' is a mental act; 'to remember' gives verbal expression to the act (TB Meg.18a). Memory in both instances is generated by way of the word, however formulated – certainly not by way of any monument or figurative image or artifact. It is equated with recall through unmediated, verbal transmission ('You shall *say* to your children. . .').

The correlation to repetition as the mode of memorisation elevates the mouth to the status of the bearer of memory: 'it is not in the heavens... No, the thing is very close to you, in your mouth and in your heart, to observe it' (Dt.30:10–14). Joshua and Isaiah drive home the point: 'let not this book of the teaching cease from your lips' (Joshua 1:8); 'the words which I have placed in your mouth, shall not leave your mouth, nor the mouth of your children, nor the mouth of your children's children, from now on for all time, said the Lord' (Is.59:21).

Through the capacity of the mouth to transmit and of the ear to receive, continuity is created: the prototypical example is the recall of the Exodus – which 'you shall expound to your son on that day' (Ex.13:8) and which, in its turn, is also incumbent on the son so that a continuous succession of transmittals is created.[36] Through this process, and also as a consequence of this process, not only does remembrance become more than memory in its engagement with the past but that past is also assimilated to the present. Each successive generation is included in the Exodus, for this wonder 'was wrought for our fathers and for *us*. He brought *us* out from slavery to freedom, from sorrow to rejoicing. . .'.[37]

Once the static monument with its capacity 'to turn pliant memory to stone' (in the same way as a statue will petrify a human being at a certain moment in time – see page 81) is done away with, then access is opened to the past in an ever-renewable manner. The argument here is that past and present inhere in each other and, whilst remaining distinguishable, can still be experienced as one unit of consciousness. This is because the original 'past' is open to the present, never, in fact, ceases to be accessible to the present and *vice versa*. Time is no longer considered in spatial terms, quantitatively, but qualitatively, in terms of a Bergsonian *durée*.[38]

The author of Deuteronomy recapitulates the covenant concluded at Sinai in these unambiguously 'open' terms: 'I make this covenant, with its sanctions, not with you alone, but both with those who are standing here with us this day before the Lord our God and with those who are not with us here this day' (Dt. 29:13–14). The second recapitulation of the Deuteronomist refers primarily to place. It answers the question: where? The instruction given to the Israelites is not 'beyond reach'. It is not in the heavens. 'Neither is it beyond the sea'. . . No, the thing is very close to you, in your mouth and in your heart, to observe it' (Dt.30:11 ff). Memory is emancipated from spatially determinate and determinative 'reminders' or 'messengers'. The past becomes mobile, portable, transmitted from mouth to mouth. The effect of these two declarations is to release the covenant from its original, now absent, setting and to make each succeeding generation its contemporary bearer.[39]

There is a certain amount of confusion and misunderstanding on this point. It is, for example, misleading for Ricoeur to describe the Covenant at Sinai simply as 'an enduring rather than a repetitive event'.[40] In its complex reality it is both; and because it is repeated through memory does it remain enduring.

Heschel clarifies the conjunction between 'enduring' and 'repetitive' in his exposition of Exodus: 'on the third new moon after the children of Israel had gone forth from the land of Egypt, on this day they came into the wilderness of Sinai' (Ex.19:1). Why '*this*' day, Heschel then asks, in echo of traditional rabbinic puzzlement? Why not *that* day? And he answers: 'this can only mean that the day of giving the *Torah* can never become past; that day is this day, every day'. The *Torah* has an existence such that it is 'as if it were given us today'.[41] The past, as it were, is freed from the past and becomes ever-present. If, therefore, the Israelite is exhorted to 'remember the days of old, consider the years of many generations' (Dt.32:7), he is always and at all times engaged in a pursuit that is strictly contemporaneous with his own situation. A unique happening of a past time both preserves its uniqueness and is also made part of a unique present. That is why R. Joseph Soloveitchik can make the individual 'the interaction of eras . . . "now" is to be anchored in "once"'. Not only do 'living figures roam from generation to generation', but their tradition accompanies them: 'theoretical innovations, abstract concepts, halakhic formulas and logical principles . . . a certain existential rhythm and experiential continuity'.[42]

This formula preserves the events and traditions of the past but also entrusts their survival to each later generation.

The absent is made present through re-experience and not through any artifact. This re-experience is distinguished both from actual re-experience – obviously – but also from the static repetition of the same re-experience. This again is the subject of misunderstanding. Connerton writes: 'The same feasts are celebrated on the same dates. With each periodical festival the participants thus find themselves as it were in the same time: the same that had been manifested in the festival of the previous year, or in that of a century, or five centuries earlier. These critical intervals are organised so as to appear and be experienced as qualitatively identical. By its very nature, therefore, ritual time is indefinitely repeatable'.[43]

But in our case, the notion of a festival being experienced as 'qualitatively identical' year after year is simply inapplicable in its failure to take account of the changing nature of the changing remembrance of which each festival is successively the subject throughout the Jewish year. Such a 'qualitatively identical' experience would be tantamount to a reification of the particular festival, the spatialisation of its time, and thus contradict the very *durée* which the festival belongs to. Take the paradigm of the Exodus from Egypt: this must be repeated differently and understood differently in each generation by each individual, to which the multitude of *midrashim* already testify.[44] To take one obvious distinction: the terror felt by the vanguard of fleeing Israelites as they approached the Sea of Reeds – to their rear the Egyptian cavalry and chariots ('Were there not enough graves in Egypt that we have to die in the desert?' Ex.14:11) – how could they know that the waters would part? But to the successors of those in flight that fear showed itself unwarranted and to that extent their own reception of the Exodus narrative must be significantly altered from that of the original participants. Another example: the phrase from the Haggadah for the festival of Passover – 'in each and every generation our enemies rise up to kill us' – now, after the Holocaust, alerts to a threat of infinitely graver import than ever before.

Still less can the contemporary Jew ever re-experience the assembly at Sinai as did his ancestors of the wilderness, for the simple reason that the events at Sinai have affected his consciousness and must separate him from those whose consciousness was not as yet thus affected.

It must be inevitable that when the events of past time are retained in the memory of one generation and then transmitted to its successors through speech or even inscription, their emphasis and resonance will change. The commemorative act of these later generations will be subjective and relative to their own condition, and therefore in a constant state of flux.

To question now whether this constant mutation of the content of memory matters is to miss the point. It must and indeed should mutate. To revert to the Exodus: what is asked of the remembrancer is that his memory should function in such a way as to recall the particular event in the only context now available and possible – his own: 'each man should feel as though he himself took part in the Exodus' (TB Pes.116b). Maimonides's formula is more extreme: 'in each generation a man is obliged to show himself as if he himself has gone out now from Egyptian slavery . . .'.[45] In either case the requirement is feasible because it does not ask of the individual that he disengage himself from his present existential situation and engage with the impossible task of identifying himself with an event beyond his experience. But to the extent that the present allows, that event can still be recalled and re-experienced. A fiction it would be were the particular individual claim to have participated, but it is not a fiction that he can experience the Exodus 'as though' he had himself been a participant. The result is a genuine pretence, that repeats the Exodus at the same time that it also emphasises the uniqueness of the Exodus.[46]

In some cases (for example the local communities of the Atlas mountains), local custom does prescribe an active simulation of the precipitate Exodus: the men leave their dwelling, bearing on their shoulders a bundle tied to the end of a stick, and run and cry – 'this is how our ancestors left Egypt'.[47]

But this and all other forms of re-capitulation are of a special type in that the actors are fully conscious of the make-believe mode required in the endeavour to re-present a unique and distant event. In fact, they are not actors in any recognised sense, in that there is no need for self-conviction nor for convincing others of a guise that is anything other than self-identification. Here is no symbolic ceremony or pretence or mimesis; rather a theatre in which the 'actors' act themselves, because this is the mode in which they do in fact experience the Exodus. It is only as a contemporary experience that the original experience can become retrievable. The 'actors' are performing in what has been happily likened to 'a non-mimetic theatre';[48] the actors concentrate on not exchanging their customary existence for the identity of another – that other who is no other than their own ancestor – and act/re-enact the past whilst in all particulars remaining themselves. Their acting is distinguished both from the original experience of the Exodus 'the real' – and from any dramatic re-presentation but, by virtue of the 'as though', combines features of both. It is a dramatic representation of the unique, whereby the past is acknowledged as past but not for that reason to be distinguished from the present. Memory alone is operative, as conveyed from the mouth of each generation to the ear of its successor.

Such materials as are made use of share in this duality of experience. The *Matzah* – unleavened bread – displayed to the assembled company on the eve of Passover makes no claim to recapitulate the past or re-present the original. It will be the product of Messrs Rakusen or Grodzinski or Manischewitz . . . and will certainly lack all resemblance to the product hastily baked in Egypt – no matter: the celebrant will still display his contemporary product as 'the bread of affliction our ancestors ate. . .'. There is no pretence, or fiction or act – merely a re-presentation of the past in terms of the present, the 'as though' mode being the only mode in which the past can be made present.

What applies here applies also to the tabernacle constructed in part commemoration of the temporary shelter used during the Israelites' desert wanderings. It is certainly no replica or reproduction of the original but also no model or symbol; it is a contemporary structure 'as though' it were the original and serves the same purpose, of providing an actual dwelling for the commemorative period in the same way as the unleavened bread of the Passover ceremony is actually consumed.

The conclusion that follows must emphasise that so soon as experience is conceived in the 'as though' mode it will create an equivalent series of props, appropriate to this mode, sharing the same quality of acknowledged pretence. But this will prevent them being regarded as static images of an unchanged-unchanging past and the whole task of remembrance is therefore made to depend on verbal communication, written or spoken. In fact, it must be so, because otherwise an intolerable discordance would be created between the transmitted narrative – of the Exodus in this case – which belongs differently to each generation of narrators, and its unchanging imagery. As it is however, to entrust the task of remembrance to memory alone ensures that its authority becomes sufficient to create its own world of representation, in its own contemporary image. Thus each repetition is a *novum*. Atlan writes 'if the rite (i.e. of remembrance) is to repeat a creative act it can only do so in not repeating it, for only once can a creative act be creative; if the rite repeats it exactly, it is no longer an act of creation'.[49]

On the ground that 'your eyes shall behold your teacher' a photographic album of Hungarian rabbis is published. But that this 'beholding' could ever teach of itself would never be maintained. What however is maintained is the indissoluble bond between memory and action.

If to remember is also to observe, then to forget is also to transgress. In the same way as remembrance is tantamount to fulfilment of the commandments, so is forgetting tantamount to their transgression: in Biblical terminology, 'following other gods to serve them' (Dt.8:19). To forget God is as much an action as to remember God, though in a negative sense.

The past is not to be recalled for its own sake but because it is the repository of a summons to action. The task of remembering joins the task of sanctification in encompassing and enunciating an imperative to action. The content of verbal memory, when deconstructed, proves to contain a factor that transcends mere remembrance.

The exegesis of the fourth commandment of the decalogue is conclusive: in the first version this is phrased: 'remember the sabbath day and keep it separate' (Ex.20:8): in the second version the same commandment is phrased: 'observe the sabbath day, and keep it separate' (Dt.5:12). From the viewpoint of Biblical scholarship, this variation in terminology

can be convincingly attributed to a change in historical circumstances. At the time of the Exodus, Israel, obviously,
has direct experience of the Covenant; but the Deuteronomist
has to take account of the passage of time and must reverse
the emphasis so that it is no longer necessary to remember
in order to observe, but to observe in order to remember.
'The role of memory has been completely reversed by the
Deuteronomist'.[50] The conclusion of the modern Biblical
critic converges with traditional commentary. R. Ḥizkiyah
b. Manoaḥ (the 'Ḥizzekuni') writes: 'in the commandments
in Exodus, when He wants to remind the Israelites about
the Sabbath, which He had already given to them at Marah,
the appropriate word is "remember". But here in Deuteronomy, when the commandments are being repeated forty
years later for the benefit of those who did not hear them
the first time, the appropriate word is "observe" since the
matter was not new to them'.[51] In either case, whether it is
to 'remember' or to 'observe', the intents coincide. Both
words were said 'in a single word', according to the Talmud (TB Shab.20b). (Their conjunction is beautifully displayed in the two wicks that R. Meir b. Baruch (the Maharam
of Rothenburg), prepared for his two Sabbath candles: one
denoted 'remember', the other 'observe' – see Y. Z. Kahana
(ed.), *Maharam mi-Rothenburg: Tshuvot, Psakim, Minhagim,* I,
Jerusalem, Mossad ha-Rav Kuk 1957, No.210, p.208).

Thus when the mouth issues its summons: remember 'you
were a slave in Egypt' (Dt.24:18 ff), it is in fact enunciating
a normative demand: to protect the economically weak
(stranger, orphan, widow) by not taking the widow's garments as pledge for a loan; by not completely clearing a
field at harvest-time; by leaving surplus grapes and olives
for the poor to glean.

To unpack the injunction to remember/observe the Sabbath day yields a content that is similarly rich: not only in
the demand for a cessation from labour but also in the
demand for a certain social order.[52]

No static, figurative monument to the past will speak in
this way. A *lieu de mémoire* it might well be, but this *mémoire*
is one-dimensional and quasi-inarticulate as compared with
the capacity of the mouth to transmit a remembrance that
is also an imperative.

5 Art in the Shade

When Marcel Brion ascribes to 'Mosaism, Islam and the Reformation', 'the absolute proscription of every image' he is wheeling out an old canard.[1] Talk of 'iconophobia' is no less misleading.[2] Between the innocent image and the illegitimate idol that is indeed deserving of utter destruction, especially if erected in the land promised to the Israelites (Dt.12:3), the Bible is well able to distinguish. A comprehensive policy of iconoclasm has no part in the Biblical aesthetic.[3]

This follows from the argument that the prohibition of images is primarily a consequence of the prohibition of service to other gods (see Chapter 1), which other gods are considered to exist predominantly by virtue of their existence in relation to some material form. This is their mode of being. But precisely because the image-ban is secondary, merely a by-product, as it were, of the over-riding need to vanquish those other gods, it follows that where an image is not expressive of any 'theology', it is wholly legitimate. Ouellette writes: 'basically, it is the symbolism attached to this or that image which determined its licit or illicit character'.[4] Where there is no symbolism the image is theologically indifferent. Image-making *per se* the Bible does not proscribe, simply because not every image is an idol.

The sole exception to the relevance of intention is the depiction of the human being, where special considerations do indeed apply (see Chapter 6); otherwise the context of the prohibition is always and everywhere that of worship. Remove this context as a qualifying factor and the prohibition falls away. What applies to the image of an existing and visible entity applies no less to the depiction of a non-existent and purely imaginary entity – a dragon, for example, again provided that it does not serve as an object of worship. A permissive attitude is *a fortiori* acceptable in the case of an imagined entity because under a prohibition applying only to those entities already in being it obviously can not fall. It is neither in the heavens nor on the earth nor under the seas.[5] Perhaps for this reason Jewish art (for example, in manuscript illumination) has a marked welcome for the image that is freakish, grotesque, distorted and hybrid.[6]

The Renaissance commentator R. Obadiah Sforno seems to be entirely isolated when he understands 'You shall not make for yourself a sculptured image' (Ex.20:4) to denote the manufacture of an image 'even if not (intended) for worship'. Sforno applies the same principle in interpreting 'you shall not make molten gods for yourself' (Ex.34:17). He understands this to denote 'talismans' with which their fabricator would hope to satisfy his material demands, perhaps unaware that although he does not himself accept the object as a god this would still be 'rebellion' against God. In other words, according to Sforno, to make the artifact *per se* constitutes a transgression, quite irrespective of any intent attached to it.

Undoubtedly, however, the general view is that formulated by Nahmanides in his comment on the first commandment: 'in this verse (Ex.20:3) there is no injunction against the making of images that are not to be worshipped'.[7]

The distinction between an image that is worshipped and another – or perhaps even the same image – not intended for worship illustrates the subjective and relative nature of idolatry. The individual 'makes' his own idol: one man's idol is another man's image, the history of religion being itself testimony to the multitudinous variety of entities that have been invested with worshipful attributes at one time or another. This is possible because to be an idolater is to succumb to certain conceptions of reality that invest an object with certain attributes. It is a subjective relationship;[8] similarly, two Jews may be ostensibly engaging in the same action, bowing to a statue, say, but only the one who accepts it as a god is liable to punishment by stoning; the other Jew, who is engaged in merely showing respect, is performing a theoretically inconsequential action.[9] The subjective nature of idolatry is also evident in the interpretation given by some commentators to the apparently redundant warning not to make 'molten gods' (Ex.34:17). Why is the warning repeated? 'On account of the episode with the calf, so that even when thinking heavenwards, they should not place that scene before them' (Biur, ad loc.).

The same object will be an idol at one time and/or place and something utterly inconsequential and innocent at another; R. Johanan, for example, argued in Roman times that contemporary gentiles outside the land of Israel were not idolaters but 'merely following the customs of their forebears';[10] in sixteenth-century Poland R. Moses Isserles argued on similar lines: 'the form to which they (gentiles) bow belongs to the legal category of idolatry and it is forbidden (to a Jew to have any benefit from it) unless it is nullified, but those that they have round their neck as a remembrance are not regarded as idolatrous and it is permitted (to a Jew to have benefit)'.[11] Maimonides dismissed out of hand any suggestion that contemporary Islamic worshippers at the Ka'aba were idolaters, whatever might have been in the past the case: 'those who kneel towards it today have no other intention save towards heaven'; and he equates such Moslems with those who see an idolatrous shrine but take it for a synagogue and bow down – 'surely their heart is to heaven' (TB San.61b).[12]

Rabban Gamliel provides two familiar illustrations of contextual importance: how could it be proper for him to patronise, (that is, to have benefit from) a Roman bath at Acre sporting a statue of the goddess Aphrodite, he was asked. This is no goddess, he retorted: 'I did not enter her domain, she entered mine'. 'This (statue of Aphrodite) stands by a conduit and everyone urinates before it. (In the *Torah*) it is only stated their gods, meaning what is treated as a god is prohibited, what is not treated as a god is permitted' (TB AZ 44b). The second example: Rabban Gamliel's preparation of models of the sun and moon. This would usually be interpreted as falling under the prohibition contained in the second commandment, no matter whether the models were raised or sunken. But in this instance Rabban Gamliel's purpose was to determine, by questioning witnesses, the phases of the sun and moon as a means to fix the calendar – thus 'if the purpose is to be instructed to understand and to teach, they (these models) are all permitted'.[13] Another Talmudic example: in villages idolatrous statues (of Roman emperors) are prohibited because they are conceived simply as gods. But those in towns are permitted for they were certainly manufactured as decoration, unless they stand at a territorial border and hold in their hands symbols of sovereignty, such as a sceptre, a bird, a globe, a sword, or a crown and ring (TB AZ 41a).

Perhaps also the physical image can be redeemed by its conversion into a concept. It is seen, not as a re-presentation of that which it purports to represent, but as an exercise in the presentation of an idea. In these 'ideal' terms Michelangelo's statue of the horned Moses had for Jewish thinkers a peculiar fascination. 'If there is any work of art that the cultured Jews of Central Europe adopted, it is this vision of the Hebrew leader'.[14] The lure of forbidden fruit, perhaps? In any case, the statue, as 'read' by Freud and Hermann Cohen, lent itself to an intellectual transposition – of strikingly different connotation, it is true, but the point is that in each case not a statue is seen but an idea. To Freud, the artist has 're-written' the Biblical text so as to depict a Moses who is engaged in 'the highest psychical achievement which is possible for a man, in the subjection of his own passion in favour of, and in the fulfilment of, a calling to which he has dedicated himself'.[15] Hermann Cohen's version follows the text and therefore contradicts the Freudian reading; here the 'lawgiver . . . the founder of the moral state order through the law of the Ten Commandments' is depicted 'in the transitional stage to a mighty upsurge, the calm before the tempest. . .'.[16] Schönberg's version of the statue is aural and not verbal, and, in reference to his opera *Moses und Aron*, 'not at all human'.[17]

A very different example: R. Abraham Kuk, an exile in London during the First World War, regularly visited the National Gallery for the sake of the Rembrandts: they reminded him of the legend about the creation of light. 'We are told that when God created light, it was so strong and pellucid, that one could see from one end of the world to the other, but God was afraid that the wicked might abuse it. What did He do? He reserved that light for the righteous when the Messiah should come. But now and then there are some great men who are blessed and privileged to see and I think that Rembrandt was one of them, and the light in his pictures is the very light that was originally created by God Almighty'.[18] A visual panorama could also become a concept: the Talmud takes up Balaam's exclamation of delight – 'how fair are your tents, O Jacob/Your dwellings, O Israel' (Nu.24:5) – and asks for the meaning of 'fair' in this context. The answer presents the spectacle in terms of an exemplary moral display. Balaam saw, says R. Johanan, 'that the openings of their tents were not facing each other and he said, they (i.e. the Israelites) merit that the divine presence rests on them'. The rabbi transvalues a visually attractive 'fairness' into an appreciation of the privacy required by the demands of a modest morality.[19]

To sum up: what must not be fabricated is an idol but what constitutes an idol depends on no inherent attribute, solely on its context and relationships, so that in certain contexts a statue of Aphrodite is a goddess, and in others a mere decoration; in the countryside the statue of a Roman emperor is an idol but not in the town. In this respect *ars gratia artis* must be the leitmotif of the Jewish artist. A fabricator or admirer of 'secular' images incurs no guilt, to which the whole history of Jewish art testifies. Through a rabbinical pun on the Hebrew word for 'rock', God is himself designated an 'artist'.[20]

The understanding of the prohibition of images limited to this permissive and relative sense makes it possible to distinguish between the image that is an idol and the image that is an innocent adornment (even though they are interchangeable). Further: it establishes a role for adornment that can perhaps be regarded as a medium, in Freudian terms, to reconcile the pleasure-principle with the reality-principle.

This has a most important corollary: obviously there can be 'sacred art' only in the limited and utilitarian (but commendable) sense of beautifying a religious appurtenance. In such a context it is even possible to talk of adorning God. This follows from reading Exodus 15:2 as, 'this is my God and I will adorn Him'. There is a problem here: how to adorn what is perfect?[21] The answer is found in reading 'Him' as 'to Him' and this enables R. Ishmael, when discussing the verse, to refer beauty to the commandments: 'I will prepare before Him a beautiful *lulav*, a beautiful booth, beautiful fringes, and beautiful phylacteries'.[22] These are all of course visible appurtenances. The Talmud also marries embellishment to a purposeful object that is the primordial repository of the divine: the Scroll of the Law. To the same verse, a response is found in a Scroll, written with a fine pen by a skilled scribe and wrapped in beautiful silk (TB Shab. 133b).

But with this exception all artifacts are either idolatrous or a 'secular' and permitted means of adornment and delight. The appreciation of an artistry limited to the anthropocentric purpose of decoration is central to the disenchantment of the artifact and its artificer. This is thoroughly in concert with Mendelssohn's view that 'the final end of the fine arts is to please'.[23] This gains a further dimension from the appreciation of physical beauty, both in nature and man. It provides occasion to recall the work of the creator. Those who behold a particular seat of natural wonder are called on to utter a special blessing: 'blessed are you, O Lord our God, king of the universe who has made the creation'. The phraseology is appropriately varied to meet individual circumstances, e.g. mountains, seas, etc.[24]

Admittedly, to the author of Proverbs, 'grace is deceptive, beauty is illusory' (31:30); and romantic love is no Jewish value – 'Eros and Dionysos are Greek and not Jewish heroes'.[25] But here is no reason not to salute, with reservations, the reputed beauty of figures such as Sarah, Rahab, Abigail and Esther. For the handsomeness of their colleague R. Johanan, the Talmudic sages had nothing but admiration.[26] At times circumcision was in part considered a token of God's concern for the enhancement of male beauty. A Midrash reads: 'R. Judah said: in the case of a fig its only defect is its stalk. Remove it and the blemish ceases. Thus, the Holy One blessed be He said to Abraham, "Your only defect is this foreskin. Remove it and the blemish is cancelled. Walk before me and be perfect"' (Gen.17:1).[27]

But there is a stage when the appreciation of beauty, or the distinction between an entity intended for worship – an idol – and an innocuous image becomes problematic to the point of virtual collapse. The theory of *ars gratis artis*, the entity that is theologically meaningless, can no longer be sustained. The innocuous entity – which, as I shall hope to show, need by no means be figurative or material or plastic – proves to exert a hostile power and take on independent life.

This is exemplified in the decoration of synagogues. On the one hand, synagogue decoration with murals, for example, dates at least from as early as the third century CE; in the days of R. Yoḥanan: 'people began to paint pictures on (synagogue) walls and he did not forbid them'.[28] In sixteenth century Poland, particularly in synagogues constructed by renaissance masters (as in Cracow and Lwow, the 'Nahmanowitz'), murals of Biblical scenes were displayed.[29] In the wooden synagogues of the Ukraine, especially at Mogilyov, the painter El Lissitzky found walls painted with giant lions and peacocks: 'in the sky above (i.e. the ceiling) stars are strewn around in the form of flowers'; there are birds, bears, foxes which are in fact human beings, 'through the masks of animals and birds they are looking with human eyes'.[30] The third-century synagogue at Dura Europos even showed human figures adorning portals and niches, to say nothing of frescoes and wall panels depicting virtually every Biblical character.[31]

On the other hand, why did Maimonides find all adornment to the synagogue unacceptable and close his eyes when confronted with any decorated wall or curtain before the Ark.[32] In his law code, the Tur, why did the medieval authority, Rabbenu Jacob b. Asher b. Yehiel, demand of a synagogue that nothing, save for the Ark and reading desk, intervene between the worshipper and the wall?.[33] In sixteenth-century Padua, why did R. Samuel Archivolti deride the painted walls of synagogues which, he complained, made them resemble a tavern or theatre?[34] Why, according to a famous Talmudic anecdote, would R. Ammi and R. Assi pray in Tiberias only 'between the colonnades, where they studied', although the town had thirteen synagogues? (TB Ber. 30b).

I would suggest that an understanding of these clashes of opinion is to be found not so much in diversity of taste or legal considerations but far rather in a differentiated appreciation of what degree of decoration would encroach on the primary purpose of the synagogue.

The name of Bezalel, the principal craftsman/artist mentioned in the Bible (Ex.31:2) is a guide. This is a proper name but means literally 'in the shade of the Lord' and could therefore signify the artist's subordinate relationship to the *Torah*. He is to remain in its shade. This subordinate position can however, be threatened and the fear aroused lest the artifact take on an independent role and, as it were, escape from beneath 'the shade of the Lord'.

The effect of this escape is not to create a focus of idolatrous concern. Nowhere is it suggested that the images are at all likely to be treated as objects of worship. It is surely not idolatry that is at stake – rather, the presence of a certain barrier, created by an artifice of one sort or another, in one medium or another, that has interposed itself between the teaching and the taught. This is the crux of the matter: not idolatry *per se* constitutes the focus and rationale of rabbinic concern but the effect incidentally produced by an entity that in another context might well be of no great moment. The closest to an affirmative judgement is probably that expounded by R. Zvi Hirsch Schpira: he disapproved of a pair of lions embroidered with gold and silver thread on the covering of a Scroll of the Law, ruling that this was 'akin to a trace of idolatry', on the grounds that lions formed one of the four faces of Ezekiel's chariot (and thus their representation breached divine transcendence).[35]

The balance as between text and adornment must remain unequal. It is only too possible to imagine a continuing process of embellishment so that its status moves from subordination to paramountcy. The artistry can indeed change the text and thus frustrate the intention of the text, even whilst the latter retains its original form. The particular process in question then shows itself to be quasi-indispensable to the development of an unambiguous impediment. It functions as a necessary cause, even if not as a sufficient cause and this validates rabbinic concern a priori. So long however, as the process is contained, as it were, within a limited context, creating no more than an adornment, then no harm is done (though it is certainly potentially present). This can not be made actual unless and until a change in status has taken place. But when this does take place then the subordinate has substituted itself for the principal, wrongfully attracting the attention demanded by the latter. Adornment has 'taken over'. It will then arouse susceptibility towards some inappropriate entity in a particularly sensitive setting. The fear is that adornment will introduce some alteration

into the text, such as will eventually degrade it to a spectacle and thus mute its summons to action and thought.[36]
Beguiling but wrong messages might be conveyed and they
must therefore be rendered harmless, not necessarily removed,
only confined 'in the shade of the Lord'.

Normally, as we have seen, it is possible to classify artifacts as either innocently decorative or idolatrous: this is a
useful hermeneutic principle of division but it certainly may
not be used as a pair of mutually exclusive and opposing
categories. They can well inter-penetrate and, if so, create a
potentially dangerous indeterminate aura. This pre-occupation is not of course exclusive to the Jews and the latter
might well concur with the Platonic equation of artist and
sophist in condemning their common predilection for jug-
gling with images.

In Platonic terms, the phenomena of this type – adornments, embroidery, animal statuary, literary artifice, tunefulness, illuminated books – lead the best part of the soul
to 'lower its guard'.[37] From a Jewish point of view, although
there is certainly some overlap with the Platonic, there is
also a significantly different emphasis on the impediment
to action that untoward decoration creates: that is, when it
escapes from 'the shade of the Lord'.

Frequently, synagogue draperies, especially those covering the Scroll of the Law are objects of concern. The centrality of the institution, together with its status as a truly
sacred and revered entity requiring some form of obeisance,
would in any case command attention. But with what intent? Should the drapery covering the Scroll be embroidered
with, say, birds and doves, then the obeisance might be
misconstrued as a mark of respect to the adornment rather
than to the Scroll. This would apply both to the worshipper, who might imagine that the birds and doves shared in
the sanctity of the Scroll, and/or to any beholder of the
action who might attribute the wrong motive to the worshipper. This is why, to R. Mashash of Tlemsin (North Af-
rica), certain decorations on the coverings of the Scrolls of
the Law, were inadmissible: '. . . . for the people all bow
towards the Scroll of the Law and pour out their thoughts
before God when the Scroll passes before them, and if so it
is certain that it is absolutely forbidden to place on it any

figure. And it is clear and evident that the birds and doves must be removed. . . .'[38] For the same reason, R. Judah the Pious, in the medieval German Rhineland, strongly deprecated the installation in the synagogue of any figure or image, especially before the Ark (where the Scrolls were housed when not in use), 'so that it would not appear as though one were bowing to these images'.[39]

But a complaint in regard to a curtain hanging in front of the Ark (*parochet*), bearing coloured images of Noah's Ark, figures of David and Jonathan and 'indications of sun-worship' was dismissed by R. Ezekiel Katzenellenbogen. He ruled that no 'negation of prayer' was involved, all the less so as the cloth of the curtain was cut and sold by measure irrespective of the patterning.[40] A negative judgement also emerged from a medieval dispute submitted by R. Joel Halevy of Mainz to R. Ephraim of Regensburg. This became in fact something of a *cause célèbre* and was repeatedly alluded to by later rabbis: were synagogue draperies decorated with birds and horses permissible, given the possibility that they might distract the congregation at prayer? R. Ephraim gave an unambiguous denial: 'men do not worship the images of birds and horses even when they are depicted separately and all the less so if they are shown on draperies . . . there are therefore no grounds for suspicion'.[41] Sometimes, the answer to this sort of problem concerns itself not only with the distraction to prayer that might result from a prominent and excessive adornment or even with its possible offensiveness but also with artistic quality. All these factors were relevant to the reply by R. Abraham Geiger (Germany, nineteenth century) to certain members of a congregation desirous of installing an oil-painting of Moses in a synagogue window. Not only must 'the aesthetic sense' not be affronted, he argued; also, that this demand, however artistically executed, be reconciled with an incapacity 'to divert from the religious thought' or to provoke 'independent, distracting contemplation'. Moses is revered as the man who gave Israel the divine law but 'his image is something indifferent', Geiger maintained, 'and should therefore remain as distant as an other from the house of God. He stands for us too high to be employed as indifferent adornment; he stands too low, that his image should be significant'. But Geiger refrained from outright rejection of the adornment and appealed for 'a peaceful understanding' between the contending parties.[42]

If synagogal adornment had always to be scrutinised and sometimes inhibited, then so must be that of the prayer-book: was it fitting to illuminate prayer-books with the painted figures of animals and birds? This was a question submitted to the medieval authority, R. Meir b. Baruch (the Maharam) of Rothenburg. The practice was 'certainly not attractive', he commented, 'for in looking at these pictures, people are not directing their heart to their father in heaven'. R. Meir nonetheless ruled that the illuminations were visually of so little account that on grounds of supposed idolatry there could be no question of any prohibition.[43] In the case of a manuscript Bible, R. Judah the Pious in the *Sefer Hassidim* insisted on a contract with the scribe that excluded decorative figures of birds and animals, either in text or margin – 'how will one see', he asked?[44] In an illustrated Bible R. Samuel Aboab in seventeenth century Venice saw 'no benefit or increase in understanding of the *Torah*'.[45]

R. Jacob Mölln, in fifteenth-century Germany, associated himself with other contemporary scholars (such as R. Jacob Segal) in condemning illuminated prayerbooks – he distinguished between those books written in fulfilment of a religious commandment and those where the scribe's aim was 'to glorify himself'. He was at one with Segal who refused to pray from 'pleasing' (that is, illuminated) prayer books.[46]

A literary artifice or conceit, no less than visual appeal, might also create disturbance. This was the case presented by R. Isaac Arama (Tarragona and Catalayud, fifteenth century): he objected to the inclusion in the liturgy for the Day of Atonement of a poem by Solomon ibn Gabirol in which the poet spelt out his name in acrostic form. This ingenious device might well disturb devotion.[47]

What is at issue here? No variety of asceticism. On the contrary, Maimonides, who was certainly amongst the more 'restrictive' teachers in respect of the physical, explicitly appreciated the role of appropriately determined sensuous satisfaction in securing the health of the soul.[48] Also not at issue is idolatry in any obvious sense such as obeisance to a stained-glass window or a synagogue drapery, which is in one case at least explicitly disclaimed. Rather, the justification for rabbinical censure and exclusion derives from the awareness of two inter-dependent threats. The first is grounded in the apprehension that the presence of aesthetic appeal has the capacity to obscure and ultimately to silence the text; the second, and dependent threat, arises from the alarm that because the text is silenced, those to whom it is directed will fall unaware of its normative demands, or, at the very least, be rendered inattentive to those demands. Ultimately, the actor is converted into an uninvolved spectator. This degeneration is closely akin to the position reached in Nietzsche's presentation of 'the aesthetic, purely contemplative will-less mood'.[49] Not only does the aesthetic make no claim on action but it actually obscures and thereby weakens an existing claim. This is paralleled in Kierkegaard's theory of the aesthetic which is sometimes presented in terms of opposition between the sophist and the religious, and sometimes in terms of opposition between art and existence: 'When you fix your gaze on poetry and art it is not reality you are looking upon, and that is what we should really be talking about'.[50] But if one is not so talking and holds to the view that art facilitates entry into reality, then 'this is just as misguided as to believe that the more artistically perfect a sermon, the better it is able to transform life. Ah no: the more aesthetic is its effect, away from the existential'.[51] In the distinction made by Hermann Cohen between aesthetic love and religious love, the same juxtaposition of values is displayed. The former is 'no more than fantasy', 'mere abstraction', 'a play with ideas burning with heart-felt fire'; the latter has 'an earnestness' that discloses itself as 'the discovery of the individual in the suffering human being' and thereby of the correlation with God.[52]

Let the Bible be read as literature and, for all its unchanged form, it ceases to be the Bible of Moses and the Prophets: 'certainly', Danto writes, 'it can be read as such, its poetry and narrative responded to as poetry and narrative, its images appreciated for their power and its moral representations as a kind of drama. But to treat it so is to put at an important distance the Bible considered as a body of revelations, of saving truths and ethical certitudes . . . So some fundamental relationship to the book will have changed when it sustains transfer to the curriculum as "living literature"'.[53]

The Zohar, the mystical classic, echoes this, with an additional nuance of condemnation: 'woe to the man who declares the *Torah* is just a story-book'.[54] Likewise, the Song of Songs must not be understood as a secular poem – this would 'bring evil to the world'. The *Torah*, personified in this passage, laments that it is not 'a harp on which men might frivolously play' (TB San. 101a).

If however, these warnings are not heeded, then not only have principal and subordinate concerns been inverted but the latter have supplanted the former. The principal has not simply been dethroned but it has also been lost and subsumed in the inferior.

This inversion of values results from the unwillingness, for whatever reason, to take normative demands seriously and therefore to relegate them to a less demanding – perhaps entirely undemanding – frame of reference. In effect, when they are transferred from one frame of reference to another, the demands are neutralised, and the tension created is lost, for the aesthetic as real is tantamount to an acceptance of the status quo, especially when it is mediated through the eye (see Chapter 8).

Because of the relative, contingent and subjective expression and nature of the aesthetico-idolatrous impulse, this is not immediately apparent. If a statue is in one context an idol and not in another; if a synagogue may be adorned, in the view of one rabbi, and in the view of another, should be bare – does it then matter which? But an argument on these lines misses the point – that even if no definition of an idol, still less of idolatry, is forthcoming, then the criterion whereby to gauge the artist's emergence from out of 'the shade of the Lord' must operate in terms of its anticipated consequence: does it lead to the loss of contact with the norm, through the dominance of an aesthetic world whence the divine imperative has been dismissed? But this is an empirical question, demanding an answer derived from experience. Only this can determine whether the *Torah* is to become a song, harp or story-book, as aesthetics would make it, the synagogue a theatre, transforming the God in whose name the *Torah* speaks into a non-god. The ethical and the aesthetic would then become confused, precisely as though the Bible were to be read as 'literature'; to equate the two involves and positively requires the transgression of a barrier. Two *ultimately* incompatible worlds of discourse are brought together in a self-destructive combination, in which only an ethical void survives. The use of aesthetic appeal solicits the very acme of 'alien worship', eventually to create a universe of reified entities.

This is the crucial factor that turns the synagogue itself into an arena where contradictory values may find themselves in conflict. The sophistic and the aesthetic confront the rabbinic in a conflict that Kierkegaard would easily recognise. Whether this would lead him to speak of idolatry is of course another matter but in the rabbinic combat this is certainly implicit; for to turn the Bible into literature is all but to destroy it, through removing the factor of 'existential' commitment to action. It becomes an object of contemplation, so soon as aesthetic appeal brings about a discontinuity between commandment and action. The genre is changed, even though the text has formally remained intact. The text has become as dumb as any idol or statue.

With unique acuity the art of music and the lyric brings all these matters to the fore: the reason is that only to these arts does Biblical, rabbinic and Jewish thinking in general extend a welcome; so much so, that Hermann Cohen (whose works include a study of Mozart's libretti), juxtaposes aversion for plastic art with 'the alliance' that, in lyric poetry, 'monotheism made with art'.[55] In actual fact, in respect of this 'alliance' – the only one of its type – lyric poetry is extended into song and music in general.[56]

Martin Buber and Hermann Cohen were certainly at odds over most things Jewish. But over music they meet to some degree in a common accord, for, in the context of Buber's engagement with Wagner (see page 161) it is maintained that music is 'the art of time', that to 'the God without form and name' musicality is 'the parallel-phenomenon', and to God 'the strongest and most immediate equivalent'.[57]

This language is turgid but Cohen's 'alliance' stands out at all levels: in, for example, the prominence given to musical accompaniment on social and festive occasions – 'die Fiedel macht das Fest', sings Heine;[58] and in the intense and continuing rabbinic interest in musical theory – relative to such themes as melody, composition, harmony and genres. Isaac Abrabanel, Arama, Archivolti, Judah Messer Leon, Falaquera, Judah Halevi, and Moscato are noteworthy exponents from medieval and renaissance times.[59] The Hispano-Jewish curriculum in the twelfth and thirteenth centuries included the study of music.[60] There is, to the best of my knowledge, no case where youthful interest in music was discouraged in the way that students of the plastic and figurative arts were discouraged.[61]

It is indeed the case that a distinction, in accord with that made by Schopenhauer and Nietzsche, where the Dionysiac confronts the Apollonian, separates music from all other arts. In a Jewish context, this particular confrontation is certainly irrelevant, Dionysius being as little a model as Apollo. Even so, their voice, appropriately varied, is audible in the bells, lyre, timbrel, viol, harp and horn of priest and Psalmist.

In God's preference to hear first the songs and praises of Israel before those of the ministering angels is shown his love for Israel, an ancient Midrash declares (in the name of R. Yishmael). Each and every angel and seraph 'that I have created must be silent until I have first heard and listened to the voice of the songs and praises of Israel, My son'. Not before 'all the angels of the firmament' have heard the songs and praises from below may they, from above, intone their own praise.[62]

If this is the case, it is clear that those prayers 'from below' must be animated by an intent that takes precedence over all else, and especially so in the case of the individual worshipper. The medieval *Sefer Hassidim*, for example, concerns itself, in its guidance and instruction for worship, almost exclusively with the matter of individual intent and has virtually nothing to say of tunefulness or melody, still less of synchronised prayer (even though worship is normally communal).[63]

The therapeutic value attributed to music also deserves a word: as a means, for example, to dispel melancholia. This is recommended by Maimonides, as an adjunct to pleasing the eye in surveying things of beauty (gardens, buildings, forms).[64] Thus, in his capacity as court physician to the Sultan of Egypt – a sufferer from constipation, dejection and poor digestion – Maimonides prescribed a regime which required his patient to spend at least two hours daily listening to music on a stringed instrument.[65] The classical case is the success of David's lyre-playing in removing 'the evil spirit' that afflicted King Saul (1 Sam.16:23). This case may well have served as a precedent to influence Maimonides, it is suggested.[66]

The singular sympathy extended to music and song alone, amongst all the arts, derives from their exclusively aural character. This is not so trivial as it may sound for, as I hope to show later (Chapter 8), crucial to the distinction between time and space and thereby also to the struggle against idolatry, is the distinction between aural and visual apprehension.

Even in its own terms however, music can be abused. In the synagogue for example, it demands to be rendered in its own terms by the person to whom it addresses itself lest it become pretext for performance and display by another. A synagogue is not a concert hall, theatre or opera house. In order to hold idolatry at bay, the aesthetic appeal must be confined to 'the shade of the Lord'.

The criteria governing the qualifications of a *hazan* (cantor) exemplify the care taken to exclude any untoward aestheticism. As codified in the Shulḥan Arukh (1563) these require the cantor to be free from transgressions, enjoy a good repute, be of modest demeanour, acceptable to the people, possess a pleasant voice and be familiar with the reading of the *Torah*, Prophets and Writings. Obviously, such a paragon of the cantoral virtues is rare; so that, if no one candidate proves to possess all these qualities, the community should choose the best man in the congregation in wisdom and good deeds. He must in any case be bearded. R. Moses Isserles (Cracow, sixteenth century) glosses the text to give priority to a boy of thirteen (the age of majority) who understands what he is reading and lacks a pleasant voice over an older, bearded, ignorant person who is acceptable to the congregation but does possess a pleasant voice.[67] Despite these precautions it is not unusual to find rabbinical censure directed against cantors not only unfamiliar with the cantillation of the *Torah* but who also compound their ignorance by the introduction of tunes taken from secular life and 'theatres'.[68] Only later, in conditions of emancipation and assimilation, was vocal performance *per se* esteemed. Then, in mid-nineteenth century Vienna, it did indeed become possible for the cantor to engage in *bel canto* and, like the famed Salomon Sulzer, a friend of Schubert, make it his task 'to free and purify ancient, traditional tunes . . . from later arbitrary and tasteless flourishes'.[69] Louis Lewandowski in Berlin took a similar role. But in both cases strong Protestant and (Jewish) reform influences were at work.[70]

Maimonides found potential for abuse in music's capacity to arouse 'the sensuous faculties', all the more likely should the performance take place in a wine shop and involve either a stringed instrument and/or a woman singer.[71]

More usual is the situation however, where aural appeal might echo visual in serving to dissociate the listener from due attention to the teaching of the *Torah*. This is the perception that has conditioned the presence of music, whether vocal or instrumental, as an adjunct or accompaniment to prayer. As we shall see, David himself is not spared rabbinic censure on this score. But the context it is, as ever, that determines what is permissible. At the inauguration of an orthodox synagogue in Bratislava in 1863 the chant *Ma Tovu* ('how goodly are your tents, O Jacob') could happily be sung to a popular air from Flotow's opera *Martha*.[72] But only because this chant did not form part of the liturgy proper. More daring was the inclusion of the 'Halleluyah' chorus from Handel's 'Messiah' at a service to rededicate the Hampstead synagogue (London, 1901).[73]

At Senigallia, near Ancona, in the seventeenth century, the issue of musical participation took a different and very controversial turn. The introduction of a choir to sing certain of the prayers aroused turmoil; first, because the choristers, in the course of their polyphonic chanting, each repeated the name of God in certain prayers; this, it was held, either implied the existence of a composite rather than a single being or infringed the notion of uniqueness. A defender of the innovation distinguished 'between the reprehensible repetition of words evoking the Divinity, and the (permissible) repetition of other words or of entire verses . . .'; but it was also held that during the recitation of prayers singing was impermissible, and, further, that singing interfered

with prayer. This was substantiated in those London synagogues which, from about 1840, introduced choirs, only to
find, by the end of the decade, a decline in the audible
participation of the worshippers.[74] This is indeed the nub
of the matter for it exemplifies the power at the artist's disposal to divert an attention that belongs to the individual's
relationship to the service in which he is an engaged participant – not merely as member of an audience. This is
precisely the point of the disdain expressed by R. Esriel
Hildesheimer for 'the magnificent "Temple" (in Brünn)
decorated with an organ *comme il faut* (which) is nothing
more than a theatre'.[75]

The same point is made even more forcefully by the Talmud when it accuses David of converting normative demands
into an aesthetic value. This is read into Psalm 119:54 where
David declares: 'Your statutes have been my songs in the
house of my pilgrimage'. But is a statute a song? There is
no reason of course why a 'statute' should not be formulated in pleasing, gracious terms; also, that the 'statutes' have
the capacity to beautify Israel is a familiar idea (see page
191, fn. 22); there is also no reason why a 'song' should
not be expressed with earnestness. 'Why should the devil
have all the best tunes?', a band-leader in the Salvation Army
once wanted to know. But David has in fact changed the
text and that is why his Talmudic critics censured him for
diminishing 'words of *Torah*' (TB Sotah 35a); that is, he
had degraded 'statutes' with their normative authority to
'songs', a species of *belles-lettres*.

The argument is this: that at some point, uncertain and
indeterminate but not for that reason any the less decisive,
a created entity in a sensitive environment will obscure the
'statute' that that environment is attempting to convey and
thereby deprive the 'statute' of its force. In other words, it
loses the characteristic of a statute – its character as imperative – and is transformed into a statement of something
that is dumb and inert. This does not need to be beautiful,
which is probably a misnomer in this context, but it does
need to have acquired that characteristic of beauty that calls
for nothing more than admiration and lacks all power to
address any capacity for volition. Does a statement, meta-
morphosed in this way, then degenerate into an object of

idolisation or merely, in an undemanding limbo, occupy some intermediate niche? The difference does not seem significant, insofar as both situations denote a state of neutralisation: the sole difference is the degree of passivity inherent in this neutralisation. But no matter what degree of passivity has been introduced into an imperative, the latter is to that extent disarmed and therefore, in its summons to the beholder, emasculated.

6 Man in His Image

Of almost any object a representative artifact intended solely and exclusively for decorative purposes, can be made. But not if that object be a man, still less if God be the object of the purported representation. At any *soi-disant* portrayal of God Jewish tolerance of the image stops absolutely short; and at any portrayal of the human being, relatively short. In each case the argument is similar; it is also grounded in such inter-dependent terms as to disclose ethical relevance to an apparent matter of aesthetics. Here, and more so than in any other context, artistic autonomy is circumscribed; the artist would otherwise, like Medusa, turn to stone whatever his gaze alights on. In Jewish terms, Medusa removes the distinction between man and inert nature.

The first of these prohibitions, and its rationale, finds no better formulation, mutatis mutandis, than in the iconoclastic argument presented by the Byzantine emperor Constantine V (741–75): 'how is it possible that there can be a drawing, that is an image, made of Our Lord Jesus Christ, when He is one person of two natures in a union of the material and the immaterial which admits no confusion? Since He has another immaterial nature conjoined to the flesh, and with these two natures He is one, and His person or substance is inseparable from the two natures, we hold that He cannot be depicted. For what is depicted is one person, and he who circumscribes that person has plainly circumscribed the divine nature which is incapable of being circumscribed'.[1] To the latter proposition any rabbi would assent without demur, distinguishing however between the incarnation of God in man and man created 'in the image' of God.

The iconoclasts went down to defeat, of which one consequence is dramatised in the Sistine Chapel which can serve – negatively – to epitomise one theme of this chapter; for Michelangelo's painting in the Sistine Chapel purporting to depict God breathing life into Adam exemplifies a category-mistake and amounts to no more than what has been felicitously likened to a painting of Zeus.[2] No visitor to the Sistine

Chapel is likely to confuse what he sees with God, still less to worship what he sees, but this depiction is still the product of a category-mistake in that creative power has been conceived in terms of inert matter, paint; and thereby, as Schwarzschild writes, 'made susceptible to fetishization'.[3] The painting constitutes an exemplary warning of the danger incurred when the verbal imagery of the Bible is transposed into figurative. Further, the artist has confused the uniquely incomparable with the comparable and to that extent demeaned it. 'To whom can you liken Me, so that we seem alike?' Isaiah asks rhetorically. He then makes merry at those who hire a metal-worker to make their gold and silver into a god. 'I am divine and there is none like Me' (Is.46:5,9).

Even at the level of verbal discourse the Bible takes care, in describing its theophanies, to emphasise their surroundings rather than God himself.[4] This is not to say that the temptation of immanence has always been resisted, but this is virtually so. It seems that in the whole history of Jewish art no more than four works purportedly display an image of God and of these only one appears to be the work of a Jewish artist. This is part of the frontispiece of a rabbinical work printed in Frankfurt (1698); it is described as 'nothing more than a face with indifferently depicted features, a sketchy hand and arm and 'shoulders' wrapped in some sort of nebulous drapery, possibly an attempt to indicate a *tallit* (prayer shawl)'.[5] It is also exceptionally rare to find God's presence indicated even through a depicted hand, though such cases do exist; for example, in the synagogues of Rawitsch and Ragozen;[6] and in miniature illustrations to the *Haggadah*, also of extreme rarity.[7]

Where God's presence is sought in a representational context, angels become an expedient solution, as in depictions of the creation of man.[8] But there are also instances where an angel is found *de trop* and it will be reduced to an arm and hand, or to a wing.[9] In an illuminated Pentateuch of the tenth century this procedure went so far that the artist used foliage patterns to replace even cherubim.[10] Resort has also been had to rays of light as an indication of the presence of the divine, in an explicitly anti-anthropomorphic gesture (for example, in the famous Serajevo *Haggadah*). This parallels Islamic practice. The denial of any anthropomorphic image to God is met with at its most extreme in the Talmudic exegesis of Exodus 33:23: 'I will take away My hand and you will see My back'. 'This teaches', argued R. Ḥana b. Bizna, 'that the Holy One blessed be He showed Moses the knot of the phylacteries' (*tefillin*) (TB Ber. 7a). But since the phylacteries house salient extracts of the Biblical text and are a nullity if they do not, when this scene is 'unpacked', it is in the guise of his teaching that God is effectively showing himself to Moses.

If God may not – and indeed, can not – be shown in material form, then neither may man, except in certain conditions. Absolutely and unconditionally disallowed is the three-dimensional statue of a human being. The temptation is certainly there but also the resistance: manifest, for example, in Ben Gurion's refusal to countenance the erection of stone monuments to the fallen heroes of the Israeli war of independence, and in Ernst Simon's opposition to a monument in honour of the great humanitarian, Henrietta Szold.[11] In 1860, a *cause célèbre* united three rabbinical authorities – S. R. Hirsch (Frankfurt), Z. Frankel (Breslau) and N. M. Adler (London) – in the collective condemnation of a proposed statue in New Orleans to Judah Touro, the American patriot and philanthropist: not only did it contradict 'ancient Jewish custom and usage'; also, it was 'according to Jewish law, prohibited'.[12]

To Blumenberg the prohibition of images 'is much more general than a mere prohibition of the divine image; it is above all prohibition of the copying of man' – attributed to fear lest the copy be abused by magic.[13] Be that as it may, the Talmud reads 'You shall not make with Me gods of silver, gods of gold' (Ex.20:20), to include also the human form (TB AZ 43b). In his Talmudic commentary, the medieval exegete, R. Abraham ibn Daud, utilises the ambiguity in the unvocalised text of the Pentateuch to conjoin 'not to make Me'/ 'not to make with Me', from which he deduces that the conjoined reading denotes 'the form of a man', especially the human countenance.[14] This introduces the familiar dichotomy, distinguishing that which may only be visually depicted from that which may be made the object of verbal description: in his verbal portrayal of the male and female form the author of the Song of Songs is unsparing of such detail as would certainly render impermissible a physical portrayal of these forms.

But the prohibition does more than enunciate the familiar; it also emphasises the unique status of man. Traditional and later Biblical exegesis already makes clear (see Chapter 1) the generosity with which the fabrication of well-nigh any image is regarded, provided alone that it has no association with worship. To the human being however, this freedom does not apply, even where there is no association with worship and where the artifact consequently falls into the only other aesthetic category; that of adornment or decoration.

This limitation brings the human form into a category distinct from all others. To the human figure *per se*, especially in three-dimensional or even embossed form, liberty of representation (as distinct from the depiction of an animal or flower, say) is strictly qualified, irrespective of circumstances. The singular status of man is emphasised in his exclusion from the general rule (as summarised by Maimonides) that permits the manufacture of any of these other forms for decorative purposes: 'the only image that must not be made for decoration is solely the image of man' and this refers to the image of a whole man with all his limbs.[15]

There is an interesting gloss to this, arguing that Maimonides referred only to fixed forms of the human being and not to casual and incidental forms such as the masks with human faces used in children's games or by actors.[16] But this hardly makes an overall difference. Man's exceptional status in the scale of the permissible is underlined in the *Ḥinukh*, a thirteenth century exposition of the 613 commandments in the *Torah*; in addition to the general commandment prohibiting the manufacture of graven images etc., the author identifies 'a prohibition with special reference to the form of a man that we should not make it/him at all, even for decoration', and this is because there is a sense in which the human intellect partakes of the divine (ref. to Gen. 1:26–27). This passage in the *Ḥinukh* also validates the inclusion in the image-ban of a human representation (subject to certain safeguards) in that it attributes to such a representation an idolatrous outcome by virtue of the human relationship to God.[17]

Where, specifically, does the objection lie, in the case of a human being? After all, it is not an idol that is at issue – merely, it would seem, a statue in an alcove, say. The question is this: if, by definition, this particular image makes not the slightest reference to any idolatrous intent or practice, whence arises the prohibition? Why may a human image be not even an adornment, *tout court*? I am tempted to answer without further ado – does not a human being deserve better? But before that point is reached, two arguments need to be considered: the first will refer to the human relationship with God; the second to the effect generated when the human is reproduced in material form.

As to the first: a central theme is grounded in the creation of man as a partner with God 'in the image' and 'after the likeness' of God (Gen.1:26–27; 5:1–3; 9:6). The exact purport of these passages is certainly not clear; likewise, R. Joshua b. Levi's reference to man as 'the icon of God' (Deut. Rabbah 4:4).[18] How is this to be reconciled with Isaiah's reference to the 'incomparability' of God?

It is generally agreed however, that between God and man some sort of correlation must exist so that, for example, it makes sense for God to summon the Israelites to model their own conduct on his (Lev.19:20; 20:26). In this case the correlation is ethical. This is wide in scope: it makes the care of the body an obligation imposed by respect for its creator. Hillel, one of the leading Pharisaic teachers, saw in the human body some sort of repository of the divine, which involved an appropriate degree of hygienic concern. Where are you going?, Hillel was once asked by his students. 'To perform a commandment, he answered. They asked, what commandment is it? He replied: to bathe in the bathhouse. They asked, is this a commandment? He said, yes; if the statues of kings which are set up in public places are entrusted to someone whose job it is to wash and polish them . . . how much more so is it true for me, who was created in the image and likeness of God'.[19] The correlation extends to the comparable possession of, and capacity to, exercise moral attributes: for example, to clothe the naked, visit the sick, comfort the bereaved, bury the dead. That is how R. Hama understood walking in the steps of God (Dt.13:5).[20] In whatever way man is treated there is repercussion on the divine: 'the oppressor of the poor affronts His maker; he who favours the needy gives honour to His maker' (Prov.14:31). In the most extreme case, murder diminishes the divine image; one source makes a comparison, in principle, between the destruction of a royal image in its impact on royal status and that of murder in diminishing the status of the divine.[21] R. Meir developed this argument in his exposition of the Biblical prohibition against leaving the body of a hanged man suspended overnight on a tree (Dt.21:23) (TB San. 46b.).

We may even perceive the correlation of God and man in the power ascribed to Rava, a Talmudic sage, to create a man as a means to come closer to God (TB San. 65b). Idel writes: 'by creating an anthropoid, the Jewish master is not only able to display his creative forces, but may attain the experience of the creative moment of God . . . we may describe the Golem practices as an attempt of man to know God by the art He uses in order to create man'.[22]

The simple answer, therefore, to the question at the outset is this: if God may not be depicted, then neither may man, by reason of their very correlation and partnership in the governance of the natural polity. To depict man is simultaneously an attempt to depict him who is the 'icon' of God. This will be *a fortiori* the case if it is in the guise of the semblance of a human being that God appears to the prophets – as in Ezekiel's vision of the heavenly chariot, surmounted by 'the semblance of a human form'.[23] Obviously, also the anthropomorphic language of the Bible in reference to God must strengthen the association with and, by extension, the prohibition of, the human image.

The closeness to God, mediated through conduct, and the 'cleaving' to God of the Jewish mystics must both be distinguished absolutely from identification with God;[24] and no less from the concept of God's incarnation in man. That is why between a Jewish and Christian aesthetic in this respect, there is a certain asymmetry. If, in the former, the image of God in man makes man's depiction impermissible, it is in the latter the dogma of the Trinity and the Incarnation that legitimises and encourages the possibility of figuring God in the image of man. In the one case it is because God and man are partners and share an 'image' that the depiction of either is prohibited; in the other case, it is through God's incarnation in man that the depiction is positively welcomed. In Gadamer's view, interpreting the controversy in the light of neo-Platonism, this made possible 'the development of the plastic arts in the Christian west'.[25]

But if, through the 'image' shared by God and man, and, consequently, through the conduct this imposes, God, so to speak, is already 'incarnate' in man, then these arts must exclude the depiction of either.

What, now, of the effect produced on the original by its reproduction? To anticipate, albeit crudely – the original, to a greater or lesser extent, forfeits its quality of uniqueness, in one way or another, and is devalued, not to say degraded, through multiplication in a material representation. A modest diversion will help to explain the refusal to accept jeopardy to human uniqueness: I have in mind the *Torah*'s method of counting votes in an assembly – not heads are counted but each member is required to deposit a token coin in accordance with his decision. Only the tokens are then counted.[26] Similarly, in describing the procedure for selecting the thirteen priests (from a much larger number) required to service the daily offerings in the Temple, the procedure was to take *pars pro toto*: Rashi explains that the selection was made not by counting individual priests but by using their outstretched fingers as token of selection (TB Yoma 22a). In ascertaining whether a quorum of ten adult males is present for public prayer, the custom is not to count by a digit per head but by each of the ten words constituting verse 9 of Psalm 28. The divine punishment visited on King David for calling an unauthorised census makes the point yet more dramatic (2 Sam.24:10 ff.). In other words, human beings are not digits in a series or sum total, without personality.[27] But to treat them as such is to flout their individuality and only by the exercise of coercion is this possible, as any army commander or prison governor will confirm. In dystopias it is customary for the protagonists to lack names and be known by their digital reference (for example, D-503, the chief protagonist of Zamyatin's 'We').

If the aspiration to safeguard the individual is held in mind, it becomes easier to appreciate the affront inflicted on the human being when, in three-dimensional form, it is reproduced as a totality. Why, first, does the complete diminish? Nietzsche, with a characteristic *soupçon* of malice, takes the eulogy as his illustration: the eulogist 'needs precisely an enticing incompleteness, as an irrational element, which conjures up to the fantasy of the listener a sea, and like a fog conceals the coast opposite, i.e. the limitation of the object to be eulogized. When one mentions the known virtues of a person and does so in detail and expansively, then this always arouses the suspicion that these are the only virtues. The total eulogist places himself above the eulogised, he seems to look down on him from above. That is why the complete diminishes'.[28] It deprives the depicted object of the capacity to make its full impact. Conversely, the 'suggestive veiling' familiar to erotic art confirms the argument: 'the more vital the feature that is indicated by the context and yet omitted, the more intense seems to be the process that is started off'.[29] Second, obviously, the uniqueness is ipso facto jeopardised. Was Jane Morris 'an original or a copy?', Henry James asked himself, bewildered by her appearance in a multitude of pre-Raphaelite paintings; third, by virtue of the fact that the process of jeopardy is implemented through matter, the materialised human being loses his life.

Only in relation to man can the whole of this *Problematik* arise at all and this is because of man's iconic status in relation to God. To make this icon present in wood, marble, stone or whatever is to petrify that divine image, to present 'life' in terms of inert, inanimate matter, which is tantamount to a form of intellectual self-destruction.[30] (The satire in prophetic merriment at this contrast is paralleled, albeit without the moral chastisement, in Bergson's theory of the comic. This too has its ground in the perceived contrast between the rigidly static and the living: monsieur Perrichon is at the railway station, nervously counting his pieces of luggage: '. . . four, five, six, my wife seven, my daughter eight, and myself nine . . . we are nine').[31]

By no means is it necessary to be Jewish thus to argue. The crucial point is the limitation inherent in matter which leads Hegel, for example, to anticipate from this defectiveness, and even welcome, an end altogether to art: this follows his leitmotiv that the medium of depiction must be consonant with that which is to be depicted. Broadly speaking, this can be exemplified in the contrast that Hegel makes between the classical art of the Greeks, to which the three-dimensional medium of sculpture is appropriate, and the romantic art of the Christian West, to which the two-dimensional art of painting is appropriate. Appropriateness is here determined by the notion that the stage of the spirit embodied in the sculpture of the classical god 'should stand before us in blissful tranquillity in its bodily form and in immediate unity therewith'. But in the case of the Christian divinity, Christ's body is secondary to his spiritual characteristics, serves only as a vehicle for the Incarnation and is ultimately transcended so that these characteristics can be made manifest. But 'this cannot be portrayed in the form of Greek beauty'. In terms of this progression Hegel envisages as climax of the romantic altogether 'the contingency of both inner and outer and the separation of these two sides whereby art annuls itself and shows the necessity for consciousness to acquire higher forms for the grasping of the true than art is in a position to supply'.[32] At this point in the unfolding of spirit, the medium in which the artist works shows itself inadequate and unequal to the task.[33] But the point at which the Hegelian aesthetic culminates in its own self-destruction is for the Jewish its actual *point de départ*.

The theme is not that of idolatry in the narrow sense – the statue, say, may do no more than occupy some innocent alcove or niche, but in the sense that this statue spuriously metamorphoses matter into life and spirit, it is indeed an idolatrous object.[34]

Any attempted reproduction will be vitiated by the material used. Matter, which is, as the prophets argued, inert (see Chapter 1), cannot, by virtue of its very nature, become the repository of any semblance of human life. In fact, as Mendelssohn points out, it is only to a sort of connivance between the artist and the spectator that the artifact owes its credence and power of conviction. This derives from 'the bond between the sign and the signified' which itself derives from the habit- and convention-bound capacity for illusion and self-deception. We know that the actor is not the jealous Moor who kills Desdemona; that the Laocoon of marble feels no pain from the snake bites –

nevertheless, 'if only we bring with us the intention to allow ourselves to be pleasantly deceived, then sensuous awareness (Erkenntnis) will play its usual game . . . and cause us to interest ourselves in persons who are not present. We take genuine sympathy in non-real feelings and actions because from the non-reality, for our pleasure, we intentionally abstract'.[35]

The 'bond' however, of which Mendelssohn speaks, is imperceptible to the spectator and that is why he can assimilate the sign to the signified in such a way as, for example, to attribute life to inert matter – which is precisely the target and a theme that never departs from Jewish thinking, spanning the centuries. In the carved image of wood and stone, encased in gold and silver, 'there is no life', proclaims Habakkuk (2:18–19, seventh-sixth century BCE); from nineteenth-century Vilna the prophet's words re-echo in Abraham Paperna's denial to the sculptor's artifact of 'the attribute of spirit and the inner movements of the soul';[36] and from twentieth-century Paris in the words of Lévinas: 'within the life, or rather the death, of a statue, an instant endures infinitely'. Laocoon will never escape from the serpents' grip: the Mona Lisa will never stop smiling. The future of either will never arrive.[37]

The photographer's camera achieves the same effect, as Bergson argued.[38] Proust argued likewise, though circuitously; his is the argument that so long as she is observed the loved one lives; when unloved, she is immaterialised; but of the former, 'on n'en a jamais que des photographies manquées'.[39] Only by bringing movement to a halt can the camera capture movement (hence the term 'shoot'). (It is curious to note however, that earlier Jewish thinkers were in the main quite unconcerned with the one-dimensional, 'still' portrait, treating it as of no account – see below, pages 127–8.)

In effect the human subject is petrified and it is here, no doubt, that the Biblical, and particularly the prophetic, rejection of idolatry directs its thrust – in an attempt to save life from extinction at the hands of the artist. This fate is beautifully conveyed – all the more so because it is done innocently and inadvertently – in the argument that occasionally the artist can achieve 'the perfection of arrest'.[41] But to be in a condition of 'arrest' is scarcely to be alive, which could, even in the most favourable of circumstances, hardly be expected if, as the author also writes, the artist's material is by nature 'inanimate'.[41]

This line of thought, with its aim to safeguard life and movement, ramifies into, and has certain parallels with, the reluctance of the Talmudic sages to sanction the writing down of the Oral Law save in exceptional circumstances, on the grounds of 'the lesser evil' (TB Git. 60a; Tem. 14b). Their fear derives from a view that sees the written state as a delimitation of oral discourse, reducing the flexibility of textual interpretation and the concomitant possibility of dialogue with an interlocutor. If so, there would be a further close parallel with the Socratic argument: '. . . writing is unfortunately like painting, for the creations of the painter have the attitude of life, and yet if you ask them a question they preserve a solemn silence'.[42]

But to the hazard of material reproduction it is the human being who remains most vulnerable. Obviously, no convincing reproduction can be made. Even a Talmudic sage could fabricate no more than a dumb homonculus. But it is not arbitrary or merely a matter of convention that the three-dimensional statue of a human being should constitute the acme of the idolatrous, for this mode of depiction purveys visual and tactile qualities accessible to no other mode. It has uniquely life-like attributes, which is undoubtedly the reason why the rabbinic aesthetic makes a very sharp distinction between the three-dimensional (even the merely embossed) and any other mode of depiction (see below, page 128). It serves as an object-lesson and bench-mark in the demonstration of the impermissibly idolatrous.[43]

At this point it is necessary to attempt to separate two inter-dependent arguments. First, if the statue is anathema it is because it denotes an attempt at a totalising, annihilating aesthetic; second: to the extent that this attempt succeeds, the more the mind of the beholder is deprived of its reflective capacity. Conversely, if this nexus is to be broken, the less totalising the attempt, the less deprivation will be suffered by the beholder's mind.

Psalmist and prophet point to the confusion suffered by the person who takes his figured idol to be in some sense alive. He is in an authentic state of befuddlement. This will range all the way from those who take seriously a material symbol as a medium of communication to those who perceive a statue move or shed a tear.[44] It is not necessary to engage in detail with all these varied phenomena. But I can try at least to indicate the nature of the frustration engendered by the statue (to which the above reactions can be regarded as a 'creative' but mistaken response).

The aesthetic theories of the late eighteenth and nineteenth centuries are helpful, in that they affirm the stultification of the capacity for reflection exercised by the image and indicate also how, through its diminution, this might be overcome. Schopenhauer locates the argument for diminution/incompleteness in the framework of a vision that sees 'satisfaction' as 'genuinely and essentially always only negative. . .'.[45] Conversely, to withhold satisfaction has for Schopenhauer a positive value. He quotes Voltaire: 'le secret d'être ennuyeux, c'est de tout dire'. Schopenhauer takes as an exemplar the wax model of a human being, and maintains that its very capacity for *vraisemblance* removes its aesthetic effect and thereby exposes an incapacity to affect the beholder. Its very completeness is its undoing. Such figures, Schopenhauer writes, 'although precisely in them the imitation of nature reaches its highest degree . . . leave nothing over for the imagination to do . . . we are wholly satisfied with the impression of a work of art only then when it leaves something behind, that we, with all our reflection on it, cannot bring down to the clarity of a concept'.[46]

But it is *par excellence* in Kant's Third Critique where mimesis, mediated through the sensible, is rejected for its constricting effect on the imaginative and ratiocinative capacities, that a close approach to the conceptualisation of a Jewish approach will be found.[47] Kant shows both the obstacle to reflection created by the sensuous and also the means to its removal. Obviously, the Kantian aesthetic (no less than that of Hegel or Schopenhauer) lacks that relationship to the divine characteristic of the Jewish. In fact, all three philosophers took, for different reasons, a distinctly negative view of Judaism. But this must not obscure the varied paths which led, in some degree, to their convergence with a Jewish aesthetic.

In the case of Kant this is all the more marked by reason

of his appreciation for the second commandment: 'perhaps there is no more sublime passage in the law book of the Jews'. What this eulogy has in it that is both striking and meaningful is its association with the abstract mode of the presentation of the sublime, 'which is altogether negative as to what is sensuous. For though the imagination no doubt, finds nothing beyond the sensible world to which it can lay hold, still this thrusting aside of the sensible barriers gives it a feeling of being unbounded; and that removal is thus a presentation of the infinite'. The presentation is indeed negative, Kant concludes, 'but still it expands the soul'.[48]

The basis for this dismissal of the sensuous as 'inadequate' in relation to reason is to be found in Kant's earlier distinction between 'free beauty' (*pulchritudo vaga*) as compared with 'dependent beauty' (*pulchritudo adhaerens*). The former is exemplified in flowers, birds, fishes, designs à la grecque, foliage for wallpapers, and, in music by fantasias (music lacking a theme). This type of beauty owes its superiority to the fact that it allows of a 'pure judgement of taste' – 'no concept is here presupposed of any end for which the manifold should serve the given object, and which the latter therefore should represent – an encumbrance which would only restrict the freedom of the imagination that, as it were, is at play in the contemplation of the outward form'.

By contrast, 'dependent beauty' (of a human being, building, house) is less pure because in this case the beauty of the object's presentation has to be considered in relation to the concept of the internal end that the object serves, 'and is thus placed under a restriction'.[49] This restriction or limitation inherent in 'dependent beauty' is primarily mimetic in character whereas Kant's concern is with a sublime which is to be found 'in an object even devoid of form, so far as it immediately involves, or else by its presence provokes, a representation of limitlessness, yet with a superadded thought of its totality'. 'The sublime . . . cannot be contained in any sensuous form, but rather concerns ideas of reason, which, although no adequate presentation of them is possible, may be excited and called into the mind by that very inadequacy itself which does admit of sensuous presentation'.[50] This denial to the sublime of the possibility of representation brings the Kantian aesthetic into convergence with the rabbinic insofar as for both art now takes on the task of decoration.[51]

What Kant and Schopenhauer are concerned with is the power of 'sensible barriers' to inhibit the reflective imagination; conversely, with the 'limitlessness' that the removal of such barriers encourages or at least, allows of. Hegel speaks of art having to 'annul itself' in favour of a higher form of comprehension; Nietzsche, of the diminution imposed by 'the complete'. Foss writes: 'completeness, perfect totality is something finished, limited . . . Totality is limitation'.[52]

These considerations are all to be found in a Jewish aesthetic even though this concerns itself only with man, and, more specifically with man as 'the icon of God'. Notwithstanding its very different pre-occupations – or perhaps, because of them – a Jewish aesthetic must also take account of the danger inherent in the complete, having regard to its power to dominate the beholder.

The response is found in the intimations of a negative aesthetic, comparable to the theology of negative attributes constructed by Maimonides and his predecessors, which made it possible to formulate the notion of a God devoid of Biblical anthropomorphisms and anthropopathisms. Man also ceases to be anthropomorphic. The attribution to God of negative predicates brings *pari passu* a closer apprehension of God, in the same way, conversely, as the attribute of positive predicates would obfuscate and distort that apprehension, in the opinion of Maimonides (Guide, I:59). This negativity, tantamount to a theology that purifies the notion of God to one of absolute simplicity, would then be parallelled in the progressive need to purify the presentation of the human form. In such a case the latter's 'purification', that is, its loss of dimension, could also be analogous to the position that is reached when all that can positively be known of God is indicated through his identification with his actions.[53] If 'silence (with regard to God) is praise', as Maimonides reads Psalm 65:2 (Guide, ibid.), then this 'silence' would correspond to the complete absence of the human form.

Omnis determinatio est negatio: this dictum of the Scholastics and Spinoza serves to gloss the Maimonidean argument. Every determination imposes a negation by reason of the fact that a corresponding possibility is thereby annulled. Every possibility that becomes actual is *ipso facto* one less possibility to be actualised. To add is therefore to subtract, both in respect of the artifact and in respect of the beholder of the artifact. In order that the model be preserved entire, this aesthetic requires that it be presented defectively. The fewer predicates made of the model, the more 'the essence' of the latter will survive.

The beneficient effect of diminution is exhibited at its most spectacular in the power to make an idol *kosher*: all that is needful is to chip a bit off. Not that this alone is sufficient: the idolater must make some deliberate show of repudiation or insult to his idol. This must also be accompanied by the deliberate infliction of some form of incompleteness; in conjunction the two acts remove the idol's holy status.[54] This is not, strictly speaking, an act of iconoclasm for though the 'icon' is indeed deconsecrated and thereby its status radically changed, it is by no means destroyed but now can happily enter the only other category of artifact – the decorative. The essential has been achieved in that incompleteness has broken the bond between sign and significand and 'the ordinary materiality of the sign made plain'.[55]

The negative aesthetic with its call for incompleteness, its rejection of totality, applies equally to the human form, of which only a defective presentation is permissible. 'For a Jew to be entire', said a witty Frenchman (Eméric Deutsch), 'he must always feel that something is lacking to him'.[56] This emphasis on the need for incompleteness applies above all to the human countenance. The Talmud itself maintains: 'all countenances are appropriate for depiction except for that of a man'.[57]

R. Joseph Caro expounds the reason for this limitation: 'You shall not make with Me, not make Me, i.e. the image in which I became visible to the prophets' (the face of a man).[58] It is facial imagery that between man and God establishes a bond. It is here that 'the image of God' in man shows itself and here, consequently, that the bond must be broken, through limiting the depiction of the human face. The human countenance alone makes manifest what is divine in man.[59] If the human being is to be depicted this must therefore be accomplished in such a way as absolutely to remove any reference to its divinity and for this purpose the face offers itself as the paramount cynosure. At the 'secular' level this is true in another sense. Simmel writes: 'aesthetically, there is no other part of the body whose wholeness can as easily be destroyed by the disfigurement of only one of its elements'.[60] The face is expressive as no other part of the body. The face speaks, whereas other parts of the body, though they too can speak, cannot, to quote Simmel again, 'signify the *kind* of personality'.[61] The face then, is uniquely vulnerable and expressive: not to mention that the fate of the face enhances or diminishes the dignity of the whole person. This insight is the stock-in-trade of any portrait painter or caricaturist;[62] not to mention the paramount value attached to human individuality and differentiation.[63] That is why the practice of Jewish artists has sometimes been to leave facial features blank; or the human figures are shown only from the rear; or grotesque and hybrid figures are depicted that combine human and animal features. A noteworthy example is the Sarajevo *Haggadah* showing human beings with birds' heads; a thirteenth-century manuscript of the Book of Ruth has miniatures depicting human figures surmounted by grotesque animal heads.[64] Rabbis and others, admittedly, have at times raised objections to the presence of such imagery but not on account of any supposed idolatrousness – only that it might operate as a factor of disturbance (above page 101 ff.).

If, however, the face is to be depicted at all, then this must normally be effected in such a manner as to be recognisably unrecognisable. The means to this end is portrayal in the flat: tapestry portrayal, for example, is discussed in these terms by the Tosafists: 'those forms of a man which are dyed on to cloth or embroidered are permitted since the countenance is not complete but only half'.[65] This is a statement of the twelfth century approximately. Support was by no means wholehearted. Rabbi Moses of Coucy (thirteenth century) found that to depict 'the countenance of a man by itself' was not prohibited but since there was 'no clear proof' either way, he must err (if err it be) on the side of stringency.[66] The laws – or perhaps directives would be more apt a term – kept pace with aesthetic developments so that subsequently portrait painting can also be dealt with: in his commentary to Caro's Shulḥan Arukh, R. Shabtai Ha-Cohen (the 'Shakh') writes: '. . . all forbidden forms are forbidden only if they represent complete forms, such as a man with two eyes, a complete nose, a complete body, etc. but not half-images in the way that some painters draw only one side of a form. The latter is not forbidden'.[67]

These are examples where the incomplete or *non finito* is depicted in two-dimensional form. The problem arises however, so soon as even the *non finito* is depicted in three-dimensional form. To ask whether the same latitude extends to a raised/embossed form of the *non finito*, for example to a sculptured head or a bust of head and shoulders, is to enter an area fraught with the utmost tension. Caro ruled, following the argument of one of the most distinguished medieval authorities, Rabbenu Asher: 'there are those who hold that the prohibition (of the image) does not refer to the human shape or a dragon but only the shape when it is complete in all its parts, but the likeness of the head, or the body without the head is not forbidden, neither to him who finds it nor to him who makes it'.[68]

But there is no doubt that any three-dimensional sculptural presentation, *finito* or not, affronts Jewish aesthetic sensitivity, even though no explicit legal objection may be sustainable. Thus the Tosafists maintain that 'a complete human face carved in lacquer' does infringe the Second Commandment.[69] It was not therefore arbitrary for R. Moses Schreiber (the 'Ḥatam Sofer', Pressburg, nineteenth century) to prohibit prayers at a grave marked by a tombstone that bore the statue of a man in relief – the figure must first be removed or 'squashed', he demanded.[70] The tension between what is shown and the mode of showing is truly palpable in a responsum (of 1931) sent by R. Abraham Kuk, the Ashkenazi chief rabbi in mandatory Palestine, to Professor Klein of the Hebrew University, Jerusalem. The latter had consulted Kuk in regard to the proposed presentation of a bust to a retiring colleague. The first part of Kuk's response considers those authorities (such as Caro, Rabbenu Asher and the Tosafists) whose teaching was reconcilable with the making of the bust. He next considered the contrary views of the 'Mordecai' and R. Moses of Coucy and of R. Jacob Emden who denied the legitimacy of a bust on the grounds that the countenance depicted would be recognisable and raised, even though a complete human form was certainly not part of the proposed artifact. Kuk at length concluded: 'it is impossible for me to protest at those who permit the retention (of a bust) if it is not made by a Jew'. But the very terminology suggests he is not happy with his conclusion, and he continues: 'after all this I do say that although it is possible to find permission for this in accordance with the law the spirit of the sages is not happy with this and the spirit of pure Judaism is opposed to all statues of a man and happy is the portion of he who can dissuade those who wish to erect a statue even in the form of a bust; although I found it my duty to explain the arguments as they are and to show the permissive view, but, for all this, I maintain that a blessing will fall to him who refrains from this and will erect to a dear colleague some lasting memorial in keeping with the spirit of our people and the *Torah*, in its full understanding'.[71]

To introduce into the determination of a legal decision such factors as the 'spirit of the sages' or 'spirit of our people' is undoubtedly unusual. Clearly however, Kuk's conclusion conforms to empirical fact and has virtually the status of customary law: whereas the number of portraits (and photos) of rabbis, say, is legion,[72] I find it almost impossible to recall a single bust, still less a statue.

The thrust of Kuk's argument, though not his conclusion, is supported by an earlier case: Rabbi Joseph Mitrani had to rule on the use of candelabra bearing complete human faces. ('Complete' is not defined but it must certainly denote raised or embossed in some manner.) Mitrani, like Kuk, recounted the arguments for and against, and came to a negative decision, not on the basis of an appeal to 'spirit' but on the legal principle that where the authorities held conflicting views (as in this instance) and since the issue at stake involved a prohibition proclaimed by the *Torah* and not simply by the rabbis, it was incumbent on the decisor to be stringent rather than lenient in his interpretation of the law.[73]

Given this uncertainty and undeniable inhibition, it is clear why rabbinic aesthetics should in certain instances require additional precautionary diminution – even where the arti-

fact is already *non-finito*. If, for example, the seal on a sig-
net ring bears the embossed likeness of a man, then it may
not be worn but can be used as a seal, for it will produce
only a sunken and hence innocuous impression. If the seal
is sunken, then the ring can be worn but may not be used
as a seal, for it will produce an embossed human image.
R. Judah, it appears, had a ring of the latter type. He was
accordingly admonished by his colleague, Samuel, a third-
century sage of Babylon, to 'take out its eyes'. Rashi explains this to mean: 'diminish its form'.[74] The Tosafists add
that in this way R. Judah would be exonerated from the
suspicion that he had transgressed the prohibition 'not to
make Me. . .'.[75] Theodor Reik, the early psychoanalyst, records
this anecdote: when his widowed grandfather left a ghetto
environment near the Austro-Hungarian border to join his
children and grandchildren in Vienna, one of his first actions was to strike away the nose from a marble bust of Jove
or Apollo that stood on the family sideboard.[76] To avert
misunderstanding – the fact that a Greek god formed the
object of the depiction is immaterial. In a precisely analogous case Moses and Aaron met the same fate: R. Moses
Schreiber required a silversmith who had fashioned two
figurines of Moses and Aaron as adornment to a Scroll of
the Law to remove from the figures the tips of their noses.[77]

Perhaps also, a truncated Moses on a wood-carved *mezuzah*
responds to the same demand for de-formation.[78]

The extreme mode in the de-formation of a three-dimensional depiction is reached when the actual face of the bust
is dispensed with. I have already referred to the case where
a statue in relief on a tombstone had to be 'removed' or
'squashed' (see page 128). It is now maintained, however,
that the approval given by Rabbenu Asher to a human bust
(see page 128) did not extend to the inclusion of the facial
features: a style reminiscent of Henry Moore's was demanded
by R. Abraham Zvi-Hirsch Eisenstadt (Lithuania, nineteenth
century): he argued that only to the depiction of a head
'without the form of a recognisable face' did the permission extended by Rabbenu Asher to human statuary apply:
'it is not enough that it be without a body'. Eisenstadt also
disallowed even 'a smooth head' if set on a complete human body.[79]

It is not only man who must not be permitted to suffer from replication. The relevance of the prohibition in this respect gains further emphasis from the fact that the holiness of the Temple in Jerusalem and its appurtenances extends to them also the same protection from any exact reproduction. This again may only be defective or imperfect. A candelabrum, for example, must not be made on the model of that in the Temple (which had seven branches) but only with five, six or eight branches. Even if of a different metal no seven-branched copy might be made.[80] This would make the unique arbitrarily renewable and ephemeral. Rashi quotes a source that would also debar reproductions of the cherubim in the Temple from installation in synagogues.[81] In his much-quoted discussion of the loss of aura and disrupted tradition suffered by a unique object when it is mechanically reproduced, Walter Benjamin has rationalised the Talmudic rabbinic argument. The latter is of course far more stringent, for Benjamin was concerned only with mechanical reproduction; the Talmud with reproduction by any means.[82]

To revert to man: here the negative aesthetic of the rabbis finds its rationale in terms of the unique status of man as the sole being to be created 'in the image of God'. The means whereby to reconcile this status with the plastic depiction of man is the technique of the *non finito*, the fragmentary. There may also be affinity here with Benjamin's notion of *das Ausdruckslose* (the expressionless) and *das Bilderlose* (the imagelessness).[83]

The rabbinic presentation of the *non finito* in its varied forms relevant to the human being – as two-dimensional painting, as bust of head and shoulders, with perhaps a 'smoothed' or 'diminished' or absent countenance – enjoys support from the philosophers.[84] It frees the imagination and reflective capacity from domination at the hands of the sensuous (Kant); it exposes the incapacity of matter to contain ultimate spirit (Hegel); it meets with Schopenhauer and Nietzsche in the reminder that the effort at totality contained in the *finito* is ultimately unsatisfying and perhaps even self-destructive. The work is deliberately 'open', awaiting completion, finality and stability, which all are in fact withheld.[85]

The technique of incompleteness had to await the late nineteenth and twentieth century for its full implementation. It hails 'Picasso, but not Titian, Ingres or Poussin'.[86] To Scholem, Picasso's 'Woman with Violin' had 'something Jewish about its look' (*mutet jüdisch an*) and he grounds this judgment in the view that 'the prohibition of the "portrait" in Judaism means precisely this: disintegration in the symbol'. 'The art of Judaism seems to me in fact to rest on the symbolic disintegration of space';[86a] and to Picasso I would add Henry Moore, in view of R. Eisenstadt's remarks (see page 130).

For all that, the limits of this convergence and support must be retained. Kant, it is true, does indeed associate his anti-mimetic aesthetic with the 'sublime' Second Commandment and there his understanding of the political and religious control of iconography certainly meets with a Jewish echo; also Hegel's contrast of the lyric and the plastic in the Jewish approach to God is consonant with the demands of the Second Commandment. But neither, it seems, is centrally concerned with the need to suppress idolatry, that is to avert the identification of spirit – 'the image of God' – with matter, and to this end the concept of the *non finito* is crucial. The effect is twofold: first, the face of the image is in some way changed, which necessarily differentiates it from the original whose uniqueness as an image of God is thereby preserved; second, the de-facement is tantamount to a mode of incompleteness which demonstrates positively the eschewing of illusion and a breach in continuity. It constitutes some sort of challenge to *determinatio*. The mimetic rupture, which, as I have shown earlier, may amount to no more than an indeterminate degree of breakage, draws attention to itself as a self-aware, ironising distortion that declares what it is not at the same time that it also declares the original of that which it declares itself not to be. In so doing, the original is revealed at the same time as the deliberate incompleteness (not to create an illusion) is made apparent, and this, I hope to show, also operates dialectically in favour of movement and life. Obviously, this type of incompleteness must be distinguished from the incomplete that is complete.[87]

There is already a strong suggestion of this aesthetic in a rabbinic comment on a matter remote indeed from the

human image but cognate through its mode of presentation – Herod's Temple: 'he who has never seen the Temple
of Herod has never seen a beautiful building . . . He originally intended to cover it with gold, but the rabbis advised
him not to, since it was more beautiful as it was, looking
like the waves of the sea' (TB BB4a).

Gold can indeed shimmer but it certainly can not suggest
the movement of the waves; into an ever-mobile, ever-changing
vision it can not transform a fixed and earth-bound edifice.
This notion can also be perceived in Kant's reference to
'the changing shapes of the fire or of a rippling brook: neither
of which are things of beauty', he adds, 'but they convey a
charm to the imagination because they sustain its free play'
(Kant, op. cit., p.89).

To revert to the image of the human: in so far as it is in
a state of *non finito* it will alienate the beholder and by the
same token emphasise the distinction between the model
and the copy. In other words, the image of God, present in
the living human being, is saved from confusion with, say,
even that statue that lacks all facial features. The integrity
of the original is preserved inviolate and in its transcendence, which must now be sought.

It is being maintained that something incomplete, perhaps even distorted, can more adequately preserve the image of God in man than a totalising image. But this is so
because it will alienate the beholder, engage his interest
and create dissatisfaction with the existent. The sign will
not exhaust the signified to such an extent that the element of *non finito*, by deliberately drawing attention to itself, will signal that here no pretence of completion or illusion
is sought. This is a task the beholder must achieve for himself. Gombrich makes a similar point: 'Rembrandt could dare
to leave the eyes of his most moving portraits in the shade
because we are thus stimulated to supplement them'.[88] The
negative aesthetic of the *non finito* – 'limitlessness', Kant would
have said – eo ipso permits of the entry of life, the divine
image, into a medium that is inert. This can also denote an
opening, through its very negation of the status quo, towards the future. The countenance that is deliberately left
defective not only negates its exemplar, rescuing that exemplar from duplication, but also makes it possible to regard

this defectiveness as a means whereby the contours of the existent are enlarged.

It is at this point that it becomes possible to discern the association between the *non finito* and the passage from space into time. Mendelssohn's old-fashioned aesthetic would certainly not have countenanced the former in the Kantian sense but he already introduces the notion of 'the before' and 'the after' in relation to a painting or piece of sculpture. This follows from the contrast with a work of architecture, of which one feature must be 'solidity' (Festigkeit). Painting and sculpture, on the other hand, have no such concern with 'the perfection of external state and with the attribute of endurance ... the lines of beauty in painting must exercise themselves more freely than in architecture'. Hence follows the paramountcy of the artist's choice – that pregnant moment of a whole action which can be gathered into 'one single point of vision ... Everything must in this moment be rich in thought and so full of meaning that each lesser concept (*Nebenbegriff*) makes its own contribution to the required significance'. This will enable the imagination 'to discern the past from the present and confidently anticipate what is to follow'.[89]

This aim will be achieved in part at least, if, as Mendelssohn requires, the artifact is considered not as a self-contained work, complete in itself, but also as participant in a movement that has a 'before' and 'after'. To this extent it does remain incomplete, and this is of course an enduring condition because the succession of 'befores' and 'afters' knows no finality.

Should this be so then the image lacks all claim to static finality in order to become part of a process in movement, so it has entered into the dimension of time. Because it calls incessantly for completion it no longer belongs wholly to the world of matter and subsists also in a state of anticipated realisation. A cogent and similar contrast is made between Rembrandt's work and a Byzantine icon: whereas 'unchangeableness and therewith supra-temporality lies in the essence of the icon, temporality and therewith changeableness are bound up with the fragmentary, no matter in what meaning we may grasp it'.[90]

In a twentieth century context, the work of Pissarro,

Modigliani, Chagall and Soutine is said to point to 'a meeting' between modern art and the Jewish condemnation of 'the image as an arbitrary fixation of appearance outside time, as a blasphemous attack on the majesty of time'.[91]

Take the assault on 'static' time a stage further, making use of Hugo Bergmann's bold reading of the answer given by God to Moses in response to the enquiry for God's name (Ex.3:23–24): 'I am what I am'. The 'am' of the latter translation, writes Bergmann, is 'an imperfect, expressed in the tense of the uncompleted being . . . God makes himself known as the I in a state of being but at the same time the uncompleted I, to be realised'.[92]

The world also is in a similar state of becoming, 'created in order to be made' (Gen.2:3). In such a case, the rejection of *determinatio*, the embrace of the *non-finito*, establish a tripartite cosmic correspondence amongst God and the unfinished world and the unfinished image, in their common challenge to the idol and the fixity of reification, no less than to any form of pantheism. To leave unfinished the 'image of God' is therefore to bring to mind the God who is also in a state of becoming: R. Abbahu interprets 'one of the hardest passages in Scripture', Psalm 91:15–16, to connote: 'the salvation of the Holy One Blessed Be He is the salvation of Israel'.[93]

It is also in this sense that the three-dimensional statue of a human being, through its very totalising endeavour, obscures the God in a state of becoming. By the same token as the statue annihilates the human original into 'the perfection of arrest', so too would it now impose on God a static finality. God and his followers once again find themselves in conflict with the idolater's assent to the present.

7 Time, Time and Time Again

Biblical, and to some extent rabbinic, Hebrew requires six words to connote 'time': *et, pa'am, mo'ed, olam, ketz, zman.*[1] This follows from the varied conceptions of time that Jewish thought makes use of and which are not always compatible with each other. But in the rejection of time as inexorable fate and in the acceptance of time as a human construct, susceptible in the human interest, to human manipulation and understanding, there is general agreement. This differentiates any Jewish conception of time from the idolater's submission to fate, in what Bloch calls 'the astral-mythic' religions of paganism.[2]

The Bible must also challenge and define itself against the impersonal Platonic idea of time as 'the moving image of eternity' (Timaeus, 37), or the Kantian 'pure form'.[3] There is an even more telling rejection when the counterpart to the Bible is a 'cold', totemic-mythological society, the institutions of which, writes Lévi-Strauss, aim 'to annul the possible effects of historical factors on their equilibrium and continuity in a quasi-automatic fashion' and consequently do indeed accept 'a before and an after, but their sole significance lies in reflecting each other'.[4] Lévi-Strauss sees in the aim of mythology an attempt 'to ensure that as closely as possible . . . the future will remain faithful to the present and the past'.[5] But this aspiration is the precise antithesis to the Biblical which, as I hope to show, denies autonomy to the present and looks to a future as different as possible from the present.

Speaking more generally now, the Bible must also define itself against a generalised and diffuse atmosphere of concern at the passage of time. 'But at my back I always hear/ Time's wingèd chariot hurrying near'. Marvell was doing no more than appealing to his coy, reluctant mistress (let her not tarry till the 'conversion of the Jews'), but the conflict with time is widespread. Marvell's chariot gallops through

136

the ages, beginning say, with Kronos, the Greek god of time, who devours his own children. Schopenhauer visualises time in the likeness of an endlessly turning wheel, separate from the individual's particular destiny; and occasionally the burden of that destiny becomes heavy to the extent that the individual strives to unburden himself, that is to 'kill time'.[6]

Time might also be annihilated in the repetitive process conceived in Nietzsche's 'eternal recurrence of the same'. Here too time is hypostasized as a supra-historical force, at odds with man and impervious to his aspirations. It is akin to Eliot's meaningless cycle of 'birth, copulation and death'. Spengler, in his *Untergang des Abendlandes*, a work avowedly indebted to Nietzsche, gives historical substance to the thesis of repetition.

Time conceived as beyond human control is one important form of hostility. It is complemented in a most drastic form by the pervasive conjunction of death and the sentiment of extinction with the passage of time. This assumes exemplary iconographic form in a multitude of images; in Holbein's *Dance of Death* the skeleton of death bears an hour-glass; and in the image of Old Father Time the aged figure customarily bears an hour-glass and also a scythe. Faust, in Goethe's version, acknowledges that were he to call on a moment of bliss 'to tarry', then he would willingly perish. Death is the price that must be paid when time is halted. Were it possible to bring about the cessation of time, then also the individual must cease to be – such is the pre-supposition.

The Bible is of course familiar with this mode of thinking. Ecclesiastes espouses a fatalistic cyclical outlook: 'one generation goes, another comes. But the earth remains the same forever'; and does not this author also echo Zarathustra: 'only that shall happen which has happened, only that occur which has occurred. There is nothing new under the sun' (1:4,9)?

A second objection: if the Biblical author is correct in declaring that 'the transgression of the fathers is visited on the children' (Ex.20:5), then does not time show itself to be an inexorable, ineluctable force, punishing the innocent for the errors of the past? Is there not at work an unbreakable chain of causation? But such a proposition is challenged by

Ezekiel, who indeed does not deny that today the innocent
do suffer but who also ascribes to man the capacity to exercise his freedom to break from the chain, so that 'a child
shall not bear the transgression of a parent' (18:20). Jeremiah
looks forward to an era when it will no longer be said 'that
parents have eaten sour grapes and children's teeth are
blunted. But everyone shall die for his own sins and whoever eats sour grapes, his teeth shall be blunted' (31:29–
30), Ecclesiastes too, can be read in an optimistic spirit – if
there is a time to die, there is also a time to live.[7] A notion
of time as an entity that is either hostile or indifferent to
human effort, or, through death, brings human effort to
nought, the Biblical and rabbinic struggle against idolatry
must contest. In all its guises, time must be rejected when
represented as inexorable, unresponsive to human interest
or inimical to man. Notions of determinism, totemistic stagnation, temporal circularity and repetitiveness fall victim to
dissolution and disenchantment. Old Father Time is laid low.

To Biblical and rabbinic thought the epitome of these
phenomena is astrology, so much so that 'star-worship' is a
very frequent synonym for idolatry in general (see Introduction, page 1). Its overwhelming but spurious attraction is its
supposed capacity to meet the urge for insight into the future and the capacity to influence the future.[8] Astrology is
a paradigm for the belief in the power of the stars and planets
to affect a person's character and destiny (especially their
constellation at the moment of birth), and also the belief
in the power of the stars and planets to influence human
affairs (or at least the belief in the correlation between any
particular constellation and the course of human affairs) so
that for the skilled reader of the stars it is possible to pre-
dict the course these affairs will take. By extension the belief covers other spurious means to discern the future. Here
is a lively example of the clash between a believer and his
Jewish opponent: Hecataeus of Abdera, an eye-witness and
participant in one of the campaigns of King Alexander,
describes the action of a member of an escort of Jewish
cavalry, a certain Mosollamus:

> . . . a very intelligent man, robust, and, by common con-
> sent, the very best of bowmen, whether Greek or barbarian.

This man, observing that a number of men were going to and fro on the route and that the whole force was being held up by a seer who was taking the auspices, inquired why they were halting. The seer pointed out to him the bird he was observing, and told him that if it stayed in that spot it was expedient for them all to halt; if it stirred and flew forward, to advance; if backward, then to retire. The Jew, without saying a word, drew his bow, shot and struck the bird, and killed it. The seer and some others were indignant, and heaped curses upon him. 'Why so mad, you poor wretches?' he retorted; and then, taking the bird in his hands, continued, 'Pray, how could any sound information about our march be given by this creature which could not provide for its own safety? Had it been gifted with divination, it would not have come to this spot for fear of being killed by an arrow of Mosollamus the Jew'.[9]

The derision of Mosollamus for auspices and auguries is inherent in a far broader campaign waged against occult phenomena that obscure man's perception of time and give credence to seers, as against human prevision and calculation; to 'hapless' stargazers as against God who 'annul(s) the omens of diviners and make(s) fools of the augurs' (Is.47:13; 44:25).

Augury belongs to that commerce with the occult – divination, clairvoyance, necromancy, sorcery, soothsaying, witchcraft, etc. that has no part in Biblical thinking.[10] These are all practices every whit as idolatrous as the worship of a graven image. Jeremiah associates 'portents in the sky' with impotent, inarticulate wooden images decked with silver and gold and fastened into place with nails and hammer: this is the way of the nations 'that the Israelites are not to learn' (Jer.10:2 ff.); the text equates King Manasseh's construction of shrines and altars to honour pagan deities with the same king's practice of soothsaying, necromancy and divination (2K. 21:2 ff.). Later generations make the same identification.[11] When Kimche first explains Samuel's castigation of Saul and then Samuel's comparison of the king's rebellion to 'the sin of divination' (1 Sam.15:23), he explicitly assimilates diviner to idolater.

In effect, the Jew who consults an astrologer or clairvoyant is making three statements: first, he is disloyal to God in postulating an alternative source of foreknowledge and power, irrespective of whether he hopes to influence the future or merely to discern the future. But he is deluded – 'against Jacob there is no enchantment, neither is there any divining against Israel' (Nu.23:23); second, such a Jew, acting in this way, will be abusing himself in entrusting his own power of discernment to an occult and ignorant source: Naḥmanides writes: 'to know the future it will be unnecessary for you to resort to a diviner or soothsayer who receives (the knowledge) from the stars or from the lower powers among the lords of above, whose words are not all true and who do not provide all necessary information. But prophecy informs us of God's desire and not one of its words will fall to the earth';[12] third, this person is attributing to the future some degree of fixity and ossification and thereby frustrating his own power to create a variety of possible options. In an oracle, 'what is said is immobilised'.[13]

The refutation by Maimonides of astrology has acquired classic status: it has a threefold ground: the work of 'the stargazers' (Is.47:13) can satisfy none of the epistemological demands of trustworthy knowledge; their arguments do not derive from reasoning, the senses or tradition handed down from the prophets or the righteous. Subsidiary to the argument from reason, but within the same framework, is the reference of Maimonides to the contempt for astrology shared by 'the wise men' of Greece and Persia as against the foolishness of the Chaldeans, Egyptians and Canaanites. Maimonides has a political-pragmatic argument: the Israelites' preoccupation with astrology was directly responsible for their neglect of the art of war which led in turn to the loss of kingdom and Temple. Most important, is the argument from freewill for, writes Maimonides, 'were a man compelled to act according to the dictates of predestination, then the commands and prohibitions of the Law would become null and void and the Law would be completely false, since man would have no freedom of choice in what he does'.[14] These beliefs, Maimonides writes, pollute the mind: 'cleanse your mind as one cleanses dirty clothes'.[15]

In the fate of the zodiac, the aversion to the concept of

planetary influence on human affairs can be discerned. It has been a motif of synagogal decoration at least since the third century CE. It featured prominently in the synagogue of Bet-Alpha in the plain of Jezreel.[16] Even so the zodiac suffers from two objectionable features. The first of these is the presence of human figures. These could be neutralised if they were replaced by suggestive objects, formed on the principle of metonymy: if, for example, a wedding canopy or flowers took the place of Virgo; a bow and arrow the place of Sagittarius.[17] At Khodorov in the Ukraine, Virgo took the form of hands engaged in embroidery; Gemini became two entwined figures without heads.[18] It is ironical of course, that such care was taken to remove from an idolatrous image equally offensive anthropomorphic images. Recourse was also had to a re-arrangement of the figures in an unconventional pattern, in formal pairs running in an anti-clockwise direction so that the original astrological association would be disguised.[19] But none of these devices could convincingly remove the inherent astrological taint with all its capacity to mislead. This is precisely what dismayed R. Eliezer Deitsch when consulted in regard to the proposed installation of a zodiacal decoration in a New Jersey synagogue in the early twentieth century. He condemned the suggestion outright, for did the zodiac not teach a form of planetary determinism, in denial of providence, whereas – 'Israel has no planet' (ref. to TB Shab. 156 a–b), and enjoyed free-will.

This is what the very presence of the zodiac would deny, even if only by tacit suggestion: 'what a man depicts before his eyes makes a great impression on his thought and intention', wrote Deitsch. This was no plea to banish from the synagogue all adornment. Deitsch accompanied his disallowance of the zodiac with this challenge: 'can we not embellish the house of God in a permissible way rather than in this?'[20]

Genesis makes man dominant over nature; it is he who dictates to nature and not vice versa (though this does not release man from his responsibility as nature's steward, in default of which nature retaliates). This relationship does not entail or require any particular, individualised notion of time; rather, it provides an opportunity to devise a variety of times, in correspondence with human need. These will mediate between man's mastery over nature and his dependence on nature for sustenance and the necessities and amenities of life: e.g. man is dependent on the sun and moon for lights, but does this dependence then determine the organisation of human life? To some extent 'yes'; to some extent 'no'.

If man enjoys, in the promise of Genesis, mastery over nature, he is not irrevocably bound to its rhythm. As I will explain, sunrise, sunset and even the Sabbath are not wholly fixed and precise divisions; in certain, admittedly exceptional, circumstances, it is even possible for night to be considered day and day night. Even if it is true that only a legendary river, the Sambatyon, ceases to flow on the Sabbath, nature is not wholly inert, ignorant and amoral and can be endowed with human meaning. Were it otherwise then idolatry would have successfully re-asserted itself and time have forfeited its relativity to human need. In the same way as spatial limitations have been made amenable to human need and effort, so too must the sway of natural time be undermined. The analogy is precise. The way in which space can be manipulated and made responsive to man parallels the way in which natural time can be variously understood, in sympathy with the same purpose. Space, as I have earlier shown, can, through mere designation, be chopped up through an *erub* into passable or impassable territory, into private and public areas, into 'sacred' and undifferentiated sites. Similarly with time, which can be subverted in such a way as to re-form the past; made subservient to legal deliberation; and, third, and most strikingly, be deprived of its power to separate time present from time future.

The Jewish calendar articulates a message, which, whilst taking full account of the obvious limitations to human domination of nature, also designates a temporal order separate from that of nature, but related to it in terms of an imputed message; though the moon is made 'to mark the seasons' (Ps.104:19) it is God who has designated the 'seasons' and man whom they serve. Nature's subservient status, or, correspondingly, the superior status of man, makes it possible to create a series of arbitrary and artificial institutions that together constitute a temporal system, further emphasising the elevation of man over the phenomena of nature.[21] Heschel contrasts 'the repetitive processes in the cycle of nature' with the series of 'unique events' constituted by historic time, that is, those correlated artificially by specific historical events with nature. 'Jewish ritual', Heschel writes, 'may be characterised as the art of significant forms in time, as *architecture of time*'.[22] To continue the metaphor – additions to this architectural framework are provided by the new moons, the festivals, the Day of Atonement, the sabbatical year, and the year of jubilee.

This distinction between natural time and its man-made 'architectural' structure is strong to the extent that in the calculation of the calendar it can tolerate error, whether wilful or inadvertent. Should the date of the sanctification of the new moon and the consequent designation of the calendrical festivals, all of which are celebrated in reference to the lunar calendar, be incorrectly calculated then the error holds good.[23]

The same distinction operates in a variety of contexts. If, for example, in a year when a second month ('second Adar') is intercalated, two boys are born – one at a later date in the first Adar and the other at an earlier date in the second Adar and both reach their maturity at the age of thirteen in a normal year when there is only one Adar, then, because both boys will reach their maturity in the same month, the one who is born at the earlier date will be considered the older, even though he was born in the second Adar, that is after the boy who was born in the first Adar but at a later date in the month.[24]

This power over time is – once again – not absolute. For all that, the Biblical separation of man and nature conduces to the possibility of a notion of time that brings it into the human domain and does distinguish it from impersonal time as experienced by the idolater. Generally speaking, 'a modality of time' is created, which, it is claimed:

> ... is not linked to natural cycles; it is not cyclical. Indeed such a modality of time is solely a reflex of an unconditional and unqualified divine will ... In the Bible, the category of history also determines the way older natural rhythms are assimilated and relived: the harvest festivals

memorialize moments in Israel's historical destiny (they are moments of manifest divine will); the Sabbath is no longer a term designating a moment in the lunar flux, but transcends the natural cycle. The correlation of festivals with the new and full moon is no longer emphasized. Natural bounty becomes occasions for historical credos (cf. Deut. 26).[25]

In this sense, the system is perfectly exemplified in the divine decision to proclaim a new year that will coincide with the exodus from Egypt (Ex.12:2). The occasion, the time, and the event reciprocally define each other, in opposition to a nature that knows nothing of renewal through exodus.

The transcendence by the Sabbath of the lunar cycle can be elaborated so that it is related not only to a divinely ordained determination but also to a certain 'humanisation' of the time involved. Thus, although the Sabbath and its obligations are bounded by time and also bound time, neither of these bounds is fixed. (In the case of certain other obligations such bounds may be entirely disregarded, for example the prescription to visit the sick constitutes a continuing obligation of an indefinitely recurrent duration). It is made possible for man to advance the inauguration of the Sabbath in certain circumstances, or, correspondingly, to retard its termination – especially as the end of one day could not always be clearly distinguished from the beginning of the next.[26] Neither sunset nor nightfall need be all-powerful; and this, incidentally, exemplifies the capacity to blur the distinction between differentiated ('holy') time and undifferentiated ('profane') by adding the latter to the former, thereby providing a further parallel with the same procedure in the case of space. Similarly, the arbitrary nature of the differentiation of the Sabbath – that is, its designation for the purpose of *imitatio dei* in a particular manner – is formulated in the capacity, in certain extreme circumstances, to determine one's own Sabbath; if the Jew should so lose count of time as to ignore the incidence of the seventh day, one suggested procedure is to count six days and observe the seventh as the Sabbath; another rabbi reverses the procedure (TB Shab. 69 b). The timing of the daily evening service, Jacob Katz shows, has depended in a wide range of North African and European communities 'on the mutual inter-relationship' of law, custom and life-style.[27] Uniformity is absent.

The Talmudic discussion of the criteria for or against the intercalation of an additional month ('a second Adar') in any particular year of the normal twelve months gives further emphasis to the component of human action, discretion and convenience in the fixing of the calendar: for example, so that the Passover festival with its pilgrimage to Jerusalem should not fall at a time when the roads were impassable, or a bridge in need of repair, or the corn or fruit trees were ripening unusually early. Snow, cold weather or the convenience of exiles coming to Jerusalem who had not yet embarked on their journey were, on the other hand, not considered valid reasons for intercalation.[28] The Jew need never lose control over time, be bereft of time or an occasion for *imitatio dei*. In effect he can, within certain limits, bring time into the human purview, make his own time, even if only by way of emergency action. Within certain limits, control over time is taken away from nature and entrusted to the Jew, so as to create a world that belongs to him, is part of his history and subject to his discretion.

The fabled Jewish astronaut, circling the globe in his space-capsule and, as dawn succeeded dawn, required to say his daily morning prayers every five minutes or so, knew in outermost space precisely where he was: it was time for *Shachrit.*

This man's time has become a part of his activity and, in consequence, time as determined by nature forfeits paramountcy. The astronaut makes his own time by 'filling' it with his own activities, remembrances, and so on. No sooner is this position achieved than the fear of time, as experienced by the idolater, is overcome, or can at least be faced with a degree of mastery.

The dominance of man-made time over nature and historical time is inherent also in the capacity to correlate events with a particular date, irrespective of historical fact, thereby elucidating a common significance, which becomes a source of consolation. States the Mishnah:

. . . five misfortunes took place for our fathers on the seventeenth of Tammuz, and five on the ninth of Av. On the seventeenth of Tammuz (1) the tablets of the Torah were broken, (2) the daily whole offering was cancelled, (3) the city wall was breached, (4) Apostemos burned the Torah, and (5) he set up an idol in the Temple. On the ninth of Ab (1) the decree was made against our forefathers that they should not enter the land, (2) the first Temple and (3) the second Temple was destroyed, (4) Betar was taken, and (5) the city was ploughed up after the war of Hadrian (TB Ta'anit, 26a–26b).

These two catalogues of catastrophic events, precisely because they are unhistorically aligned, may well intend to dull each individual catastrophe and deprive it of its uniqueness: 'it is absorbed into a pattern of like disasters', writes Neusner, 'all exhibiting similar taxonomic traits . . . The power of taxonomy in imposing order upon chaos once more does its healing work'.[29] As Israel has survived the one, so will it survive the others.

Counterpart to the association of disparate events is the dissociation of sequence. This marks the wall paintings in the third-century synagogue of Dura-Europos where Biblical personages and events from different periods flank each other on the same panels. The lack of respect for times and places derives, it is suggested, from the desire to assert a theological message.[30]

The ability to integrate what the anthropologists know as 'liminal time' into and with historical time, as commonly understood, also exemplifies this serious play with time that converts even disaster into hope.[31] In the course of Jewish history, the liminal period extends from the creation until the Israelites enter the Promised Land. During this period neither had circumcision – the paramount sign of Jewish identification – nor had the *Torah* been finally accepted. But to later generations, particularly those who had experienced the Hadrianic persecutions, the destruction of the Temple and the failure of the Bar-Kochba revolt, this deficiency was intolerable. As part of a revised spirituality, the *locus* of reward and punishment was transferred to a future world from its hitherto dominant position in this. This created a need to give greater and greater emphasis to the observance of the prescriptions of the *Torah* which in turn was projected onto the past and correspondingly generated 'the unification of history through the sublation of liminal time into the flux of historical time'.[32] Hence we find that Shem studied *Torah*, that Abraham already fulfilled all its prescriptions – *mitzvot* – and even that Adam, Enoch, Shem, and others were born circumcised.

The rabbinico-legal contribution to the *Problematik* of time is concerned mainly with its composition: is time to be considered an indivisible continuum, a totality, or as an aggregate of separate, discrete moments? This distinction is analogous to that between synchronic and diachronic time.

It is exemplified in two contrasting views of the temporal nature of the duration of the vow of the person who assumed nazirite status, refrains from 'strong liquor', and so on (cf. Nu.6:1–21): if the vow is for a period of time that is measured by an indifferent number of discrete units ('as the dust of the earth', 'as the hairs of my head', 'a thousand years'), then the nazirite status is considered to require confirmation every thirty days, because the undertaking is time-bounded and a priori couched in diachronic terms. But if the vow is for an undefined period, and conceived, say, in terms of the (unknown) duration of the nazirite's life, then this is considered a continuous, uninterrupted period of nazirite status not subject to a pre-determinable foreseeable conclusion; the commitment being made in terms of synchronic time, it lacks any necessity for recurrent confirmation.[33]

The distinction between time as synchronic continuum and time as diachronic discontinuity is no mere academic matter but has legal consequences; for example, when does the failure to perform a positive commandment render the offender liable to punishment? Suppose that ill-health quite legitimately debars an infant boy from being circumcised on the mandatory eighth day from birth, so that the performance of the rite must be postponed. When, subsequently, does further delay beyond the period of recovery render the person on whom the duty is incumbent liable to punishment for the failure to perform a positive commandment? According to Maimonides, although every day that the operation is delayed beyond the period of restored health constitutes an infringement of the commandment, the offender does not render himself liable to the punishment of extirpation unless and until he should die uncircumcised. Maimonides's critic, R. Abraham ibn Daud, argued that if it was a positive commandment to perform the act (following the boy's recovery), on pain of extirpation for its non-performance, then the penalty must also apply every day of that ensuing period and ibn Daud therefore maintained that every day that the performance of the injunction remained unfulfilled rendered the offender liable to punishment. In the one case time is considered a simple essence of uninterrupted *durée*; in the other an aggregate of parts.[34]

A case such as this must however, be distinguished from the superficially similar case where the issue is whether a male minor can become betrothed (such betrothal to take effect only when the minor reaches maturity). Here time cannot be regarded as a simple, indivisible entity, encompassing past, present and future during which the minor will reach maturity, the reason being that to the minor's attainment of maturity not only is time an essential but absent contributor, which thus destroys the idea of time as a simple entity, encompassing past, present and future, but time is in such a situation no more than a contributory factor to the realisation of a future the presence of which is essential and therefore its absence nullifies the projected betrothal *ab initio*.[35]

The exodus that coincides time-wise with the new year, the nazirite whose event-full status is measured by this or that measure, the rubric of catastrophes attached to a common date – these are all examples of the creation of a continuum that knows no concept of abstract time or of an event that occurs outside time. Events and the time they 'occupy' are virtually synonymous and co-dependent and qualitatively distinguished by virtue of their identity with their denotation.[36]

Already in the story of creation each segment of time – each 'day' – is conceived in terms of an event: the specific addition to creation. The upshot of this dialectic, where no moment of time lacks an event to give it body and meaning, is to create a mode of event–time continuum. Years are measured in terms of harvests (Lev.25:16). The concept is perfectly encapsulated in the customary festival benediction when the celebrants acclaim God – who 'hallows Israel and the seasons'.

In the Talmud's rhetorical question on Proverbs 3:2 ('My commandments . . . will bestow on you length of days, years of life and wellbeing') R. Joseph Rosen ('the Rogatschever') perceives another example of the event-time continuum: the Talmud asks, 'but are there years of life and years which are not years of life?' (TB Yoma 71a). Obviously not, which Rosen interprets to mean that without life, that is, event and motion, there is no time, that time and event are indissoluble, that time without an event has no existence, that the two form one unit.[37] This is supported with reference to Maimonides's argument for creation *ex nihilo* in opposition to the Aristotelian argument for the eternity of matter. Maimonides maintains that time is also one of the created entities and only comes into being with the creation (Guide, II:13); further, if time is 'an accident in that which is moved', then motion serves to unite time and matter. On the basis of this understanding of Maimonides, Rosen allows himself to conclude that matter, by virtue of its co-creation with time, is in a continuing state of movement and becoming.[38]

This continuum of time and event also allows for – as indeed it must – the relativity of time to the individual event. The individual will experience time in a mode that differs from chronological, abstract, impersonal time. Rosen quotes to this effect an earlier writer (the fourteenth-fifteenth century Shimon ben Zemaḥ Duran, *Magen Avot*, ch.5, Mishnah 21, p.93): 'and know that the sages of nature say time is not a uniform entity but a measure of movement'. The earth completes its circuit in one day but 'to him who is occupied with enjoyment and diversion it will seem that the day is short, contrary to those who are sick and suffering to whom the night will seem long'.[39] This is another mode of the coincidence of time and event.

If time has no existence and is even inconceivable, in the abstract, in the absence of events – again like space – how can it at all make sense to make a reality of future time, in advance of events? On the other hand, how can it make sense to make a reality of an event in advance of the time of its eventuation? This is the aporia produced through the

construction of an event-time continuum. A special problem is thereby created for the *Torah* in that its effort to
subvert the status quo – by which I understand the messianic
era – seems, as it were, to enunciate a reward impossible of
attainment. If the struggle of the *Torah* against idolatry, as
exemplified in astrology, philosophies of history and other
theories of determinism, has its antithesis in the conception of free human action overcoming the inadequacy of
the present, then the problem is to bring the period of struggle into alignment with the end aspired to and thereby
maintain the event-time continuum; or, conversely, to bring
the end into 'alignment' with the period of struggle.

The perplexity created by the continuity of present and
future must now be examined. The world is created in order to be made (Gen.2:3) – which already makes two points:
one, that the world is in need of 'repair' (*tikkun*, the Jewish
mystics would say); two, that the task of improving the imperfect can nowhere else be performed than in the imper-
fectly created world. There is nowhere else to begin from,
and that is why history serves as both the messiah's *point de
départ* and his *point d'arrivée*, and why the promise of the
messianic era is predicated on a confirmation of the present.

This applies whether the era replicates the (idealised)
conditions of the Solomonic monarchy when – from Dan
to Beer-Sheba – 'Judah and Israel dwelt in safety, everyone
under his own vine and under his own fig-tree' (1 K. 5:5);[40]
or whether the vision looks forward to a less localised dis-
pensation when swords become ploughshares, spears pruning hooks, and 'nation shall not take up sword against nation'
(Micah 4:3–4).[41]

In either case there still subsist such familiar entities as
nations. How will their contacts and relations be governed?
Above all, there still subsists the need to engage with nature;
why else would pruning hooks and ploughshares be needed?
No sooner is this concession to the present made, than there
necessarily follows the whole structured register of social
arrangements, precautions, and safeguards that human dependence on nature requires of man. The historical continuum persists. Here is another radical version of this
viewpoint: 'the sole difference between this world and the
messianic world is in respect of (Israel's) subjection to the

nations', declared Samuel, the third-century *amora* of Babylon; even the conquest of poverty is excluded by reason of Samuel's reference to Deuteronomy 15:11 – 'for the poor shall not cease from the land' (TB San. 91b). This envisages in contemporary parlance, it is maintained, a continuation of the class-struggle.[42] The historical emphasis is all the sharper if heed is given to Maimonides's indication that the messiah, being mortal, will die, to be replaced by his son and grandson, and, although the messianic age 'will endure thousands of years ... (and) not easily disintegrate', the unspoken implication is that indeed it is subject to disintegration.[43] Anything else would be incompatible with messianic historicity in general and that of Maimonides in particular. Maimonides, it is argued, could envisage no ideal historical conditions which would allow judges and policemen to be dispensed with.[44] To Hermann Cohen the historicity of the messianic era is apparent in the quasi-absolute refusal by the Bible to associate it with the eschatological motif: 'disregarding the one reference in Isaiah (25:8) in which "death shall forever be swallowed up", then all other instances indicate an earthly future, be it of Israel or of all the peoples'.[45] The cessation of death is 'only a parable (Gleichnis), one of the many which describe nature's peace'.[46]

The Hebrew word *olam*, though normally rendered 'eternity', denotes neither the world to come nor chronological infinity but 'a time without limits'.[47] This is the continuum which coincides chronologically with the messianic quest in historical time. It must be so, for, if what is known of the future is its capacity for human shaping, then this must necessarily limit the scene of such shaping to that world which man can indeed shape; the Hebrew word for 'history' – *toldot*, deriving from a root meaning 'engender' – already points to this option.[48] In no sense therefore, does the messianic age connote an end to history or its abrogation.

Only in a world that transcends the present will it no longer be possible to say: 'parents have eaten sour grapes and children's teeth are blunted' (Jer.31:29). The prophet is demanding that causes operate in such a way as to produce no effects. For that 'a new covenant' is required (Jer.31:31).

In its absence however, the effect of the unbroken historical continuum is to insist that human choice is not exercised in a vacuum and is not free. The Psalmist implores God 'not to remember against us our former iniquities' (79:8). But nothing is more clear than that those iniquities are indeed remembered and that no *table rase* exists such as would give absolute freedom to constitute the future. This is indeed the hope of the revolutionary; by contrast the Bible shows itself sensitive to those enduring factors that limit freedom – most obviously, in its disenchanted awareness of the constraints that one generation imposes on its successor(s) through the errors, abuses and misdeeds that it has itself perpetrated: 'our fathers sinned and are no more; and we must bear their guilt' (Lam.5:7). This is the Biblical version of Marx's argument that although men make their own history, they do so only in circumstances not of their own making and where 'the tradition of all the dead generations weighs like an incubus on the brain of the living'.[49]

This constraint is not easily accepted and this would explain why a multitude of 'jumps' from necessity to freedom has proliferated. But an unhistorical static vision of utopian perfection petrifies the future, bringing time to a stop: for were one 'to re-count the future, then one would inevitably make it into the rigid past'.[50] No model of perfection must emerge, such as would define the future and impose itself as inescapable. Here, as in the image, to define is eo ipso to limit even that circumscribed degree of possible freedom that does exist.

Likewise, to postulate a breach in historical *durée* on the basis – as do many messianic schemata – of a planetary conjunction, an historical context or the appearance of a particular individual would be to confound the idea with the very idolisation of time it is designed to overcome.[51] Messianic scenarios of this type necessarily remove human capacity to shape the future in favour of time conceived as an abstract, impersonal force, transforming them into almost a philosophy of history. They exist at two extremes: that which rejects, like Walter Benjamin, 'enlightenment from soothsayers', but also, disconcertingly, makes of 'every second the narrow portal through which the messiah could enter'.[52] At the other extreme stands the proposition that the messiah's inevitable coming will take place during the sabbatical year – so-called 'chronomessianism'. The outburst of messianic zeal that accompanied the Bar-Kochba revolt in 132/33 (by the Julian calendar) may, it is suggested, have been encouraged by the coincidence of a sabbatical and a jubilee year.[53]

In default of 'a new covenant', the means whereby the challenge to history is met and at the same time the means whereby all escape into a non-historical, metaphysical world is thwarted, involves recourse to a calculated 'fiction': a 'fiction' that ventures to locate in the present the abode of the messiah. (I use inverted commas to cast doubt on the reality of the 'fiction'). This notion will provide an exit from the aporia mentioned earlier, for time and event are now no longer at odds with each other but brought into a synchronic state of coincidence, however 'fictional'. It also circumvents the twin perils of messianic nostalgia for an unreal, idealised past, on the one hand, and the fantasy of a precipitate messianic advent, on the other.

How can it be maintained that the here and now constitutes this 'narrow portal'? For a representative answer I turn to R. David Kimche's comment on Obadiah 1:15 ('for the day of the Lord is near'). Kimche writes: 'even though it is far from the day of prophesy, it is as if it were near. If God said it would take place, it is possible to think of it as having (already) taken place'. Prophecies referring to the future are often couched in the past tense, Kimche notes, as though they had in fact already come to pass – 'for the word of the prophet is as certain as if it had already been fulfilled', he comments on Jeremiah 23:19.[54] (That, incidentally, is why the category of hope is of little account in Jewish thinking.) The operative notion of time prevalent here is the synchronic duration of historical time in that, in a certain sense, the future is already present – not in any sense of a pre-determined moment but in the sense that the cherished and anticipated 'end' must eventuate and has already done so. The sense is that in which the future can be thought of *as if* it were already present. It complements another tradition whereby the Sabbath (as well as sunshine and sexual intercourse) can be regarded as an anticipation of messianic days and their partial fulfilment in the present.[55]

A weaker version of the 'as if' mode of thought is found by Neusner in the reading of Israel's history, not in the same 'natural' terms that apply to the history of all other peoples but in terms of a 'reality that does not correspond to the perceived facts of this world'; and this is exemplified for Neusner in reading the Leviticus Rabbah of the sages as a metamorphosis of the book of Leviticus: 'instead of holy caste, we deal with holy people. Instead of holy place, we deal with holy community, in its holy land'.[56]

The most famous example of the use of the 'as if' mode of thinking must surely be Kant's categorical imperative. When Vaihinger discusses the topic (in his *Die Philosophie des Als Ob*) he is largely concerned with the differing characteristics of a hypothesis and a fiction, the first requiring to be probable and the second requiring to be purposeful, though their separate characteristics are not distinctive enough to prevent either assuming the characteristics of the other. A hypothesis may prove to be a fiction, and a fiction a hypothesis.[57] Neither of these categories quite fits our case, however, for the messianic present is not a hypothesis, still less a 'fiction', and that is one reason why Vaihinger's argument has been criticised by Samuel Atlas. A second, and more cogent attack refers to the limitation imposed on the fictitious judgement. To Vaihinger, this is 'negative in so far as the equivalence of A and B is clearly expressed as an invalid equivalence; it is positive insofar as the possibility of yet treating this invalid judgement as valid is affirmed' (Vaihinger, op. cit., p.594). But to Atlas, through fiction 'the area of reality is widened to include within itself the ideal reality created by it' (the fiction).[58] The same argument would also seem to apply to Leibniz's discussion of possible worlds (though with a slight but unimportant difference of vocabulary). It arises in connection with Leibniz's argument that 'space is something purely relative . . . an order of co-existence . . . For space signifies in terms of possibility an order of things which exist at the same time, insofar as they exist together' (*en tant qu'elles existent ensemble*).[59] This 'insofar as' implies both a present and a potential, though as yet unactualised, present: hence what has been termed 'a two-fold temporal division'.[60] But this 'insofar as' does not allow for the existence of a potential that is also actual, this by reason of the fact that its actualisation is divinely guaranteed and which can thus, in its own terms, already be considered an actuality.

The promise of the messianic present is therefore best regarded as a type of hypothesis that is unusual, to the extent that by virtue of the divine promise conveyed by the prophets and by tradition, it enjoys guaranteed confirmation. But by virtue of the fact that its realisation is guaranteed the existent is enlarged to include the as yet non-existent but certain, future existent.

Now, although this conditional/unconditional mode of thought is unaffected by the certainty of substantiation – or vice versa – it still makes a distinction between what it maintains and what it also demands. What is maintained is the validity of a promise, but this promise has still to be redeemed; for the messianic present patently lacks those characteristics enunciated by the prophets in terms of peace and plenitude. In this regard it is indeed only by a genuine fiction that the present can be considered any sort of messianic fulfilment.

But to use the term 'present' is to some extent a misnomer and therefore misleading. Given that the scene is and always remains historical, it allows for a *durée* that itself also allows for human action that creates the required *durée*.

The relationship between present and future is not that of an exchange, in which X gives an object to Y, on the pre-supposition that at some pre-determined future date Y will give to X an object of equivalent value.[61] The relationship is far more intimate and conditional in that, although the promiser (God) does indeed guarantee the fulfilment of the messianic promise, the promisee (Israel) not only has it in its own power to delay or advance the performance of the promiser's guaranteed undertaking but it lies also in its power to modify the very content of the promise.

Take for example the Talmudic tradition (San. 97a) that the world will last 6000 years – equally divided amongst eras of confusion, *Torah* and messiah. This gives R. Judah Loewe b. Bezalel ('the Maharal of Prague') the opportunity to argue that the *Torah* must be revealed. This is closed. But when and by whom? This was open: Should Moses not have been found worthy of the task, then Ezra would have been . . .; and if not Ezra, then . . . and so on. Similarly, the two millenia of the messianic era must also advene, they too are built into the divine schema. But at what point in the era? This is the open and uncertain factor, to be decided by the deserts of Israel – otherwise it is in his time that the messiah will come.[62]

It lies with man therefore, to make an authentic equivalence between 'the day of the Lord' and man's present. But because this present is historical, from which there is no escape, this history is also no more than man's own product. The capacity is enjoyed, though it is certainly qualified, to match event with time and to make of the messianic promise a messianic present. Those norms demanded if the promise is to be redeemed are identical with those that are required if the here and now is to redeem the future. Present and future are shown to be inseparable in their requirements to an extent that makes the future unnecessary to the present, for the former is already part of the latter.[63]

In this sense it is immaterial whether the messianic age becomes a reality or not – not, indeed, because the age is already a reality, but because those standards and values that inform the messianic future and alone conform to its maintenance are brought into the undeniably inhospitable present.

There is a strong intimation of this in the declaration of Socrates: whether the ideal city exists or not is irrelevant; 'he will live after the manner of that city, having nothing to do with any other'.[64]

The Kantian version of this statement is couched in terms of 'a universal regulative principle'. Kant makes a distinction between a transcendent conception of 'an intelligible world in which everything is actual by reason of the fact that, being something good, it is possible' and the fact that such a world, because it is transcendent, beyond experience, cannot yield what Kant calls: 'any constitutive principle determining an object and its objective reality'. However, it can yield 'a regulative principle' which 'converts . . . the rule of actions according to that idea into a command for every one'.[65]

Now, when into a Jewish context is brought the notion of adopting the 'manner' of the ideal city which does not exist (Socrates) or of perceiving in a transcendent, intelligible world a source of universal 'command' (Kant), that notion undergoes a degree of radicalisation and reinforcement. This is so by reason of the fact that here the transcendent is, so to speak, immanent; that in the existent is the ideal city to be found, and not in any transmundane realm. Hermann

Cohen makes three major points: that the messianic future stands explicitly in 'opposition to the empirical sensuousness of ethical values . . . the ideal in opposition to reality'; but this ideal, in the form of the kingdom of God, 'cannot be only future but it must be enduring present' and 'a personal reality for my consciousness of duty . . . I therefore do not wait for the kingdom of God to come and do not only pray for its appearance but through my own preparation (Rüstung), my own will I bring it about'.[66] This means that time takes on anthropocentric attributes of anticipation subject to human action and 'is by no means an order of succession of one thing after another (Nacheinander) but far more the *production of the sequence*'.[67]

It seems to me that, if this schema is now understood in the context of Cohen's insistence on the this-worldly intent of the prophetic message – and his rejection of eschatological doctrine – it adds a valuable gloss to the tradition enunciated by Kimche. It is indeed true that for Cohen, and for the prophets also, 'the kingdom of God is bound up with this earth'.[68]

But in no way must this imply any degree of *stasis* or finality. He points out that the Hebrew word for 'end' (*sof*) indicates, by reference to its root, 'succession' – that is, that each 'end' leads to its successor.[69] Accordingly, prophetic teaching can look to no end that is not 'in unfolding, in change, in an eternal new-origin'.[70] 'The future must never become a present, no matter how much this is yet different from the present of all historical past'.[71] Cohen's attachment to the succession of temporal 'ends' is strong to the extent that to them is assimilated the notion of eternity in a particular sense. What Cohen is here arguing is congruent with Kant's quasi-fanciful presentation of '*The end of all things*' (1794) as either unimaginable or self-contradictory. But Cohen goes further in rejecting the idea of eternity as a complement to time – it is not 'the infinite sum of all future time – that would be the eternity of standstill' (*Stillstand*) but it is 'an ethical concept', bearing on the pure will and the moral self-consciousness, both of which are directed to ensuring 'that there be no standstill for the life of the will'. Eternity thereby comes to constitute 'an infinitely distant point for every finite point'.[72]

It may well be objected that Cohen's 'consciousness of duty' with its relative neglect of the *Torah* as a body of prescriptions and laws has about it the uncomfortable ring of Kantian antinomianism and conscience; and this is perfectly true. It is also true that Cohen's aversion to the *Problematik* of space, and his thesis that freedom *vis-à-vis* the future requires that the preservation of Israel as people be combined with its loss of statehood, circumscribes the scope of action to a limited and abstract dimension.

But to Cohen, only this combination will ensure Israel's capacity to serve as 'the symbol of humanity'. There is, and must be, he writes, 'an anomaly between state and people in the history of Israel'. The consequent universalism unites the first Isaiah with the second as expressed in, 'and all peoples will stream' to the mount of the house of the Lord (Is.2:2).[73]

On the other hand, Cohen's perception of the need to 'align' time with purposive messianic action is perfectly compatible with the tradition. He exploits the 'as if' concept as a means to make of the existent the substance of a transformation. It is 'as if' another world exists – that of 'eternity' – through the influence of which the existent can be brought into a state of change and movement.

The consequence is a dynamism and urgency lacking to the Socratic or Kantian positions. Whether it is also more realistic is of course another matter. It has in any case the merit of maintaining the congruence of the present promise with its redemption.

It is a world away from Rosenzweig's vision of a people whom the *Torah* has removed 'from all the temporality and historicity of life'.[74] In the history of the Jews, according to Rosenzweig, the absence of epochs freed them from 'the power to which all other people are subject, the power of time, a unique people amongst the peoples, amongst the peoples an eternal people'.[75]

This is truly a static vision that lacks access to the determination of time and event created by Mosollamus's despatch of the augur's bird. This arrow found its target. The much more famous arrow of Zeno, the Eleatic philosopher, did not. To the implications of the 'Jewgreek' antithesis I now turn, by way of reflection on the foregoing.

8 Reflections and Echoes

'The hearing ear, the seeing eye – the Lord made them both' (Prov.20:12). The two organs co-operate, for the voice that is heard at Sinai is also 'seen' (Ex.20:19). The verbal message is put into the terms of visual perception.[1] The inference does not necessarily have to be that the exemplar of cognition is the eye, or that aural perception has attained to the level of the visual – rather that the two senses create a unity of perception. But if this vocabulary serves to recall that both 'the hearing ear' and 'the seeing eye' are part of the creation, it serves also to recall that the eye needs at times to be corrected by the ear lest what is seen becomes incitement to corruption. That the favourable relationship to sound is internally consistent with, and in fact inseparable from, the struggle against idolatry is already evident in the instructive contrast with the guarded and at times negative relationship to what is made visible, whether as image, symbol, artifact, soil, natural phenomenon or simply 'the holy'.

The common origin of eye and ear is insufficient to justify their common evaluation for, as I hope to show, in the hierarchy of the senses the eye suffers demotion at the hand of the ear, and this is simply because the ear can offer access to instruction in a way denied to the eye.

This juxtaposition, Biblical through and through, has already been touched on in Chapter 1. But its amplitude, in the way that it bears on the struggle against idolatry, is such as to demand a second look. How can it be maintained that idolatry is dependent on the work of the eye, from which the ear is fitted to offer release and redemption?

Such is the theme of the following remarks. If they are persuasive I will have shown that the empowerment of the ear is indeed of crucial importance to the struggle against idolatry, not only in itself, but also in its function as necessary pre-condition to the struggle on all fronts against the domination of the visual on which idolatry depends. There is a strong sense in which favour extended to the ear is designed to function as a means to attenuate or avert that special relationship to space and matter from which idolatry is generated; and to which not even the most tenuous relationship with matter remains immune. An accompanying degree of disfavour is appropriated to the eye.

Success will also unveil the error, perpetrated by an otherwise well-informed author, that not until the late nineteenth century was 'a concerted challenge to the hegemony of the visual . . . successfully launched' (M. Jay, *Downcast eyes*, University of California Press, 1993, p.187).

Note from the outset, however, that the differential evaluation of eye and ear incites no. denigration of nature or the visible in an ascetic or mortificatory sense. Neither organ displaces the other. Abraham is indeed required to sever himself from familiar sights and scenes – land, birthplace, father's house (Gen.12:1 ff.) – in an enforced alienation which alone will qualify him to hear the voice of God; he is nonetheless not summoned to enter into some existence that would transcend the visual; rather, he is offered a particular territory.[2] To heed the voice of God does by no means entail a disembodied existence. In fact, of course, many provisions of the Covenant can only be fulfilled through the occupation of land – most obviously those agricultural laws relating to the cultivation of the soil. Even there, where, as in the presentation of Rosenzweig, the people are sojourners in their 'own' land ('Mine is the land', God informs them – Lev.25:23); where 'the spirit of the exile' and 'the struggle of the higher life against decline into the limitations of soil and time' enforce an extreme degree of visual alienation; even there, where all 'natural' rootedness is absent, it is still through the body in whose 'natural procreation . . . it has the pledge of its eternity', that the people's future is guaranteed.[3] Hermann Cohen makes the archfathers of monotheism into 'tribal-fathers, the biological foundation of propagation and hereditary transmission (*Vererbung*)'.[4] An irreducible degree of visible and corporeal existence subsists in the most rarified presentation.

There is however, a temptation to go beyond these limits and positively to welcome the encouragement that territorial existence gives to plastic art. When the young Martin Buber engaged with this theme he did so in the context of

Wagner's allegation that among Jews 'no plastic artists' are to be found.[5] Buber did not explicitly challenge Wagner but maintained that a distinction must be made between 'the man of the ear' (the Jew of the ancient world) and 'the man of the eye' and that this distinction turned only on climatic and historio-sociological factors and would be overcome, in favour of the eye, through a resurgent Jewish nationalism.[6] R. Abraham Isaac Kuk adduces a similar argument: whilst manifesting his sensitivity to the idol on the one hand, and to the divine summons to the artist-craftsman Bezalel on the other, Kuk associates a restored interest in beauty also with the return to Jerusalem and, correspondingly, an end to 'spatial alienation'.[7]

But the point where 'spatial alienation' ends is also the point where the latent threat of the idolisation of the material may, perhaps, become actual. Whatever may in fact be the relationships whereby artistic expression is conditioned, the import of the anti-iconic struggle is blurred together with its correlated diminution of the visual. The eye will now enter into its own and it becomes more than a truism to say that the eye makes idolatry possible, so to speak, by its capacity to perceive matter: 'in visual signs it is the spatial dimension which takes priority'.[8] Even though it is also true that a certain inappropriate relationship to the visual object is required to actualise the reality of idolatrous conduct, and that the object made manifest by and to the eye – plastic image, soil or whatever – must be endowed with some immanent attribute, of holiness, say, before it can become an idol, it exists in no meaningful sense until it can be seen (or touched). This is the first point. Obviously, understanding of this sort, when the reference is to divine anthropomorphism, cannot but confront the objections of certain philosophers, especially Maimonides, by whom heresy is alleged of those who attribute to God any aspect of corporeality even though their form of worship might otherwise be impeccable.[9] Idolatry however, as understood here, requires some incorrect relationship to a corporeal entity and by no means necessarily involves the nature of the perceived object of worship.

Secondly, the work of the eye is such as to create space in an enduring mode. The effect of the visually perceived

permits of no distinction in time between the process of seeing and the object of perception. Only as a simultaneity and
therefore as static can the eye perceive the physical world.[10]

The relative status of eye and ear in their capacity as or-
ganising percepts and therefore in their respective bearing
on the theme of idolatry can be helpfully expounded in
terms of a Hebrew-Greek comparison – what to R. Isaak
Unna is a 'world- historical contradiction between Hellenism and Judaism'.[11] This is a vexed, perplexing and peren-
nial theme, of multitudinous dimensions. To Leo Strauss
the topic of Jerusalem and Athens reached classical level in
the twelfth and thirteenth centuries.[12] But it is as alive in
the contemporary work of Lévinas and Derrida as in the
Maccabean period. 'Are we Greeks? Are we Jews?' asks Derrida
in his discussion of Lévinas; and he ends this discussion
with a further question: what is the 'legitimacy' of Joyce's
copula (in *Ulysses*): 'Jewgreek is greekjew. Extremes meet'.[13]

The Talmudic sages – some at least – were ready indeed
to welcome 'the chief beauty of Japhet into the tents of
Shem' (TB Meg. 9b – ref. to Gen.9:27) because 'chief beauty'
here denotes the Greek language (cf. Rashi, ad. loc.). Others coupled their welcome for the language with a rejection of the wisdom; but also to be recalled is the presence
in the school of Rabban Gamaliel II (c. 100 CE) of five
hundred pupils studying *Torah* and an equal number studying 'Greek wisdom' (TB Sota 49b). Momigliano points out
that R. Meir remained with his teacher, Elisha b. Abuyah,
although the latter became an apostate under Greek
influence, on friendly terms (c. 200 CE).[14] Not that the relationship between rabbinical 'Greeks' and their colleagues
was always thus amicable: in early seventeenth century Poland
the highly respected R. Solomon Luria vehemently attacked
the equally respected R. Moses Isserles, on the grounds of
the latter's reference to Aristotle in a responsum. Isserles
vigorously counter-attacked, quoting illustrious precedents
and explaining, inter alia, that 'only on the Sabbath and the
High Holydays and the intermediate days of festivals, at a time
when people go for a stroll', did he occupy himself with the
reading of Aristotle; otherwise he devoted every day to the
study of the Talmud, Mishnah and their commentaries.[15] -

The particular aspect of the 'Jew Greek' confrontation here

at issue concerns the visual as a limiting factor; more particularly, the argument that knowledge is patterned after a
visual concept, that an essence beyond immediate sense-
impression is discoverable, an unchanging reality to which
sense impression gives a mere mimetic representation. But
this is precisely what a Jewish mode of thinking contests
and must reject. Hans Kohn makes the conflict explicit: the
ancient Greeks, he writes:

> . . . were the people of sight, of the spatial and plastic
> sense . . . as if they thought to transpose.the flowing, fleeting,
> ever related elements of life into rest, space, limitation,
> and to give the formless form . . . thoughts became plas-
> tic pictures. Plato's ideas were primordial images, the world
> purified of the dross of growth and based on the pure
> types of being . . . The Jew did not see so much as he
> heard; he lived in time . . . His organ was the ear . . . This
> God personified himself to the Jews, not in the image but
> in the call . . . When Elijah perceived God, he heard only
> a still small voice (1K 19:12). For that reason the Jew never
> made an image of his God'.[16]

Obviously, as indicated earlier, no Jew, or anyone else for
that matter, can in any sense be said to 'live in time'. But
for Kohn's general thesis there is widespread support.[17] The
parallel that Plato establishes between the visible and the
intelligible world (*Republic*, Bk.VI, end) leads Karl Joel rhetorically to ask: are not the Platonic ideas 'the true divine
statues of the world? Is not idea, *eidos*, literally the image,
the visible . . . For him is not true cognition precisely vision
of the idea, and is not the sensuous world the dark cave
with mere shadow-pictures of true entities which he himself
likens to statues?'. Joel expounds Plato's theory of ideas as
'an Acropolis of the mind'.[18] Bergson's terminology is not
markedly different in its reference to a modern-day 'science
and metaphysics' possessed of the 'architectural simplicity
of the Platonic theory of ideas or of a Greek temple'.[19] But
a Greek temple enshrines the cult of beauty and brings about
what to Jewish eyes denotes an idolatrous and static synthe-
sis of divinity, beauty and the this-worldly.[20] It is no more
than for the eye a feast.

It is one thing to demote the eye, quite another to promote

the ear, 'that handsome volute to the human capital'. On what grounds then, does the ear acquire its superior status? It seems that this is so by virtue of the ear's capacity to receive and apprehend a verbal message conveyed orally – all the more so if this message is at times of a detailed nature that can then, if necessary, be inscribed. The eye is limited in its power of apprehension to no more than the surface appearance of the object, its patterning, colour, shape, and so on.[21] When apprehended in this way the object's identity may still not be apparent. As a sociologist, and talking in terms of person-to-person interaction, Simmel maintains, for example, that what is seen of a person generally requires to be interpreted by what 'we hear of him'. The person who sees without hearing 'is much more confused, at a loss, disturbed, than he who hears without seeing'.[22] To this considerable extent, the visual is dependent upon the auditory for a meaningful elucidation. The ear, on the other hand, is able to receive a variety of messages ranging from the blunt to the most sophisticated. It is what Simmel calls 'an egoistic organ', passive and immobile, formed physically in such a way as to receive whatever comes within its range – unlike the eye it cannot be averted or closed.[23] Further: if, as is in fact the case, the passage of time must be endured – 'auditory signs act in a time sequence' (Jakobson, op. cit., p.340) – before a sequence of verbal events can be converted into a meaningful synchronic totality, then only the ear enjoys this relationship to time in that it can wait, as it were, does not and cannot depend on simultaneity of apprehension and is thereby fitted to receive instruction seriatim. It is necessary to await the moment when a sound (or series of sounds) is completed before its import can be evaluated. Duration, the word and the ear form an indissoluble mode of apprehension.[24] By virtue of the ear's inherent attribute, whereby it conceives of the world not as a simultaneity but as a succession, one can talk, following Merleau-Ponty, 'of a sort of Bergsonian "reduction" which reconsiders all things *sub specie durationis*'.[25]

This argument has not been found convincing by all the philosophers. Philo was persuaded to esteem the sense of sight as 'the queen of the rest . . . in the closest connection with the soul . . . the prophets being called seers'; whereas the ears 'are in some degree more slow and more effeminate than the eyes'.[26] But this is a rare exception, and in their discussion of the senses, although the medieval philosophers, with frequent reference to Aristotle, do esteem both sight and sound as agents of the intellect, it is to the latter medium that over-riding importance is ascribed by, for example, Shimon Duran, Salomo Halevi and Bahya b. Asher. They adduce four main grounds: only through oral instruction can the unlearned be taught; the intercourse of minds is of particular intellectual benefit; what enters by the ear is free from doubt and obscurity, such as self-instruction through the eye is subject to; although the eye is the source of intuition, from oral discourse the true source of illumination proceeds.[27]

The Tosafist, in a playful and punning mood, describes the oral in an exemplary mode; from Isaiah 22:18 he takes the word *kadur* (Heb. ball) and uses it as central to an image of instruction, likening oral teaching to a game in which girls toss a ball back and forth: 'thus a man transmits to his fellow and to his pupils the words of *Torah*, to and fro, and the eyes of all are opened'.[28]

The ear is the instrument through which Abraham is brought the voice of God;[29] through which God makes known his wishes to the Israelites. Thus, wilful deafness is synonymous with the refusal of instruction. Why else would prophet after prophet assail those whose 'ears are blocked and they cannot listen' (Jer.6:10); those 'rebels' who neither see nor hear (Ezek.12:2); those who 'turn a mutinous back and have hardened their ears from hearing' (Zech.7:11)? This exaltation of hearing, as against the inferior and sometimes deceptive role of vision, attains perhaps its apogee in the Isaianic concept that predicates messianic movement on 'watching' your guide but also 'heeding' the command and 'treating as unclean the silver overlay of your images and the golden plating of your idols. You will cast them away like a menstruous woman' (Is.30:20–22).

Rabbinic psychology postulates, so to speak, a chain of command, encompassing all mental and physical activity; it is exemplified in the exegesis of Psalm 119 (especially Sec. 5, vv. 35 ff.). Rabbenu Jacob b. Asher (in his legal code the Tur, Orekh Hayyim 1:1) interprets these passages as a plea by David that he may hear the word of God, that God will 'lead' him (that is, addressing David's legs), that he will 'turn' David's heart to God's decrees; and, 'avert my eyes from the sight of vanity'.[30] Ear, legs, heart and eye are brought to a unity of conduct in the service of God. But the ability and willingness to hear is the *sine qua non*.

This mode of receptive communication belongs to, and is determined by, the divine purpose. The 'signs and wonders' that accompany the Exodus are indeed called on to substantiate and illustrate divine action and purpose but Moses is also enjoined not only to retail, and thereby complement, what the Israelites have already seen of these actions but also instructed in 'the words' that will convey what God demands of the Israelites (Ex.19:4 ff.) – and, whatever may have been the vehicle whereby the words were uttered, it is to the human ear that they are addressed – 'hear, O Israel' – and the human ear by which they are received. The ear, like the eye, can certainly be deceived – hence the warning against 'false prophets' (Dt.13:2 ff.) – but it still remains the only agent capable of receiving verbal instructions in a detailed and precise form such that they can be constituted into a message, much as if the instructions were inscribed. It does not seem to me possible to imagine any other agent able to function in this way with the same degree of articulacy and precision; certainly not what Langer justly decries as 'wordless symbolism', non-discursive, untranslatable and incapable of defining or generalising.[31]

These words, made accessible to the ear, are to be inscribed (Dt.27:8). This inscription is used by Joshua as a medium of instruction (Josh.1:8; see also 23:6 and 24:26); and also by Ezra (Neh.8:1 ff.). In the reign of King Josiah there is mention of the re-discovery of a lost 'scroll of the Teaching' (2K.22:8). The precedent is of course the Tablets bearing the Decalogue. This commitment to a surface, visually perceptible as 'engraving, groove, relief', now has the essential characteristic of being 'infinitely transmissible'.[32] The oral origin of the 'engraving', as mediated through the ear, undergoes no change of course but does its altered presentation in a fixed, inscribed, transmissible and 'iterable' form entail petrifaction? Idolisation? Is doctrine now set in tablets of stone? And separated from its origin? This question is sharpened all the more by reason of the bias against reciting by heart what is inscribed (TB Git. 60b). The *Problematik* of a written text, book or scroll re-appears in Derrida's critique of western metaphysics and its hostility to the supposed fixity of the inscription. That is why Derrida can gloss Saussure's – 'the superstition of the letter' – as 'the sin of idolatry'.[33]

In the context of Mendelssohn's sympathetic relationship to Rousseau – another target for Derrida's assault – and Mendelssohn's theory of imageless symbolism, emphasis on oral instruction, disdain for 'overmuch writing' and the 'dead letter', this theme has already been touched on.[34] It would seem to relate Mendelssohn to the ranks of the logocentrics. But his recoil from an impersonal 'paper' world does not impose this conclusion and such an argument would fail to do justice to his presentation of the revelation 'through *words and script . . .* (of which) only the most essential part was entrusted to letters'. For its elucidation, unwritten and oral sources are demanded.[35] This is indeed the crucial *modus operandi* whereby the idolisation of the 'letter' is averted in favour of a plurality of meanings, all acknowledging their relationship to their origin.

The *rapport* of written and oral is modulated by the rabbis within a variety of nuances but their convergence in terms of the mutual dependence of both texts, in combination with the preservation of their independence, is clear. Having said that, oral teachings were in fact committed to inscription, as early as Talmudic times. This was justified by reading Ps.129:126 to mean: 'when it is a time to work for the Lord, they break thy Torah' (TB Tem.14b; Git.60a).[36] Better to inscribe than to forget.

Nevertheless, the Maharal of Prague (R. Judah Loew b. Bezalel) can still ask: why were the words of the sages not written down? Even though it would not be proper that they should be inscribed with the *Torah*, on account of the difference between them, even so, 'for their own sake, like all the books of holiness', they could still be inscribed. Judah Loew takes his answer from the text – 'to the making of many books there is no end' (Eccl.12:12) which he takes to mean not that there is no end to the number of books but that the books themselves have no end: 'the words of the sages do not resemble the words of the *Torah*, for the words of the *Torah* are the ground of the commandments and the words of the sages particularize the commandments and words that particularize move without end, and because they have no end they were not written down at all; for if a part of them were written, then a part would be lacking because it is not possible to write down all and therefore they were not written in whole or in part'.[37]

The absence of vocalisation to the text of the *Torah* gives R. David ibn Zimra a welcome opportunity for the consequent possibility of different readings – 'for were it vocalised, the *Torah* would have but one form and one understanding'; similarly, since the letters are not pointed and the text unvocalised and uncantillated – and here ibn Zimra quotes with approval an earlier authority, Saadya Gaon – there is all the greater possibility 'to know all the hidden wisdom and understanding (of the *Torah*)'; the Oral Law clarifies the Written and brings to light all its 'hidden aspects'.[38]

This *modus operandi*, only in the most superficial sense, fails to change the text. As the 'game' described by the Tosafist (page 165 above) proceeds, the eventual outcome is the interaction of text and bearing in an unceasing process. The manner in which the 'players' are mutually enlightened in regard to the text necessarily involves change in its respective bearing for each of them. This of course, is further predicated on the fact, as Hercenberg recalls, that 'in Hebrew the written work is conceived in such a manner that it integrates the interpretation of the reader'.[39] This activity destroys neither the text nor its interpretation but brings them together at the same time that they are distinguished. The deification of the text as image is averted; any suggestion of self-subsistence and self- sufficiency is refused; and between text and reader an expository dialogue of indefinite duration comes into existence, engaging all past readers in the way that it will also engage their successors. This is why Derrida can rhetorically ask: 'is it by chance that the meaning of meaning (in the general sense of meaning and not in the sense of signalization) is infinite implication, the indefinite referral of signifier to signifier? And that its force is a certain pure and infinite equivocality which gives signified meaning no respite, no rest, but engages it in its own *economy* so that it always signifies again and differs?'.[40]

On the other hand, none of this must in any way suggest that the written text is modified; so much so that what is written should not be recited by heart (see above, page 167). The inference must be that inscription is designed to preserve the unaltered character and integrity of the text and avert its conservation at the hands of the vagary and fallibility of human memory. Even in such a case however, 'signified meaning', in its inscribed plenitude, will still co-exist with 'the indefinite referral of signifier to signifier'. The text becomes a source of suggestions rather than of conclusions. In this way the threat of finality will be indefinitely delayed and the text retain its capacity for innovation. This is one example of the counter- argument offered by Jerusalem to the challenge from Athens, and from idolatry in general. The weapon deployed is the introduction of the notion of the unfinished into what the idolater regards as a closed and self-sufficient totality.

This process is one of enlightenment: that is, at the same time as the *Torah* diminishes the whole it also legitimises the fragment. The means whereby the *Torah* asserts its demands precisely coincide with those that are needed to achieve a state of acceptability. There is no intermediate position such, for example, that a state of enchantment might first require to be disenchanted: occupy some neutral limbo, as it were, before a second operation might then procure some legitimising effect. The passage from enchantment to legitimacy is instantaneous and no more than one operation achieves a dual purpose. What is a negation is also an affirmation.

The idolater's material image is regarded in an essentialist sense as in some way in a relationship of participant with that force which it purports to contain. What is sought in such an entity, according to Maimonides, is what is deemed to exist in it (Guide, I:1). But the supposedly transcendent attribute is solely the product of the idolater's consecration, dedication or projection. What was previously indeed lifeless is now in some sense eyed as alive. But this is an illusion, the emanation of a false consciousness, that confuses essence with becoming. So soon however, as the integrity of the image is destroyed through breakage, then immediately and absolutely it becomes *kosher*, as a form of innocent decoration. At one blow the *Torah* breaks the spell and brings about enlightenment. This simultaneity is not in any way jeopardised by the necessity for the idolater's concurrent renunciation of his image.

This example serves not only to demonstrate the coincidence of disenchantment and enlightenment but points also to the association between reification and a visual component, if not to the former's actual dependence on the latter. This is evident in the intense reserve with which the idea of sanctity is regarded, even more so its physical location; there is an equivalent wariness in respect of any material symbolism that goes beyond symbolic acts; the anti-mimetic aesthetic rejects with abhorrence the three-dimensional; primarily in oral terms is memory preserved and transmitted, as alone consonant with a perpetually renewed present, in opposition to the monument or memorial. Perhaps however, the most striking example of disengagement from the material is achieved through the operation of the 'as if' mode of thought for, simultaneously with the alternative reality that is envisaged, the negation of present reality is its precondition. To acknowledge the deficiency and imperfection of the existent (for all its exalted role as 'good' and human designation – Gen.1) does not obscure its apprehension *as if* that vastly imperfect existent were also a far improved entity.

The material and visual component to the state of reification can be at least partially undermined by the introduction of the *non finito*. But this is not exclusively a spatial operation, for it has also a temporal dimension in that the fragmented image or the imperfect world can be regarded as having entered into the anticipation of completion. The dimension of time has been restored. This has its counterpart in the incomplete portrayal of the human being, where, by contrast, completeness would signify petrifaction and the extinction of life. The symbol, through its immaterial nature, loses its capacity to signify an unchanging denotation. The holy, because it is dependent on changing circumstances, can embody no fixed, essential value. Time itself resists spatialisation and destroys the existent through its capacity as the repository of the world that is created 'in order to be made' (Gen.2:3). In the meantime however, every end marks no more than a fresh beginning.

Notes:

INTRODUCTION

1. Emeric Deutsch, 'Argent et Sexe', in J. Halpérin and G. Levitte (eds.), *Idoles*, Paris, Denoël, 1985, p.42.

CHAPTER 1

1. See B. S. Childs, *Exodus*, London, SCM Press, 1974, p.403; and H.- P. Müller, 'Gott und die Götter in den Anfängen der biblischen Religion', in O. Keel (ed.), *Monotheismus im alten Israel und seiner Umwelt*, Fribourg, Verlag Schweizer 1980, p.137.
2. *Siphre zu Deuteronomium*, ed. M. Friedmann, Vienna, 1864, Re'eh, No. 54.
3. Maimonides, *The guide to the perplexed*, Eng. trans. S. Pines, Chicago UP, 1963, III:37 (hereinafter referred to as Guide).
4. F. Rosenzweig, *Briefe und Tagebücher*, II, The Hague, Nijhoff, 1979, pp.770–771.
5. Gen. 35:1–4; see also J.-B. Frey, 'La question des images chez les Juifs', *Biblica*, 15, 1934, pp.265–300, esp. pp.267 ff.; and W. Hallo (ed.), 'Cult statue and divine image', in *Scripture in context*, II, Indiana UP, 1983, pp.1–17.
6. Rashi, Ibn Ezra and Sforno to Gen. 35: 1–4.
7. See R. Judah Loew b. Bezalel (the Maharal of Prague), *N'tivot Olam II*, repr. London, Honig, 1961, pp.121 ff.
8. S. A. Geller, 'The sack of Shechem: the use of typology in Biblical Covenant religion', *Prooftexts*, x, 1990, pp.1– 15.
9. M. Weinfeld, *Deuteronomy and the Deuteronomic School*, Oxford UP, 1972, p.92 (discussing Dt.13:13–19).
10. See also M. Halbertal and A. Margalit, *Idolatry*, Harvard UP, 1992, pp.223 ff.
11. R. Judah Loew b. Bezalel, *Gevurot Ha-Shem*, repr. Jerusalem, 1971, p.307.
12. See, for example, the variety of Biblical interpretations of the episode of the golden calf (Ex.32) discussed in M. Fox, 'R. Isaac Arama's philosophical exegesis of the golden calf episode', in M. Brettler and M. Fishbane (eds.), *Minhah le-Nahum*, Journal for the study of the Old Testament, Supplement Series 154, pp.87–102.
13. Where the verse is numbered 23.
14. See the discussion in Nehama Leibowitz, *Iyyunim Hadashim be-sepher Shemot*, 9th rev. ed., Jerusalem, World Zionist Organisation, 1986, pp.256 ff.; see also Z. Levy, 'Über Dekonstruktion, Religion und jüdisches Denken', in *Studien zur jüdischen Geschichte und Soziologie:*

Festschrift Julius Carlebach, Heidelberg, Carl Winter, 1992, pp. 37–54.
15. See S. E. Loewenstamm, 'The making and destruction of the golden calf', *Biblica*, 48, 1967, pp.481–90, here p.485; also Rashi, ad loc.
16. See Childs, op. cit., pp.402–3; G. von Rad, *Theologie des alten Testaments I*, Munich, Kaiser Verlag, 1958, p.203 fn.28; C. J. Labuschagne, *The incomparability of Yahweh*, Leiden, Brill, 1966, p. 139.
17. Ex.20:2–6, as translated and arranged in *Tanakh – the Holy Scriptures*, The Jewish Publication Society of America, Philadelphia/New York, 1988; see also M. Weinfeld, 'Aseret ha-dibrot – yihudam u-mkomam ba-masoret Yisrael', in B.-Z. Segal (ed.), *Aseret ha-dibrot*, Jerusalem, Magnes Press, 1986, pp.1–34, esp. pp.5 ff.; Leibowitz, op. cit., pp.220 ff.; and M. Friedländer, *The Jewish Religion*, London, Kegan Paul, 5651 (1891), pp.266–267; and C. Carmichael, 'The Ten Commandments', Ninth Sacks Lecture, Oxford Centre for Postgraduate Hebrew Studies, 1983, pp.13–14.
18. See T. Mettinger, 'The veto on images and the aniconic God in ancient Israel', in H. Biezais (ed.), *Religious symbols*, Uppsala, 1979, pp.5–29; and J. Ouellette, 'Le deuxième commandement et le rôle de l'image', *Revue Biblique*, vol.74, No. 4 (1967), pp.504–516; W. Zimmerli, 'Das Bilderverbot in der Geschichte des alten Israel', in K.-H. Bernhardt (ed.), *Schalom – Studien zu Glaube und Geschichte Israels*, Stuttgart, Calwer Verlag, 1971, pp.86–96.
19. Mettinger, op. cit., p.18.
20. Further discussed on pages 159 ff.; for the relationship in the late Hellenistic world, see M. Laffranque, 'La vue et l'ouïe', *Revue Philosophique*, vol.153, pp.75–82; for a modern statement, cf. N. Viallaneix, 'Soren Kierkegaard: La voix et l'ouïe', *Les Etudes Philosophiques*, 1969, pp.211–224; also J. H. Charlesworth, 'Kierkegaard and Optical Linguistics', *Kierkegaardiana*, VII, 1968, pp. 131–134.
21. For a discussion of this point, see R. Draï, *La Traversée du désert*, Paris, Fayard, 1988, p.100; also C. Chalier, *La sagesse des sens*, Paris, Albin Michel, 1995, esp. Chapter 4.
22. Prov.2:1; 22:17; 23:19; see also the material assembled in J. Muilenburg, 'The Biblical view of time', *Harvard Theological Review*, liv, no.4, Oct. 1961, pp.225–252, here p.240.
23. Sifre to Numbers, Piska 115, p.126. These references also illustrate the erotic connection with idol-worship (see also pp.4–5).
24. It is characteristic of the elaborate Temple built by Solomon that hewn stones should have been used for the altar which was even overlaid with gold (1 K.6:7,22). Samuel Krauss (*Synagogale Altertümer*, Berlin-Vienna, Benjamin Harz, 1922, pp.290 ff.) discusses these and other variations.
25. See for example, C. Dohmen, *Das Bilderverbot*, Frankfurt am Main, Athenäum, 1987, pp.174–175.
26. See R. Samuel b. Meir, Nahmanides and Sforno ad. loc.; also E. Shohat, 'Magamot Politiyot be-sipurei ha-avot', *Tarbitz* 24 (1955), pp.252–267, here p.266.
27. Ibn Ezra to Jer.10:7–9.
28. H. Graetz, 'The Construction of Jewish history', in M. Meyer (ed.

and trans.), *Ideas of Jewish history*, New York, Behroman, 1974, p.223.

29. See above p.3.
30. For references to the existence of 'other gods', see also Ex.23:23; Ju.11:24; 1 Kgs.11:5, 7, 33; 2 Kgs.23:13; Jer.2:11.
31. Rashi ad loc., quoting Sifrah to Lev.19:4; see also D. Kotlar, Ha-Omanut ve-ha-Dat, Jerusalem/Tel Aviv, Maran Books, 1971, pp.79 ff.
32. MT Book of Knowledge, Laws of Idolatry, II:1.
33. Hallo, op. cit., p.2.
34. R. P. Carroll, 'The aniconic God and the cult of images', *Studia Theologica 31*, 1977, pp.51–64, here p.53; for an analysis of the general problem involved, see J. Peel, 'Understanding alien belief systems', *British Journal of Sociology*, XX, 1969, pp.69–84.
35. E. Cassirer, *The Philosophy of Symbolic Forms*, II, Engl. trans., Oxford UP, 1955, p.241.
36. Y. Kaufmann, 'The Bible and mythological polytheism', *Journal of Biblical Literature*, Vol.70, 1951, pp.179–97, here pp.180, 183.
37. Halbertal and Margalit, op. cit., p.259, n.6. Finkelstein argues that the prophets ignore the distinction between matter and spirit, 'precisely because it might seem to provide a rational basis for idol-worship. The Prophets decline to argue the existence of a shade, independent of the human body, or a god independent of the idol, bearing its name. They generally speak and write as though there were only one realm of existence, that which is spatial, tangible and visible. They refuse to speculate on the difference between man's spirit and his body' (L. Finkelstein, 'Judaism as a system of symbols', in M. Davis (ed.), *Mordecai Kaplan Jubilee Volume*, Engl. Sec., New York, Jewish Theological Semiary of America, 1953, pp.225–244, here p.238).
38. M. Greenberg, 'Masoret aseret ha-dibrot be-ra'i ha-bikoret', in B.-Z. Segal (ed.), *Aseret ha-dibrot*, Jerusalem, Magnes, 1986, pp.80–81.
39. See the discussion in C. Dohmen and T. Sternberg, . . . *Kein Bildnis machen*, Würzburg, Echter, 1987, pp.20–21; and von Rad, op. cit., pp.214–215.
40. See C. Dohmen, *Das Bildverbot*, 2nd. ed., Frankfurt am Main, Athenäum, 1987, pp.196, 208;
41. In *The natural history of religion* (ed. A. W. Colver, Oxford UP, 1976, p.58), Hume writes: Jews and Moslems have prohibited 'all the arts of statuary and painting . . . lest the common infirmity of mankind should thence produce idolatry'. Actually, it is not correct to tar painting and statuary with the same brush since the rabbinic aesthetic makes a sharp distinction between the flat and the raised (see Chapter 6). But Hume's main point, concerning the association of imagery with idolatry, stands.
42. I. Unna, Ästhetische Gesichtspunkte im Religionsgesetz', *Jeschurun*, I, No.1 (1914), p.13.
43. J.-B. Frey, 'La question des images chez les Juifs', *Biblica*, vol.15, 1934, pp.265–300, esp. pp.269 ff.
44. J. Faur, 'The Biblical idea of idolatry', *Jewish Quarterly Review*, Vol.69, no.1 (July 1978), pp.1–15, here pp.11–12.

45. W. Zimmerli, 'Das Zweite Gebot', in *Festschrift für A. Bertholet*, Tübingen, Mohr, 1950, pp.550–63.
46. O. Grether, 'Name und Wort Gottes im Alten Testament', *Beihefte zur Zeitschrift für die alttestamentliche Wissenschaft*, No.64, 1934, p.8.
47. Carroll, op. cit., p.63; J. Hempel, *Das Bild in Bibel und Gottesdienst*, Tübingen, 1957, pp.9–10; C. Dohmen, op. cit., p.28; J. Faur, *Golden doves with silver dots*, Indiana UP, 1986, p.39.
48. L. Lévy-Bruhl, *L'expérience mystique et les symboles chez les primitifs*, Paris, Presses Universitaires de France, 1938, p.236.
49. Zimmerli, op. cit., p.561.
50. See also Halbertal and Margolit, op. cit., p.52. There is something of a parallel here to the distinction made by Hermann Cohen between music and plastic art. In a reference to Bach's St. Matthew Passion, Cohen writes: it would simply be 'aesthetic barbarism were one to ground its musical value in the faith-value of the text . . . As musician Bach is a genius, not as a hero of faith' (*Ästhetik des reinen Gefühls*, 2 vols., Berlin, Cassirer, 1912, II, pp.161–2). But Cohen also writes: 'each plastic image of God is a denial of monotheism' (*Religion der Vernunft aus den Quellen des Judentums*, Leipzig, Gustav Fock, 1919, p.63); hereinafter referred to as *Religion der Vernunft*.
51. MT Book of Knowledge, Laws of Repentance, 3:6–7.
52. See Lionel Kochan, *Jews, idols and messiahs*, Oxford, Blackwells, 1990, pp.149 ff.
53. See MT Book of Knowledge, I:8–9, and Guide I:26.
54. See H. Davidson, 'The principle that a finite body can contain only finite power', in S. Stein and R. Loewe (eds.), *Studies in Jewish religious and intellectual history*, Alabama UP, 1979, pp.75–92, here p.89.
55. D. Boyarin, 'The Eye in the Torah', *Critical Enquiry*, 16, Spring 1990, pp.532–550, esp. pp.533–4.
56. See K. W. Whitelam, 'Israelite kingship', in R. E. Clements (ed.), *The world of ancient Israel*, Cambridge UP, 1989, pp.119–139.
57. See W. Brueggemann, 'Trajectories in Old Testament Literature', *Journal of Biblical Literature*, Vol.98, No.2, 1979, pp.161–85, esp. pp.168 ff.
58. M. Weinfeld, *Deuteronomy and the Deuteronomic School*, Oxford UP, 1972, pp.191–209.
59. Von Rad, op. cit., pp.215–216.
60. Weinfeld, op. cit., p.7.
61. H. D. Preuss, *Verspottung fremder Religionen im Alten Testament*, Stuttgart, Kohlhammer, 1971, p.42.
62. See also Mettinger, op. cit., pp.23–4.
63. Faur, op. cit., (1978), p.205; Frey, op. cit., p.267.
64. For references to ceremonies of invocation, and so on, intended to animate the idol, see the material cited from Egyptian, Near-Eastern and Greek and Roman sources in J. Faur, *Iyyunim ba-Mishneh Torah le-ha-Rambam*, Jerusalem, Mossad ha-Rav Kuk 1978, pp.194–238.
65. R. David Kimche to Jeremiah, 16:18; see also R. Isaac Arama, *Akedat Yitzchak*, II, Leipzig, 1849, Sec.53, 174b–175a on Ex.32.
66. T. Jacobsen, 'The graven image', in P. D. Miller and P. D. Hanson (eds.), *Ancient Israelite religion*, Philadelphia, Fortress Press, 1987,

pp.15–32, here pp.23–4.

67. For the above, I am indebted to H. Belting, *Likeness and essence*, Engl. trans., University Press of Chicago, 1994, pp.49, 55, 62, 64, 208; see also D. Freedberg, *The power of images*, University Press of Chicago, 1989, pp.66, 90–91, 110, 395.
68. See also Labuschagne, op. cit., p.141.
69. I. M. Zeitlin, *Ancient Judaism*, Oxford, Blackwells, 1986, p.34; see also E. Fromm, *You shall be as gods*, New York, Fawcett 1966, p.37 and fn. thereto.
70. See also Ibn Ezra to Lev.19:47 and Rashi to Dt.5:3.
71. Judah Halevi, *Kitab al Khazari*, trans. H. Hirschfeld, London, Routledge, 1905, IV, 3.
72. 'Der Mann Moses und die monotheistische Religion', *Gesammelte Werke*, XIV, London, Imago Publishing House, 1950, p.220.
73. E. Cassirer, op. cit., pp.240–1; see also A. Jospé, *Die Unterscheidung von Mythos und Religion bei H. Cohen und E. Cassirer in ihrer Bedeutung für die jüdische Religionsphilosophie*, Berlin, 1932, pp.122 ff.
74. R. P. Carroll, op. cit., pp.62–3.
75. MT Book of Knowledge, Laws of Idolatry, II:1.
76. F. Nietzsche, *Werke* I, ed. K. Schlechta, Munich, Carl Hanser 1954, p.686.
77. M. Horkheimer and T. Adorno, *Dialektik der Aufklärung*, Amsterdam, Querido Verlag, 1947, pp.219 ff..
78. H. Graetz, *Briefwechsel einer englischen Dame über Judentum und Semitismus*, Stuttgart, Levy und Müller, 1883, p.76. In the contemporary world, Graetz saw 'phantoms to which even the most civilized peoples on earth continue to pray (and which) can only be banished by Judaism just as it destroyed the altars of Baal and Astarti, of Zeus and Aphrodite, and hewed down the trees of Woden and Friga – for the inspiration came from Judaism, though the agents were Christian iconoclasts . . . Rationalism has no other representative but Judaism' (H. Graetz, *The structure of Jewish history*, ed. and trans. I. Schorsch, New York, Jewish Theological Seminary of America, 1975, p.286.).
79. F. Rosenzweig, *Der Stern der Erlösung*, The Hague, Nijhoff, 1976, p.169; hereinafter referred to as *Stern*. Leo Strauss writes: 'there is no kind of rudimentary heaven and the heavenly bodies, sun, moon and stars are, according to the first chapter [of Genesis] nothing but tools, instruments for giving light to the earth; and, most important, these heavenly bodies are lifeless; they are not gods' ('Interpretation of Genesis', *Jewish Political Studies Review* I:1–2, Spring, 1989, pp.77–92, here, p.86; see also Jer.31:35).
80. H. Frankfort, *Before philosophy*, Harmondsworth, Penguin 1966, p.242.
81. H. Jonas, *Philosophical Essays*, Englewood Cliffs, Prentice-Hall, 1974, p.29.
82. E. Lévinas, *Difficile Liberté*, Paris, Albin Michel, 1963, p.259. This is also the argument of H. Schneidau, *Sacred discontent*, University of California Press, 1977, passim.
83. H. Cox, *The secular city*, London, SCM Press, 1965, pp.23, 26, 32; see also P. Berger, *The social reality of religion*, Harmondsworth, Penguin, 1973, pp.119 ff.

84. For one account of the origin of Weber's view, see J. Winckelmann, 'Die Herkunft von Max Weber's "Entzauberungs" – Konzeption', *Kölner Zeitschrift für Soziologie*, 32, 1980, pp.12–53; see also W. J. Mommsen, 'Rationalisierung und Mythos bei Max Weber', in K. H. Bohrer (ed.), *Mythos und Moderne*, Frankfurt am Main, Suhrkamp, 1983, pp.382–402.

85. M. Weber, *Gesammelte Aufsätze zur Religionssoziologie*, I, Tübingen, Mohr, 1920, pp.94–5; compare also Das antike Judentum, ibid., III, pp.242, 415; also H. Liebeschütz, 'Max Weber's historical interpretation of Judaism', *LBYB*, IX, 1964, pp.41–68; and F. Raphaël, 'Max Weber and Ancient Judaism', *LBYB*, XVIII, 1973, pp.41–62, esp. pp.51–2.

86. M. Weber, *Wirtschaft und Gesellschaft*, repr. Cologne/Berlin, Kiepenheuer, 1964, I, pp.469–470.

87. M. Weber *Wirtschaft und Geschichte: Abriss der universellen Sozial-und Wirtschaftsgeschichte*, Munich/Leipzig, 1923/4, pp.307–9, 276, 290.

88. See M. Weber, *Gesammelte Aufsätze . . .*, I, op. cit., p.571; and 'Science as a vocation', in *From Max Weber*, ed. and trans. H. H. Gerth and C. Wright Mills, London, Routledge, 1970, pp.129-56; for a succinct statement of Weber's understanding of rationalisation/disenchantment, see M. Frank, 'Two centuries of philosophical critique of reason', in D. Freundlich and W. Hudson (eds.), *Reason and its other*, Oxford, Berg, 1993, pp.72–3.

89. For Weber's presentation of 'the pariah people' see A. Momigliano, *Essays in Ancient and Modern Judaism*, University Press of Chicago, 1994, pp.171–7; and S. W. Baron, *A social and religious history of the Jews*, I, New York, Columbia UP, 1952, pp.23 ff.

90. M. Weber, *Gesammelte Aufsätze . . .*, I, op. cit., p.564; see also K. Löwith, 'Die Entzauberung der Welt durch Wissenschaft', *Club Voltaire*, II, 1965, pp.135–155.

91. Horkheimer and Adorno op.cit., p.13; see also A. Wellmer, 'Reason, Utopia and Enlightenment', in R. Bernstein (ed.), *Habermas and Modernity*, Oxford, Polity Press, 1985, pp.40 ff.; also J. Habermas, 'Die Verschlingung von Mythos und Aufklärung', in K. H. Bohrer (ed.), *Mythos und Moderne*, Frankfurt am Main, 1983, pp.405–31.

92. Gerth and Mills, op. cit., p.152.

93. See A. J. Cascardi, *The subject of modernity*, Cambridge UP, 1992, pp.20 ff.

94. See also M. Greenberg, *Al ha-Mikra ve-al ha-Yahadut*, Tel Aviv, Am Oved, 1984, pp.116 ff.

95. R. Joseph Soloveitchik, *Halakhic Man*, Engl. trans., Philadelphia, Jewish Publication Society of America, 1983, pp.20–1.

CHAPTER 2

1. For Maimonides's endorsement of the political myth, see L. Berman, 'Ibn Bajjah ve-ha-Rambam': Dissertation for the degree of doctor of philosophy, Hebrew University, Jerusalem, 1959, pp.139 ff.

2. For the concept of space in the particular context of the Sabbath,

see C. Lederer, 'Le Chabbat et l'organisation de l'espace', *Pardès xii*, 1991, pp.86–93.

3. H. Blumenberg, *Arbeit am Mythos*, Frankfurt am Main, Suhrkamp, 1979, pp.110–111. 'Temporal distinctions' are dealt with in chapter 7.

4. M. Eliade, *The sacred and the profane*, New York pb.ed., 1959, p.11.

5. See R. Otto, *The idea of the holy*, Eng. trans., Oxford UP, 1936, chapters 14, 17.

6. For a summary outline of Durkheim's views and critique, see S. Lukes, *Durkheim*, London, Allen Lane Penguin Press, 1973, pp.24 ff.

7. Quoted from L. Fine, 'The contemplative practice of Yihudim in Lurianic Kabbalah', in A. Green (ed.), *Jewish Spirituality*, II, London, Routledge, 1987, p.79.

8. See E. Reiner, Aliyah ve-aliyah le-regel le-Eretz Yisrael 1517–1099': Dissertation submitted to the Hebrew University, Jerusalem for the degree of doctor of philosophy, 1988, pp.260 ff.

9. R. Shneur Zalman, *Likutei Amarim*, Chapter 38; Chapter 1 is also rich in the equation established between nature and the immanence of the divine world.

10. See P. Brown, *The cult of the saints*, London, SCM Press 1981.

11. L. Ginsberg, *Legends of the Jews*, Philadelphia, Jewish Publication Society of America, 1911, Vol.III, p.326.

12. R. Jonathan Eibeschütz, *Ḥemdat Ḥayyim*, Sokolko, 1905, pp.120–121.

13. See Y. Eliach, *Hassidic tales of the Holocaust*, New York, Oxford University Press, 1982, pp.92–4; also the reference in the work of the twelfth century rabbi, Eliezer b. Samuel of Metz, to the custom of adding a seal or the names of certain angels to the text in the *mezuzah*, as a means to the 'greater security' of the dwelling to which the *mezuzah* was affixed. To Maimonides this custom degraded the commandment to 'an amulet' (for references see F. Landsberger, 'The origins of the decorated mezuzah', *Hebrew Union College Annual*, 31, 1960, p.154.

14. R. Joel Halevi, *Sefer Rabiyah*, ed. A. Aptowitzer, repr. Jerusalem, 1984, p.292; and M. Schlüter, *'Deraqon' und Götzendienst*, Frankfurt am Main/ Bonn, Peter Lang, 1982, p.102.

15. R. Meir-Sima Cohen of Dvinsk, *Mesheḥ Ḥokhma*, repr. Jerusalem, nd, (?1983), cols.506–7.

16. Commentary on the Mishnah, Avodah Zarah 4:7.

17. Cf. TB San. 5b; also T. Boman, *Das hebräische Denken im Vergleich mit dem griechischen*, 7th imp., Göttingen, Vandenhoeck und Ruprecht, 1983, pp.136–8. Rashi equates frontier with 'march' (TB San. 2a).

18. R. Nehemiah Nobel, *Hagut ve-halakhah*, Jerusalem, Mossad ha-Rav Kuk, 1969, p.145 ff.

19. For further detail and references, see U. Tal, 'The Land and the State of Israel in Israeli religious life', in *Proceedings of the Rabbinical Assembly*, Vol.38 (1976), pp.16–17; also D. Hercenberg, *L'Exil et la Puissance*, Arles, Actes du Sud, 1990, pp.204 ff.

20. Norman Lamm, *Faith and doubt*, New York, Ktav, 1986, pp.174 ff.

21. See Lévinas's opening remarks to the Colloquium, L'Autre dans la conscience juive, Paris, Presses Universitaires de France 1973, p.3.

22. Tos. to TB Yeb. 6b s.v. Yakhol; see also G. Hansel, '"... Et vous craindrez mon sanctuaire" (Lev.19:30)', in J. Halpern and G. Lévitte (eds.), *Idoles*, Paris, Denoël 1985, pp.109–123.
23. The above is based on Sh A, Orekh Hayyim, Laws of Blessings, par. 218, and the commentary (Biur Halakhah) of R. Israel Meir Ha-Cohen (the Hafetz Hayyim).
24. TB Ber.59b; Sh A, Orekh Hayyim, ibid., 229:2.
25. N. Polen, 'A *derashah* of R. Joseph Saul Nathanson', *Tradition*, vol.19, no.1, Spring 1981, pp.76–9.
26. See M. Buber, *Moses*, Engl. trans., London, East and West Library, 1946, p.106.
27. See Lev.11:44; 19:2, 20:7; also Sifra to Lev.19:2.
28. See, for example, Ex.19:6; Lev.11:44 ff.; also J. G. Gammie, *Holiness in Israel*, Minneapolis, Fortress Press, 1989, p.33.
29. E. Firmage, 'The Biblical Dietary Laws and the concept of holiness', in J. Emerton (ed.), *Studies in the Pentateuch, Supp. to Vetus Testamentum*, Vol.41, 1990, pp.177–97, here p.197. See also the first few pages of R. Horvitz, 'Al ha-kedushah bamahshavah ha-yehudit he-hadashah', in *Minha le-Sarah*, Jerusalem, 1944, pp.135–54.
30. This scheme also allows for varying degrees of differentiation in terms of obligations and duties as applicable to Israelites, Levites and priests (descendants of Aaron); for details, see I. Knohl, *Mikdash ha-Dmamah*, Jerusalem, Magnes, 1993, pp.179–80.
31. 2 Sam.6:1-8; cf. E. L. Ehrlich, *Kultsymbolik im Alten Testament und im nachbiblischen Judentum*, Stuttgart, Hiersemann, 1959, pp.22 ff.
32. Ex.28:43; see also H. Ringgren, *The prophetical conception of holiness*, Uppsala, 1948, pp.10–11.
33. For a different reading of this passage which emphasises the 'extra-territoriality' of the sanctuary, see G. Hansel, '". . .Et vous craindrez mon sanctuaire"' (Lev.19:30)' in *Idoles*, op. cit., pp.109–131. This is part of an outlook that spiritualises and moralises the strong denotation of sanctity and makes sanctity a mere abstraction. It is to be found in the universalist parameter enunciated by the Psalmist (Ps.24:3,4) when he maintains that in order to ascend the 'holy mountain' of the Lord no more is required than 'clean hands and a pure heart'. So long as the mountain is 'holy', this takes no heed of the danger and the requisite precautions. In a similar spirit Maimonides maintains (MT Book of Agriculture, 13:12–13) that the priest is separated and distinguished from his Israelite brethren in order that he may serve and worship God and instruct the many in His upright ways and His righteous statutes. 'Therefore they were separated from the ways of the world, they do not wage war like the rest of Israel and do not inherit and do not acquire for themselves by the force of their bodies, but they are the army of the Lord . . .' Maimonides now extends to all mankind the same possibility: 'And not the tribe of Levi alone but each and every man of all the dwellers on earth whose spirit moves him and whose knowledge gives him understanding to separate himself and stand before God to serve and worship Him, to know God, and walks upright as the Lord made him and

has taken from off his neck the yoke of the many calculations which the sons of men seek after, behold this man has made himself most holy and the Lord will be his portion and inheritance for all time, and his desert will be in this world all that is sufficient as was that of the Cohens and Levites. David said, 'the Lord is the portion of my inheritance and my cup, You uphold my fate' (Ps.16:5)'. But it is difficult to take the priests (*cohanim*) as a model in this ascetic sense if mention is not also made of their prerogatives in the system of offerings; in military campaigns (such as against Midian, Nu.31:6; also Dt.20:2 ff.); in political matters (Dt. 17:18); and in the inspection of sufferers from various skin diseases (Lev. 13). Furthermore, given that these are among the most important functions reserved to the *cohanim* it is also difficult to see how those who are neither members of the tribe of Levi nor Israelites can take as their model the designated performers of such substantially specific functions; all the less so as Maimonides also declares that 'only the offspring of one particular family can be priests' (Guide III: 32).

34. The text of Ex.19:22, 24 uses the same verbal root – *p-r-tz* – also to designate the fatal accident that overtook Uz when his zeal for the Ark's welfare led him to approach it unprotected (see page 39).
35. TB Ta'anit 21b. By *shekhinah* is meant 'the indwelling presence of God'.
36. It is not impossible that this factor applies also to the Israelites, for God, incensed by their rebelliousness and disbelief, to the extent of contemplating their disinheritance, must be dissuaded therefrom by Moses (Nu.14:11 ff.).
37. Lev.21:17ff.; see also Dt.23:2.
38. M. Zevachim, I, 1ff.
39. Sh A, Yoreh Deah, Laws of Sefer Torah, par. 282:16.
40. See the discussion in TB Meg. 26b.
41. See R. Hayyim Sofer, *Mahaneh Hayyim*, 3rd ed., repr. Jerusalem, 1974, No.12.
42. R. Ezekiel Katzenellenbogen, *Knesset Yehezkiel*, Sadilkov, 1834, No.13. The importance attributed to utility is a feature of Rashi's comment to TB San. 16b: it is use, he maintains, that makes the Temple instruments holy, not their verbal designation as such.
43. See the view of R. Shraga Zvi Tannenbaum quoted in Y. -Z. Kahana, *Mehkarim be-Sifrut ha-Tschuvot*, Jerusalem, Mossad ha-Rav Kuk, 1973, p.383; also E. Bickerman, *Studies in Jewish and Christian history*, II, Leiden, Brill, 1980, p.202.
44. The above is based on Nahmanides's comments to Ex.13:16 and to TB Meg. in R. Moses Goldstein (ed.), *Hiddushei Ha-Ramban*, Jerusalem, 1973, cols.31–2.
45. See the Responsum of R. Meir (the 'Maharam') of Rothenburg, cited by I. A. Agus, *Rabbi Meir of Rothenburg*, 2 vols., New York, Ktav, 1970, I, No.19, pp.174–175.
46. Lev.27:13 ff. and Rashi thereto; see also MT Book of Temple Service, Laws of Trespass in regard to sacred objects, Chapters 2 and 3.
47. M. Weinfeld, *The promise of the land*, University of California Press,

1993, p.183; see also E. W. Davies, 'Land: Its rights and privileges', in R. E. Clements (ed.), *The world of ancient Israel*, Cambridge UP, 1993, ch.16.

48. Z. Zinger, *Jerusalem Post Magazine*, October 20, 1967, p.3. (This article was kindly put at my disposal by Rabbi Dr. Z. Gotthold); S. S. Sered, 'Rachel's Tomb: the development of a cult', *Jewish Studies Quarterly*, Vol.2, No.2 1995, pp.103–148, esp. p.147.

49. Quoted in W. Kaufman, *Contemporary Jewish Philosophies*, New York, 1979, p.189.

50. See Wolff's contribution to 'Les Juifs dans une société désacralisée', in J. Halpérin and G. Levitte (eds.), *L'Autre dans la conscience juive*, Paris, Presses Universitaires de France 1973, pp.75–76.

51. 'Interestingly, neither the Holy Land nor the Holy Tongue has a Jewish name in the Biblical sources, as if (in traditionalist eyes) to underscore the fact that they are sacred entities held in trust rather than by absolute right and title. The land is always referred to in the Bible as Canaan . . .' (L. Glinert and J. Shilhav, 'Holy land, holy language', in *Language and Society*, XX (1991), pp.59–86, here, p.83 fn.8). See also I. Leibowitz, *Am, Eretz, Medina*, Jerusalem, Keter, 1992, pp.76–7; and Knohl, op. cit., p.176.

52. See Sh. Rosenberg, 'Ha-Zikah le-Eretz Yisrael be-hagut ha-yahadut', *Kathedra*, no.4, July 1977, pp.148–166, esp. p.156 ff.; for an exposition of views similar to those of Halevi expressed by Naḥmanides, see A. Ravitzky, *Al Da'at Ha-Makom*, Jerusalem, Keter, 1991, pp.42 ff. According to the Talmud (BB 158b) 'the climate of the Land of Israel makes one wise' as compared with 'dark, low-lying Babylon' (ibid., Pes.34b).

53. I. Leibowitz, *Emunah, Historiyah, Ve-Arakhim*, Jerusalem, Akademon, 1982, p.126.

54. H. S. Horovitz and Israel Rabin (eds), *Mekhilta de Rabbi Yishmael*, Frankfurt on Main, 1931, Parshat Bo, p.2.

55. MT Book of Agriculture, Heave Offerings, 1:23. In any case the principle of 'manure from manure' will ensure that the two soils are indistinguishable (cf. p.36 above); compare also the material cited in R. Sarason, 'The significance of the Land of Israel in the Mishnah', in L. A. Hoffman (ed.), *The Land of Israel*, Indiana UP, 1986, pp.132–3, fn.44.

56. This is based on C. Primus, 'The borders of Judaism', in Hoffman op.cit., pp.99–108.

57. That is why Moshe Greenberg can juxtapose the 'conquest and settling of the Land' to a social system. The Decalogue, Isaiah, Amos, Micah, Ezekiel and the Psalms, Greenberg writes, 'all agree that the essence of God's requirement of man does not include the national task of settlement of the land . . . but consists mainly of the establishment of a just and mutually loving society' Moshe Greenberg, ('On the political use of the Bible in modern Israel', in D. P. Wright et al. (eds.), *Pomegranates and golden bells*, Indiana, Eisenbrauns, 1995, pp.461–71, here pp.467–8).

58. Weinfeld, op. cit., pp.184 ff.

59. See U. Simon's chapter, 'Territory and Morality from a religious Zionist perspective', in D. Burrell and Y. Landau (eds.), *Voices from Jerusalem*, New York, Paulist Press, 1992, esp. pp.111–112; also Jochanan Bloch, 'Der unwiderrufliche Rückzug auf Zion', in W. P. Eckert et al. (eds.), *Jüdisches Volk*, Munich, 1970, pp.62–81.

60. See especially Lev.18:24 ff.; Dt.4:25 ff.; 1 K.9:8 ff.; also M. Greenberg, *Al ha-Mikra ve-al ha-Yahadut*, second ed., Tel Aviv, Am Oved, 1986, pp.110–124; B. and I. Greenberg, 'Land, people and faith', in J. Edelheit (ed.), *Life of covenant*, Chicago, 1986, pp.61–76; and E. W. Davies, op. cit., pp.352 ff.

61. Adapted from Weinfeld, op. cit., p.192.

62. See R. zur Lippe, 'Das Heilige und der Raum', in D. Kamper and C. Wulf (eds.), *Das Heilige – Seine Spur in der Moderne*, Frankfurt am Main, Athenäum, 1987, pp.413–27; also Menahem (Edmond) Stein, *Ben Tarbut Yisrael ve-Tarbut Yavan ve-Roma*, Jerusalem, Massada, 1970, pp.210–211.

63. M. Tohorot, Kelim, 1:6–9.

64. See the contribution by Rabbi Dr Z. Gotthold to *Jerusalem as a holy city – A tetralogue*, Jerusalem, n.d., p.76.

65. See ibn Daud's comment to MT Issurei Bi'ah, 20:1.

66. *Sepher Ha-Trumah*, Hilkhot Eretz Yisrael, Venice, 1523.

67. *Sepher Ha-Tashbetz*, Amsterdam, 1738, Pt.III, No.199; see also the comment of Rashi to TB San. 26a (s.v. *Shevi'it*).

68. Commentary to M. Zevachim 14:8.

69. For a general and comprehensive conspectus of the diversity of rabbinic arguments, see the article 'Eretz Yisrael' in *Entsiklopediyah Talmudit*, II, 3rd ed., Jerusalem, 1956, esp. pp.213–218.

70. Thus, although in an *aggadic*, rather than legal framework, R. Meir-Simha Cohen of Dvinsk warned against conceiving of the Temple and Sanctuary as 'holy things in themselves, heaven forfend. The Lord, blessed be He, rules amidst His children but if they break the Covenant, all *kedushah* is removed from them (Temple and Sanctuary) and they become like undifferentiated ('profane') vessels (*klei hol*). Invaders came and desecrated (the Temple) and Titus entered the Holy of Holies and a whore came with him and he suffered no harm. For its *kedushah* had been removed . . .' (R. Meir-Simha Cohen of Dvinsk, *Meshekh Hokhmah*, 2nd. ed., Jerusalem, n.d., p.506 (Commentary on Ex. 32:19); cf. also TB Git. 56b).

71. TB Ket. 110a–111b. This situation anticipates the status later accorded to Poland: 'the land of Poland', according to R. Abraham Isaiah Karelitz (the 'Hazon Ish' – 1879–1954), 'with its well-established *Yeshivas* and the saintly Hafetz Hayyim and other revered great men of Torah living there, has the same legal status as the Land of Israel, whereas other lands simply have the status of "outside the Land of Israel"' (quoted Glinert and Shilhav, op. cit., p.81). R. Nahman of Braslav writes: 'in a place where Israel dwells from yore, even outside the Land, it is in respect of the holiness of the Land of Israel, in respect of a "diminished holiness in the lands where they have gone"' (ref. to Ezek.11:16) (*Likutei Moharan*, repr. Jerusalem, 1990, p.74b).

72. See MT Book of Agriculture, Laws of Heave-offerings, 1:5 ff.
73. A. Oppenheimer, 'The boundaries of Eretz Israel as interpreted by the sages', in G. Sed-Rajna (ed.), *Rashi*, Paris, Editions du Cerf, 1993, pp.166–7.

CHAPTER 3

1. This theme is discussed in L. H. Brockington, *Introduction to the Apocrypha*, London, Duckworth, 1961, pp.152–3.
2. R. Jacob Anatoli, *Malmad Ha-Talmidim*, Lyck, 1866, p.68a; see also L. Zunz, *Ha-Drashot be-Yisrael*, Heb. trans., ed. H. Albeck, Jerusalem, 1947, p.546, fn.100; Joseph Heinemann in his *Prayer in the Talmud* (Engl. trans., Berlin/New York, De Gruyter, 1977, p.249) writes: 'It is a well-known fact that there are no prayers from the Talmudic period which are addressed to intermediaries of any sort – neither to angels, nor to saints or Patriarchs. "When troubles befall a man, let him not cry out to Michael nor to Gabriel – but let him cry out to Me and I shall answer him immediately, as it is written, and it shall come to pass that whoever calls on the name of the Lord will be delivered (Joel 3:5) (J. Berakot, IX, 13a)"'; for rabbinic aversion to angels, see R. Elior, 'Mysticism, magic and angelology', *Jewish Studies Quarterly*, I, No.1 (1993/1994), pp.3–53, esp. pp.41–42; also the material cited in P. Hayman, 'Monotheism – a misused word in Jewish Studies', *Journal of Jewish Studies*, Vol.XLII, No.1 (Spring, 1991), pp.1–16, esp. pp.6ff.
3. See especially Abrabanel's comment to Ex.20.
4. E. Lévinas, *Au-delà du verset*, Paris, Editions de Minuit, 1982, p.174; *Religion der Vernunft*, pp.236 ff. and pp.262 ff.; also Jospe, op. cit. pp.50–1.
5. M R Song of Songs I:12.
6. M R Exodus 28:4.
7. See A. Halkin and D. Hartman (eds), *Epistles of Maimonides*, Philadelphia, Jewish Publication Society of America, 1985, p.103, and the material quoted p.136, n.71.
8. H. Künzl, 'Zur künstlerischen Gestaltung des portugiesisch-jüdischen Friedhofs in Hamburg-Altona', in *Festschrift Julius Carlebach*, Carl Winter, Heidelberg, 1992, pp.165–74. The 'hand' of God is also a feature in a floor mosaic of the binding of Isaac in the synagogue of Beth-Alpha (sixth century CE).
9. S. Lieberman, *Hellenism in Jewish Palestine*, New York, Jewish Theological Seminary of America, 1962, p.126.
10. E. Rosenzweig, *Briefe und Tagebücher*, II, The Hague, Nijhoff, 1979, 770–1.
11. R. Moses Isserles, *Torat Ha-Olah*, repr. nd, Tel Aviv, Pt.I, ch.16, pp.18b–19.
12. R. Judah Loew b. Bezalel, *Tiferet Yisrael*, repr. Jerusalem, 1970, ch.46, p.140.
13. R. Nahman of Braslav, *Likutei Moharan*, repr. Jerusalem, 1990, 62:6.

14. Philo writes in a similar strain of the need to transpose Biblical discourse of God into 'human' terms: of anthropopathisms, for example, that they are used 'for the sake of admonishing those persons who could not be corrected otherwise. For of all the laws which are couched in the form of injunction or prohibition – and such alone are properly speaking laws – there are two principal positions laid down with respect to the great cause of all thing: One that God is not as a man (Nu. 23:19), the other that God is as a man. But the first of these assertions is confirmed by the most certain truth, while the latter is introduced for the instruction of the many. In reference to which it is said concerning them "like a man He shall train His son" (Dt. 8:5)': *Works of Philo Judaeus*, Engl. trans., London, 1854, I, p.353).

15. MT Book of Knowledge, Laws of Repentance, 3:6–7.
16. Guide I:36. ('Image' is defined here as 'the notion in virtue of which a thing is constituted as a substance and becomes what it is').
17. MT Book of Knowledge, Laws of Idolatry, ch.1.
18. Ibid.
19. See also J. Faur, *Iyyunim be-Mishneh Torah le-ha-Rambam*, Jerusalem, Mossad ha-Rav Kuk, 1978, pp.222 ff.
20. Guide, II:12.
21. Ibid., I:73.
22. H. Cohen, *Ästhetik des reinen Gefühls*, 2 vols., Berlin, Bruno Cassirer, 1912, I, pp.185–6. (But this work contains no mention of Dilthey by name.) *Einfühlung* can be roughly translated as 'emotionally sympathetic identification'.
23. P. Tillich, *Systematic theology*, London, Scm Press, 1978, I, p.241.
24. See A. J. Heschel, *Man's quest for God*, New York, Scribners, 1954, pp.121–136; also A. L. Mackler, 'Heschel's rejection of a Tillichian understanding of religious symbols', *Judaism*, vol.40, no.2, 1991, pp.290–300.
25. See L. Lévy-Bruhl, op. cit., pp.225 ff.
26. *Religion der Vernunft*, p.495.
27. See U. Berner, 'Der Symbolbegriff in der Religionswissenschaft', in M. Lurker (ed.), *Beiträge zur Symbolforschung*, Baden-Baden, Koerner, 1982, pp.17–27.
28. E. R. Goodenough, *Jewish symbols in the Greco-Roman period*, IV, Princeton, UP, 1954, ch.3. The arguments and conclusions of this work have been much disputed: see, for example, J. Neusner, *Method and Meaning in Ancient Judaism*, 3rd series, Brown University, 1981, ch.9; and Morton Smith, 'Goodenough's "Jewish Symbols" in Retrospect', *Journal of Biblical Literature*, Vol.86, Pt.I, March 1967, pp.53–67.
29. See S. Stern, 'Synagogue art and rabbinic halakhah', *Le'Ela*, no.38, Rosh Hashanah, 5755 (Sept.1994), pp.33–37.
30. G. Tsarfati, 'Luhot ha-Brit ke-semel ha-Yahadut', *Tarbitz*, vol.29, no.4 (July 1960), pp.371–393, esp. pp.384 ff.
31. Sh A, Orekh Hayyim, Laws of phylacteries, 32:44; see also the commentary thereto of R. Israel Meir Ha-Cohen (the Hafetz Hayyim) in his *Mishnah Berurah*.

32. See J. Stern, 'Modes of reference in the rituals of Judaism', *Religious Studies*, vol.23 (1987), pp.109–28.
33. S. L. Goldman, 'On the interpretation of symbols and the Christian origin of modern science', *Journal of Religion*, vol.62, no.1 (1982), pp.1–20, here p.18.
34. For examples, see M. Bar-Ilan, 'The hand of God – a chapter in rabbinic anthropomorphism', in G. Sed-Rajna (ed.), *Rashi 1040–1990*, Paris, Editions du Cerf 1993, pp.321–335.
35. Stern, op. cit., p.117.
36. N. Goodman, *Languages of Art*, Oxford UP, 1969, p.5.
37. See A. Steinsalz, 'The imagery concept in Jewish thought', *Shefa*, I, no.3, 1978, pp.56–62.
38. See also S. B. Finesinger, 'The Shofar', *Hebrew Union College Annual*, VIII–IX, 1931–32, pp.193–228 for the historical role of the *shofar* in the inauguration of a king, as alarm signal in time of war, and so on.
39. Guide III:54.
40. E. Cassirer, *The Philosophy of Symbolic Forms*, II, Eng. trans. (slightly modified), Yale UP, 1955, p.245.
41. There is some convergence between this argument and that informing A. Eisen's 'Divine Legislation as 'Ceremonial script': Mendelssohn on the Commandments' (*AJS Review*, XV, No.2, Fall 1990, pp.239–267) where Mendelssohn's treatment of the commandments (*mitzvot*) as 'symbolic script' is related to the modern context of religious observance – 'voluntarist, individual, and thus dependent to a large degree upon rational argument, rather than communally coerced in a culture dominated by traditional authority' (pp.256–7).
42. M. Mendelssohn, *Über das Erhabene und Naive in den schönen Wissenschaften*, Gesammelte Schriften, Berlin, 1929, I, pp.456–7.
43. All the above is based on M. Mendelssohn, *Jerusalem*, Engl. trans., University Press of New England, 1983, pp.102 ff. Judah Halevi underlines the superiority of teaching by oral means, quoting the adage, 'from the mouths of scholars, but not from the mouth of books' (Kitab al Kharizi, II:72); see also Judah Messer Leon, *Sefer Nofet Tsufim – The book of the honeycomb's flow*, ed. and trans. Isaac Rabinowitz, Cornell UP, 1983, p.131; see generally B. Gerhardsson, *Memory and manuscript*, Uppsala, 1961, pp.157 ff. For the presentation of Mendelssohn's argument in the eighteenth century context, especially with reference to the contemporary interest in Egyptian hieroglyphs, see A. Funkenstein, *Perceptions of Jewish history*, Californian UP, 1993, pp.226–7. There is also the likelihood of influence from Rousseau whose second *Discours* Mendelssohn had earlier translated into German (see A. Altmann, *Moses Mendelssohn*, London, Routledge, 1973, pp.544–545).
44. M. Mendelssohn, *Jerusalem*, op. cit., p.119.
45. See also Julius Guttmann, 'Mendelssohn's *Jerusalem* and Spinoza's *Theologico-political treatise*' in A. Jospe (ed.), *Studies in Jewish thought*, Wayne State University Press, 1981, ch.15, esp. p.375.
46. Die Psalmen, übersetzt und erläutert von S. R. Hirsch, Frankfurt-am-Main, Hermon, 1924, p.379.

47. See Hirsch's commentary to Chapter 4 of Pirkei Avot in his *Israels Gebete*, Frankfurt am Main, J. Kauffmann, 1921, p.476.
48. S. R. Hirsch, *Neunzehn Briefe*, Frankfurt am Main, J. Kauffmann, 1889, pp.79, 98.
49. S. R. Hirsch, *Horeb*, Vol.I, ed. and trans. Dayan Dr Grunfeld, London, Soncino, 1962, p.clxi.
50. For all the above, see Hirsch, *Horeb*, I, pp.62, 170–1; and S. R. Hirsch, *Judaism Eternal*, ed. and trans. Dayan Dr Grunfeld, London, Soncino, 1956, I, p.111.
51. S. R. Hirsch, *Timeless Torah*, ed. and trans. J. Breuer, New York, Feldheim, 1969, p.316.
52. Hirsch, *Neunzehn Briefe*, op. cit., pp.67–8. (Italics in original.)
53. Commentary to Pirkei Avot, chap.5, p.506.
54. H. Cohen, *Religion der Vernunft. . .*, op. cit., p.494. (The original runs: 'der Jude treibt keine Symbolik mit seinem einzigen Gott'.)
55. Ibid.
56. H. Cohen, *Religion der Vernunft. . .*, op. cit., p.405.
57. H. Cohen, *Jüdische Schriften*, I, Berlin, Schwetschke, 1924, p.301; ibid., III, p.172.
58. Ibid., p.184; see also H. Cohen *Religion der Vernunft. . .*, op. cit., pp.401–2.
59. H. Cohen *Jüdische Schriften*, I, pp.140–4.
60. Ibid., III, 173 ff., 184 ff.
61. See E. Berkovitz, *Major themes in modern philosophies of Judaism*, New York, Ktav, 1974, pp.8 ff.; and A. Altmann, *H. Cohens Begriff der Korrelation*, in H. Tramer (ed.), *In zwei Welten*, Tel Aviv, Verlag Bitaon, 1962, pp.377–399.
62. H. Cohen, *Religion der Vernunft. . .*, op. cit., p.103; see also M. Dreyer, *Die Idee Gottes im Werk Hermann Cohens*, Königstein, Anton Hain, 1985, pp.229 ff.
63. H. Cohen, *Religion der Vernunft. . .*, op. cit., p.111. (Cohen's version in German has been followed for the purpose of the English translation above.)
64. Guide, I:54.
65. For many examples of such memorabilia from the early years of the Zionist movement, see M. Berkowitz, *Zionist culture and West European Jewry*, Cambridge UP, 1993, ch.5.
66. T. Herzl, *Tagebücher 1895–1904*, I, Berlin, Jüdischer Verlag, 1922, pp.33, 165.
67. T. Herzl, *The Jews' State*, Engl. trans., London, Rita Searl, 1946, p.72.
68. See E. Don Yehiya and C. Liebman, 'The symbol system of Zionist socialism', *Modern Judaism*, I, no.2 (1981), pp.121–48; also M. Berkowitz, op. cit., ibid.
69. G. L. Mosse, *Confronting the nation*, University Press of New England, 1993, p.128.
70. See Stuart Cohen, *The three crowns*, Cambridge UP, 1990, passim.
71. Quoted from K. W. Whitelam, 'Israelite Kingship', in Clements, op. cit., pp.119–139, esp. pp.132 ff.; see also Chapter 1.
72. A. Ravitsky, *Ha-ketz ha-meguleh u-medinat ha-yehudim*, Tel Aviv, Am Oved, 1993.

73. See I. Leibowitz, *Siḥot im Michael Shashar*, Jerusalem, Keter, 1988, pp.26 ff.
74. See S. Weitman, 'National flags', *Semiotica*, 8, 1973, pp.328–367, esp. pp.337–338. There has been criticism of this article (see A. Hill, 'Hitler's flag: a case study', ibid., 38, 1982, pp.127–137) but not of its main thesis.
75. E. Durkheim, *The elementary forms of the religious life*, Engl. trans., 4th imp., London, Allen and Unwin, 1957, pp.228–9.
76. For a cogent criticism of Durkheim in this respect, see Z. Bauman, *Modernity and the Holocaust*, Cambridge, Polity Press, 1989, pp.170 ff.
77. L. Finkelstein, 'Judaism as a system of symbols', in M. Davis (ed.), *Mordecai Kaplan Jubilee Volume*, New York, Jewish Theological Seminary of America 1953, Engl. Sec., pp.225–44, here p.227.
78. See Stern, op. cit., p.116.
79. *Sefer Ha-Ḥinukh*, ed. R. Hayyim Dov Chavel, Jerusalem, Mossad ha-Rav Kuk, 1977, p.73; see also, G. Appel, *A philosophy of Mitzvot*, New York, Ktav, 1973, pp.87 ff. This argument is widespread in rabbinic psychology; for an expansive account of Hirsch's version, see I. Heinemann, *Ta'amei Ha-Mitzvot II*, Jerusalem, Jewish Agency, 1956, pp.134 ff.; for that of Maimonides, Guide II:31; Eight Chapters, chap.IV; and MT Book of Knowledge, Laws of Study of the Torah, 1:7.

CHAPTER 4

1. F. Nietzsche, *Werke I*, (ed.) K. Schlechta, Munich, Carl Hansen, 1954, p.213.
2. E. Renan, *Qu'est-ce qu'une nation?*, Paris, 1882, pp.7ff.
3. See also the remarks by Jean Halpérin in his introduction to J. Halpérin and G. Lévitte (eds.), *Mémoire et Histoire*, Paris, Denoël, 1986, p.7.
4. The 'double-bind' situation that results is examined in J. Elster, *Ulysses and the Sirens*, revd. ed., Cambridge UP, 1993, pp.50 ff.
5. Certain authorities include also the binding of Isaac in this list; see the commentary of Joseph Caro ('Bet Yosef') to the Tur, Orekh Ḥayyim, I, no.13. This list, however constituted, shows how mistaken it is for Lucette Valensi to limit remembrance to two categories of events: those that illustrate the cruelty of the Jews' enemies and those of liberation through divine intervention (See L. Valensi, 'From sacred memory to historical memory and back', *History and Anthropology*, II (1986), pp.283–305, esp. p.289).
6. See also A. Funkenstein, *Perceptions of Jewish History*, University of California Press, 1993, p.17.
7. See L. L. Honor, 'The role of memory in Biblical history', in M. Davis (ed.), *Mordecai Kaplan Memorial Volume*, English Section, New York, 1953, pp.417–35.
8. See also B. S. Childs, *Memory and Tradition in Israel*, London, SCM Press 1962, ch. 3.
9. T. Adorno, *Ästhetische Theorie, Gesammelte Schriften VII*, Frankfurt am Main, Suhrkamp, 1972, pp.416–417; F. Nietzsche, *Werke I*, ed.

K. Schlechta, Munich, 1954, p.546. Danto speaks of 'the dark powers' of the artist whereby his image of X is thought actually to capture X: 'something of this magical theory, I am certain, enters into the intent of the death portrait, and into the explanation of the fact that mourners characteristically and unreflectingly seek to establish an image of the departed, as though death were magically overcome if the persona could be preserved.

And how otherwise explain the worship of images – which would not be idolatry at all if the saint were literally *in* the picture – of the powers ascribed to various statues of the Virgin, of the *sacri bambini* to be found throughout Christendom, transradiated by the sort of holy presence that relics are supposed to house: as though one's form *were* a relic in this sense?' (A. Danto, *The philosophical disenfranchisement of art*, New York, Columbia UP, 1986, pp.127–8 ff. Italics in original). This is supported from the side of the psychologists: 'according to theory, one of the functions of the appearance of an introjected object during mourning is to enable the mourner to carry on the relationship, rather than to accept totally the reality of death' (M. H. Spero, 'Object relations theory and the rabbinic concept of "Demut De' Yukon"', *Journal of Psychology and Judaism*, XI, No.4, Winter 1987, pp. 222–238, here p.234).

10. E. Fulchignoni, *La Civilization de l'image*, French trans., Paris, Payot, 1969, pp.40–41.
11. See the material assembled in D. Freedberg, *The power of images*, University Press of Chicago, 1989, pp.299 ff.
12. P. Nora, 'Between memory and history', *Representations*, No.26 (1989), pp.7–25, here p.19.
13. See also B. S. Jackson, 'Ideas of law and legal administration: a semiotic approach', in R. E. Clements (ed.), *The world of ancient Israel*, Cambridge UP, 1993, ch.9, esp. pp.189 ff.; and S. Trigano, 'Les monuments d'une alliance', *Monuments Historiques*, no.191, Feb., 1994, pp.7–10.
14. Giovanni Leoni, '"The first blow": projects for the camp at Fossoli', in G. Hartman (ed.), *Holocaust remembrance*, Oxford, Blackwells, 1994, pp.204–214, here p.205; see also ibid., p.294 fn.14 for the concurring, though qualified, views of Primo Levi and Jean Améry. The names of the killed are also the sole feature of the Vietnam Veterans' Memorial, Washington.
15. D. G. Roskies, *Against the Apocalypse*, Harvard UP, 1984, p.301.
16. Ibid., p.297.
17. D. Polinker, *Varsha*, Jerusalem, Mossad ha-Rav Kuk, 1948, p.9.
18. M. Azaryahu, 'War memorials and the commemoration of the Israeli war of independence, 1948–1956', *Studies in Zionism*, Vol.XIII, No.1 (1992), pp.57–77, here, pp.64–5; see also Mosse, op. cit., p.129.
19. J. E. Young, *The texture of Memory*, Yale UP, 1993, p.13; see idem, 'La Biographie d'une image mémoriale: le monument du ghetto de Varsovie de Nathan Rapoport', *Pardès*, xiii, 1991, pp.57–85. There is an important review of Young's work by S. D. Ezrahi in *Jewish Social Studies*, NS. Vol.1, No.3, Spring 1995, pp.161–173.

20. Pirkei Avot, 4:25.
21. R. Naḥman of Braslav, *Likutei Moharan*, repr. Jerusalem, 1990, No.110, p.99a.
22. See the introduction to Avigdor Katzburg, *Tmunot Ha-Gedolim*, New York, 1925. The portraiture of rabbis first became current in the Sephardi world of the sixteenth century and spread fairly rapidly, eventually joined by the photograph. See the most interesting article by Y.(R.) Cohen, '"Ve-hayu eynekha ro'ot et morekha": ha-rav ke-ikonin', *Zion*, Vol.58, No.4, 1993, pp.407–452.
23. See F. Yates, *The art of memory*, London, Routledge, repr. 1972, pp.233 ff.
24. See Honor, op. cit., pp.428–9.
25. Judah Messer Leon, *The book of the honeycomb's flow* (first published Mantua, 1475/76), ed. and trans. Isaac Rabinowitz, Cornell UP, 1983, pp.141–143.
26. Yates, op. cit., p.158; for a general account of Modena's treatise in its Renaissance and Jewish context see G. Bos, 'Jewish traditions on strengthening memory and Leone Modena's evaluation', *Jewish Studies Quarterly*, vol.II, no.2 1995, pp.39–58.
27. R. Judah of Modena, *Lev Aryeh*, Venice 5372 (1611/1612), I:4.
28. This recalls R. Huna's dictum: 'let not a man take leave of his friend except amidst a word of *halakhah* for in that way he will remember him' (TB Ber. 31a).
29. *Lev Aryeh*, I:4, 9, 10; II:8; III:5. In certain mystical and kabbalist circles not even the Tetragrammaton might be written down in ink on paper or parchment: 'a great catastrophe is the result. He who does so thinks that he has fulfilled the verse: "And he gazed at the likeness of the Lord", whereas, in reality, he has offended against: "for ye saw no likeness". The truth is that the wise man, even when he reads the Torah, depicts for himself black fire on white fire in order to dread and fear His name, blessed be He, as it is said, "and was afraid of My name" (Mal.2:5)' (Zvi Hirsch Eichenstein, *Turn aside from evil and do good*, ed. and trans. Louis Jacobs, London-Washington, Littman Libary, 1995, p.55).
30. R. Jacob Rosen, *Zafnat Pa'aneah*, 2 vols., Jerusalem, 1979, p.120.
31. M. Friedmann (ed.), *Seder Eliyahu Zuta*, repr. Jerusalem, 1960, p.8; see also M. Kadushin, *Organic thinking*, New York, Jewish Theological Seminary of America, 1938, pp.52–3, for similar views.
32. See Maimonides's Preface to the Mishneh Torah.
33. See, for example, TB San. 26b, 27a; and the material cited in Gerhardsson, op. cit. pp.143 ff.
34. TB San. 99a–b; Meg. 32a.
35. See Abrabanel's commentary on Isaiah and Allemanno's on the Song of Solomon (Heshek Shlomo), excerpted in I. Adler (ed.), *Hebrew writings concerning music*, Munich, Répertoire International des Sources Musicales, 1975, pp.3, 43.
36. See also R. de Vaux, 'Les sacrifices de l'Ancien Testament', *Cahiers de la Revue Biblique* I, Paris, 1964, p.25.
37. M. Pesaḥim, 10:5 (italics added).

38. This is a recurrent theme in T. Boman, *Das hebräische Denken in Vergleich mit dem griechischen*, Göttingen, Vandenhoeck und Ruprecht 1983; see also J. Epstein (ed.), *Shiurei HaRav: a conspectus of the public lectures of Rabbi Joseph B. Soloveitchik*, New Jersey, Ktav, 1994, pp.14 ff. For a classic statement of Bergson's position, see his *Essai sur les Données immédiates de la conscience*, Paris, Presses Universitaires de France, 1948, Chapter 2.
39. See Hermann Cohen, *Jüdische Schriften II*, ed. B. Strauss, Berlin, Schwetschke, 1924, p.206.
40. P. Ricoeur, 'History of religions and phenomenology of time consciousness', in J. M. Kitagawa (ed.), *History of religions*, New York/ London, Macmillan, 1985, pp.13–30, here pp.27–8.
41. A. J. Heschel, *God in search of man*, New York, Harper and Row, 1966, p.215.
42. Soloveitchik, op. cit., p.52; Rosenzweig had converse and debate with men from the past (*Briefe und Tagebücher*, II, The Hague, Nijhoff, 1979, pp.790–1.
43. P. Connerton, *How societies remember*, Cambridge UP, 1989, p.66.
44. This does not mean of course that any and every interpretation is possible e.g. to write of the Exodus as 'a paradigm of revolutionary politics' (M. Walzer, *Exodus and revolution*, New York, Basic Books, 1984) entirely distorts the purport of the Exodus as God's authority to claim as his people the Israelites and with them to conclude his Covenant; for a similar misconception of freedom under divine law see also H. Brunkhorst, 'Exodus – der Ursprung der modernen Freiheitsidee und die normative Kraft der Erinnerung', *Babylon*, no.6, 1989, pp.22–35.
45. MT Book of Seasons, 7:6.
46. See pp.153 ff. for a discussion of the 'as if' mode of thought.
47. H. Zafrani, *Mille ans de vie juive au Maroc*, Paris, Maisonneuve et Larose, 1983, p.241.
48. M. Govrin, 'Ha-pulhan ha-yehudi ke-zhanre (*Genre*) shel teatron kodesh', in D. Kotlar (ed.), *Omanut ve-Yahadut*, Bar-Ilan UP, 1989, pp.243–63, here pp.244 ff.
49. H. Atlan, 'La Mémoire du rite', in J. Halpérin and G. Lévitte (ed), *Mémoire et Histoire*, Paris, Denoël 1986, pp.29–49, here p.39.
50. B. S. Childs, *Memory and Tradition in Israel*, London, SCM Press, 1962, p.55.
51. Quoted by E. Z. Melammed, in B. -Z. Segal (ed.), *The Ten Commandments in history and tradition*, Engl. trans., Jerusalem, 1990, p.202.
52. See also p.48.

CHAPTER 5

1. M. Brion, *L'Art Abstrait*, Paris, 1956, p.268.
2. For example, M. Carmilly-Weinberger, *The fear of art*, New York, Bowker, 1986, ch.1; M. Rosenthal, 'Ein Beitrag zur Erforschung der jüdischen Ikonophobie in Mittelalter', in L. Kötzsche and P. von der Osten-

Sacken (eds.), *Wenn der Messias kommt*, Berlin, Institut Kirche und Judentum n.d., pp.77–103.

3. Incidentally, what *did* contemporary Jewish observers make of icono-clastic movements? I have been unable to find any references at all to events in Byzantium; as to the Reformation, the only contemporary reference I have been able to find is a comment in the historical chronicle of R. David Gans, first published in Prague in 1592. Luther is hailed as 'a great scholar in their writings', a follower of Hus, author of many works 'who made the religion of the Pope odious and divided the heart of the Christians and wanted to burn and destroy all images, and they should no longer pray to Mary, mother of their anointed, and not to his twelve apostles and that bishops and clergy should take wives...' (R. David Gans, *Zemach David*, ed. M. Breuer, Jerusalem, Magnes, 1983, p.386).

4. J. Ouellette, 'Le deuxième commandement et le rôle de l'image', *Revue Biblique*, vol.74, no.4 (Oct. 1967), pp.504–516, here p.516.

5. For a discussion of this point, see the Tur, Yoreh Deah, Laws of Idolatry, 141, and the comment of R. Joel Sirkes (the 'Bakh') ad loc.

6. See E. N. Adler, 'Jewish Art', in B. Schindler (ed.), *Occident- Orient: the Gaster anniversary volume*, London, Taylor's Foreign Press, 1936, pp.37–49; also pp.99, 127.

7. See also H. Schreckenburg and K. Schubert, *Jewish Historiography and iconography*, Maastrict/Minneapolis, 1992, pp.147 ff.; and M. Simon, *Verus Israel*, Paris, Boccard, 1964, p.42.

8. See Rashi to TB AZ 43a.

9. KB Keritot 3a and Rashi ad loc.

10. TB Ḥulin 13b. When this ruling is followed in early medieval times there are economic motives at work – see Sh. Eidelberg (ed.), *Tshuvot Rabbenu Gershom Me'or Ha-Golah*, New York, Yeshiva University 1955, No.21.

11. See R. Isserles's comments to Sh. A, Yoreh Deah, Laws of Idolatry, 141:1; also his comments to the Tur (note 2), ibid.

12. J. Blau (ed.) *Tshuvot Ha'Rambam*, II, Jerusalem, 1960, p.726.

13. Sh A, Yoreh Deah, Laws of Idolatry, 141:4.

14. E. H. Gombrich, 'Freud's aesthetics', *Encounter*, Jan. 1966, XXVI, no.1, pp.29–40, here p.33.

15. S. Freud, *Der Moses des Michelangelo*, Frankfurt am Main, Insel Verlag, 1964, p.38.

16. H. Cohen, *Aesthetik des reinen Gefühls*, 2 vols., Berlin, Cassirer, 1912, II, pp.301–2; in Cohen's aesthetic is embedded the argument that 'the object of plastic art must first become words, not only in order to be able to become concepts, but also the corresponding "thought-feelings" (Denkgefühle) depend on words' (ibid., I, p.366).

17. Quoted in K. H. Wörner, *Schönberg's 'Moses and Aaron'*, Engl. trans., London, Faber and Faber, 1963, p.42.

18. *Jewish Chronicle*, Sept.13, 1935.

19. TB BB 60a; see also Rashi, ad loc.

20. Mekhilta de Rabbi Yishmael, ed. H. S. Horowitz and I. A. Rabin, repr. Jerusalem, 1960, p.144, to Ex.15:11

21. See D. Daube, 'Duty and beauty', in A, M. Rabello (ed.), *David Kotlar Jubilee Volume*, Tel Aviv, Am ha-Sefer, 1975, pp.xiv–xx; also Unna, op.cit., p.15.
22. Mekhilta 3 on Ex.15:2. The laws can also beautify Israel; see C. G. Montefiore and H. Loewe (eds.), *A Rabbinic anthology*, repr. New York, Meridian, n.d., p.118.
23. M. Mendelssohn, *Über die Quellen und die Verbindungen der schönen Künste*, Gesammelte Schriften I, Berlin, 1929, p.170.
24. Compare Singer's Prayer Book, 14th ed., London, 1929, p.287.
25. A. Rosenfeld, 'Ha-Estetika shel ha-ahava', in D. Cassuto (ed.), *Omanut ve-Yahadut*, Bar-Ilan UP, 1989, pp.301–316, here, p.309. An Eros who converted to Judaism would have to be concerned with marriage, fertility, progeny, and the satisfaction of feminine sexual needs – see D. Biale, *Eros and the Jews*, New York, Basic Books, 1992, passim.
26. See the material quoted in Y. Y. Lesheim, *Ha-hakarah be-yofi phizi beyahadut*, in Cassuto op. cit., pp.75 ff.
27. MR Genesis, 46:1.
28. See E. L. Ehrlich, op. cit., p.86, fn.228.
29. D. Davidovitz, *Omanut ve-umanim be-vatei knesset shel Polin*, Jerusalem, 1982, p.18; these illustrations refer to a collective experience and do not serve as objects of worship or instruction (B. Kern-Ulmer ed., *Rabbinische Responsen zum Synagogenbau I*, Hildesheim, Olms, 1990, p.12). The illustrations serve no instructional purpose in the fashion of the *Biblia Pauperum*.
30. Z. Yargina, *Wooden Synagogues*, Jerusalem, Image Publishing, n.d., pp.40 ff.
31. See the extensive analysis in P. Prigent, *Le Judaïsme et l'image*, Tübingen, Mohr, 1990, pp.174–263; also A. Kanof, *Jewish Symbolic Art*, Jerusalem, Gefen Books, 1990, figs.53, 54. The unhistorical sequence of some of these paintings is discussed in Chapter 8.
32. *Tshuvot ha-Rambam*, ed. J. Blau, Jerusalem, 1947–1960, II, No.215.
33. Tur, Orekh Ḥayyim, Laws of Prayer, No.90 (end).
34. See the reprint of this responsum in D. Kaufman, 'Art in the Synagogue', *Jewish Quarterly Review*, IX (Jan.1897), pp.254–269.
35. R. Zvi Hirsch Shpira, *Zvi Tiferet*, Munkacs, n.d., no.36.
36. A. Altmann, 'Zum Wesen der jüdischen Aesthetik', *Jeschurun*, XIV, Nos.5/6, May–June, 1927, pp.209–226, esp.pp.222 ff.
37. *Republic* Book x, 600–605.
38. R. Mashash, *Responsa Mayyim Ḥayyim*, Fez, 1913, No.80. To R. Abraham Isaac Kuk 'distraction of [prayerful] intent' was more likely to be provoked by images of birds and animals, which do not figure in the prayers, than by images of the planets which do (R. Abraham Isaac Kuk, *Da'at Cohen*, Jerusalem, Mossad ha-Rav Kuk 1969, No.64).
39. *Sefer Ḥassidim*, ed. J. Wistinetzki, Berlin, 1891, p.396.
40. R. Ezekiel Katzenellenbogen, *Knesset Yeḥezkel*, Sadilkov, 1834, No.10.
41. Quoted Kahana, *Mehkarim be-Sifrut*, p.354.
42. A. Geiger, 'Das Mosesbild in einem Synagogenfenster', *Jüdische Zeitschrift für Wissenschaft und Leben*, Breslau, Vol.3, 1864/5, pp.136 ff.
43. See the gloss of the Tosafist to TB Yoma 54a–b s.v. *kheruvim*.

44. *Sefer Hassidim*, p.184. There is now empirical evidence to suggest that pictures accompanying a text 'may divert attention from the critical task of attending to the printed words' (see S. Jay Samuels, 'Attentional process in reading', *Journal of Educational Psychology*, 1967, vol.58, no.6, pp.337–42, here p.337; also idem, 'Effects of pictures on learning to read', *Review of Educational Research*, Vol.40, No.3, pp.397–407. Both these articles deal with those learning to read; but, even if to a lesser extent, it seems likely that pictures would produce the same effect on the skilled and mature reader.

45. *Dvar Shmuel – She'elot u-Tshuvot*, Venice, 1702, No.247.

46. *Sefer Mahani, Hilkhot Yom Kippur*, Hanau, 1628, p.35b.

47. See S. Heller-Wilensky, *R.Yitzhak Arama u-mishnato*, Jerusalem/Tel Aviv, Mossad Bialik, 1956, p.201.

48. See the extract from his 'Eight Chapters', in *A Maimonides reader*, ed. and trans. I. Twersky, New York, Behrman, 1972, pp.361–86; also H. G. Farmer, 'Maimonides on listening to music', *Journal of the Royal Asiatic Society*, II, 1933, pp.867–84.

49. F. Nietzsche, *Werke I*, Munich, 1954, p.43; see also H. Hultberg, *Die Kunstauffassung Nietzsches*, Arbok, University of Bergen, Oslo, 1964, No.2.

50. S. Kierkegaard, *Either/Or*, Engl. trans., Harmondsworth, Penguin, 1992, p.560.

51. S. Kierkegaard, *The Last Years – Journals, 1853–55*, ed. and trans. R. G. Smith, London, Collins, 1968, pp.179–80; cf. also p.312.

52. H. Cohen, *Der Begriff der Religion im System der Philosophie*, Giessen, Verlag Töpelmann, 1915, pp.92 ff.

53. A. Danto, *The philosophical disenfranchisement of art*, New York, Columbia University Press, 1986, p.137.

54. Commentary on Nu.8:1–12:16.

55. *Religion der Vernunft*, p.494. The juxtaposition, in a 'secular' sense, is presented by Abraham Paperna (*Kankan Hadash Maleh Yashan*, Vilna, 1867, p.53) in terms of movement and articulacy: all other arts, save poetry, are limited by the material they employ. The sculptor can show no more than the external appearance of a man and nothing of his spirit and emotions. The range of the graphic artist is less limited but he too can only depict his subject at any one moment in time whereas the subject is in a state of constant change so that the static and unchanging is of very limited help to acquaintance. Music can convey a person's 'inner world at different stages' but only by way of sound and not in that 'clear language' which is the prerogative of poetry alone; for its medium is the word, 'a combination of design, melody and lucidity'.

56. H. Cohen, *Aesthetik des reinen Gefühls*, 2 vols., Berlin, Cassirer, 1912, I, pp.186–187.

57. H. Berl, *Martin Buber und die Wiedergeburt des Judentums aus dem Geiste der Mystik*, Heidelberg, 1924, pp.23–25; for a similar argument see S. Kierkegaard, *Either/Or*, Engl. trans., I, Oxford UP, 1944, pp.54 ff.

58. See H. Pollack, *Jewish folkways in Germanic lands (1648–1806)*, Massachusetts Institute of Technology Press, 1971; P. V. Bohlman, 'Musical

life in the Central European Jewish village', *Studies in Contemporary Jewry*, IX, Oxford UP, 1993, pp.17–39, and the more recent study devoted entirely to Jewish performers – W. Salmen's *Jüdische Musikanten und Tänzer*, Innsbruck, Helbling, 1991.

59. See the material excerpted in I. Adler (ed.), *Hebrew writings concerning Music*, op. cit.
60. I. Abrahams, *Jewish life in the Middle Ages*, London, Macmillan, 1896, pp.365–6.
61. See, for example, Marc Chagall on his youth in Vitebsk: *My life*, Engl. trans., London, Peter Owen, 1965, pp.21, 26, 58.
62. *Bet Ha-Midrash*, III, ed. A. Jellinek, Leipzig, 1855, p.161.
63. *Sefer Ḥassidim*, ed. Judah Wistinetzki, II, Berlin, 1892, Nos.440 ff., esp. Nos.442 and 481.
64. See the fifth of Maimonides's 'Eight Chapters'.
65. M. Meyerhof, 'The medical work of Maimonides', in S. W. Baron (ed.), *Essays on Maimonides*, New York, AMS Press, repr. 1966, pp.265–299, here pp.283 ff.
66. Meir Shimon Geshuri, 'Musikah u-poeziyah be-sifrut ha-Rambam u-tekufato', in R. Hacohen Fishman (ed.), *Rabbenu Moshe b. Maimon*, Jerusalem, n.d., pp.288–302, here p.290.
67. Sh A, Orekh Ḥayyim, Laws of Blessings, 53:4–6.
68. R. Benjamin Aaron bar Abraham Solnik (or Slonik), *Mas'at Binyamin*, repr. Jerusalem, 1980, no.6; see also I. Adler, *La Pratique musicale savante dans quelques communautés juives en Europe aux XVII et XVIII siècles*, Paris, Mouton, 1966, pp.15 ff.
69. From Sulzer's introduction to his *Schir Zion* I (1838), quoted in H. Avenary, *Kantor Salomon Sulzer und seine Zeit*, Sigmaringen, Thorbecke, 1985, p.92; see also pp.154 ff. for Liszt's admiration of Sulzer as singer and choir-master (but not for Jews in general). There is a short translated extract of Liszt's comments in M. Grunwald, *Vienna*, Philadelphia, Jewish Publication Society of America, 1936, p.355. But Sulzer's work lacked a future; thus, 'Schoenberg enjoyed the advantage of a logogenic melodic heritage perpetuated less by reform-minded cantors like Solomon Sulzer and his disciples than by the old-fashioned prayer-masters, the orthodox *ba'ale tefilla*, who chanted their daily prose-texts with often dramatic inflexions deviating rarely, if ever, from the traditional prayer-mode ... And the prayers sung in Jewish homes reflected, though inevitably at a simpler level, the same essentially rhetorical, non-metric tendencies that determined much of Schoenberg's musical stance.' (A. L. Ringer, *Arnold Schoenberg – the composer as Jew*, Clarendon Press, Oxford, 1990, p.12).
70. M. Breuer, *Jüdische Orthodoxie im deutschen Reich 1871–1918*, Frankfurt a.M., Athenäum, 1986, pp.42, 52. These influences also effected a transition from the traditional *Derashah* to the edificatory sermon (A. Altmann, 'The new style of preaching in nineteenth-century German Jewry', in his *Essays in Jewish Intellectual History*, University Press of New England, 1981, pp.190–245. For a nineteenth century reform attack on the 'contributions of the miserable ballad-mongering (Bänkelsängerei) of the later middle ages', with a suggestion

that the religious music of Bach and Handel be introduced into the synagogue service, see S. L. Steinheim, *Die Glaubenslehre der Synagoge*, Leipzig, Leopold Schnauss, 1856, pp.446–447.

71. See the analysis and translation of Maimonides's responsum in Farmer, op. cit., pp.878–880. In the sixteenth century, R. Samuel Archivolti discriminated between 'excellent (or distinguished) music', that of the Levites in the Temple, which is not devoted exclusively 'to the pleasure of the ear but also to give spirit and soul to the words pronounced' and 'vulgar (or common) music' concerned only with the pleasure of the ear, in disregard of word and content (I. Adler, *Hebrew writings concerning music*, Répertoire International des sources musicales, p.97).
72. This is reported in the journal *Ben Chananya*, VI, 1863, p.719.
73. Raymond Apple, *The Hampstead Synagogue, 1892–1967*, London, Vallentine Mitchell, 1967, p.56; see also I. Adler, 'Music in the Italian ghetto', in A. Altmann (ed.), *Jewish medieval and renaissance studies*, Harvard UP, 1967, pp.321–364.
74. The above is based on Israel Adler, op.cit.; also on S. Simonsohn, 'Some disputes on music in the synagogues in pre-reform days', *Proceedings of the American Academy for Jewish Research*, xxxiv, 1966, p.102; and on S. Sharot, *Judaism – A sociology*, Newton Abbot, David and Charles, 1967, pp.84–5 (quoting *Jewish Chronicle*, November 3, 1848).
75. R. Esriel Hildesheimer, *Briefe*, ed. M. Eliav, Jerusalem, Rubin Mass, 1965, p.21; for some indication of the varying fate of the organ in synagogues in Venice, Leghorn and Prague, see Simonsohn, op. cit., pp.104–105.

CHAPTER 6

1. Iconoclasm – Spring Symposium of Byzantine Studies, No.9, Birmingham 1977, ed. A. Bryer and J. Herrin, No.18, pp.182–3.
2. Z. Levy, 'Erkhei ha-estetika ve-ha-masoret ha-yehudit', in T. Dreyfus and Y. Elstein (ed.), *Tarbut Yehudit be-Yomeinu*, Bar Ilan UP, 1983, pp.25–35, here p.29. The early ethno-psychologist Moritz Lazarus (1824–1903) made the same comparison – see S. Schwarzschild, 'The legal foundation of Jewish aesthetics', *Journal of Aesthetic Education*, IX, No.1, Jan. 1975, pp.29–42, here, p.37.
3. Schwarzschild, ibid., p.33.
4. For a discussion of this point see J. M. Miller, 'In the "image" and "likeness" of God', *Journal of Biblical Literature*, vol.91, no.2, 1972, pp.289–304.
5. E. Saltman, 'The "forbidden image" in Jewish art', *Journal of Jewish Art*, viii, 1981, pp.42–59, here p.49.
6. A. Grotte, 'Die Kunst im Judentum und das 2. mosaische Gebot', *Der Morgen*, IV (June, 1928), No.2, p.178.
7. M. Carmilly-Weinberger, *Fear of art*, New York/London, Bowker, 1986, pp.7–8; see also M. Metzger, *La Haggada Enluminée*, Leiden, Brill, 1973, p.307.

8. See W. Schubert, 'The continuation of ancient Jewish art in the middle ages', in C. Moore (ed.), *The visual dimension*, San Francisco-Oxford, Westview, 1993, p.43.
9. M. Metzger, op. cit., p.283.
10. J. Leveen, *The Hebrew Bible in art*, Oxford UP, 1944, p.67. (It is not at all necessary to attribute this 'to the exigencies of Muslim law and practice'.)
11. M. Azaryahu, 'War memorials in Israel, 1948–56', *Studies in Zionism*, vol.13, No.1 (Spr. 1992), pp.57–77, here p.65, fnn.34, 35.
12. See the material cited in Moore, op. cit., p.2, and in Schwarzschild, 'The legal foundations...', op. cit., p.41, fn.25. In 1786, there was a proposal for a monument in Berlin to the four philosophers – Leibnitz, Lambert, Sulzer and Mendelssohn, and in 1829 (the centenary of his birth) for a monument to Mendelssohn, but nothing came of these endeavours, for reasons unknown (see the letter of David Friedländer to Moses Moser (ed. A. Wolf), *Monatsschrift für die Geschichte und Wissenschaft des Judentums*, Vol.50, 1906, pp.370–373).
13. Blumenberg, op. cit., p.245.
14. See Abraham Schreiber (ed.), *Perush ha-Rabad al Massekhet Avodah Zarah*, New York, 1960, pp.99–100.
15. MT Book of Knowledge, Laws of Idolatry III:10, with reference to the Tur Yoreh Deah, 141, and Caro's commentary thereto.
16. R. Joseph Mitrany, *She'elot u-teshuvot*, Book II, Fürth, 1768, No.35.
17. *Sefer Ha-Ḥinukh*, ed. Rabbi H.D. Chavel, Jerusalem, Mossad ha-Rav Kuk, 1977, No.39.
18. For a discussion of some of the issues involved, see Koehler, K. L. Schmidt and Miller, op. cit.; also James Barr, 'The image of God in the book of Genesis – a study of terminology', *Bulletin of the John Rylands Library*, Vol.51, No.1, Autumn, 1968. The *Problematik* from the anthropologist's angle is raised by H. Eilberg-Schwartz in his 'The problem of the body', in H. Eilberg-Schwartz (ed.), *People of the body*, State University of New York Press, 1992, pp.17–46.
19. MR Leviticus, 34:3; cf. also B. L. Sherwin, 'The human body and the image of God', in D. Cohn-Sherbok (ed.), *A traditional quest*, Sheffield, JSOT Press 1991, pp.75–85; and A. Hultgard, *Man as symbol of God*, in Biezais, op. cit., pp.111–112.
20. TB Sota 14a; cf. also Pirkei Avot, III, 13; and the material assembled in A. J. Heschel, *Torah min ha-Shamayim*, 2 vols., London/New York, Soncino Press, 1962, I, 220–3.
21. *Mekhilta de'Rabbi Yishmael*, ed. S. H. Horowitz and I. Rabin, repr. Jerusalem, 1960 (Yithro, 8).
22. M. Idel, *Golem*, Albany, State University of New York Press, 1990, p.xxvii. (The Golem is an anthropoid compounded of dust kneaded with water and is animated by pronouncing the appropriate verbal formula.)
23. Ez.1:26; see also R. David Altschul (Metzudat David), ad loc.
24. See A. Altmann, 'Homo Imago Dei in Jewish and Christian theology', *Journal of Religion*, Vol.48, No.3, 1968, pp.235–259.

25. H.-G. Gadamer, *Gesammelte Werke*, I, Tübingen, Mohr, 1990, p.145. There is a reference here to the work of St. John of Damascus (675–749), a leading protagonist of the iconodule party at the time of the great Byzantine controversy. It is worth quoting at length: 'these injunctions (i.e. against idols)', St. John writes in opposition to the iconoclasts, 'were given to the Jews on account of their proneness to idolatry. We on the contrary are no longer in leading strings . . . The Scripture says, 'Ye have not seen his likeness'. . . . How depict the invisible? How picture the inconceivable? How give expression to the limitless, the immeasurable, the invisible? . . . . It is clear that when you contemplate God who is pure spirit becoming man for your sake, you will be able to clothe him with the human form. When the Invisible One becomes visible in flesh you may then draw a likeness of his visible form. When he who is without form or limitation, immeasurable in the boundlessness of his own nature, existing as God, takes upon himself the form of a servant in substance and stature and a body of flesh, then you may draw his likeness and show it to any one willing to contemplate it.' 'Of old, God the incorporeal and uncircumscribed was never depicted. Now, however, since God has appeared in the flesh and lived among men I make an image of the God who can be seen' (From A. Bryer and J. Herrin (eds), op. cit. No.20).

26. Rashi (to Ex.30:12) refers to a view from the mystical tradition that in the census process 'the evil eye' is at work and that is why the Israelites, in the passage discussed, each deposit a half shekel as token of their presence.

27. The blessing on beholding a multitude of people acknowledges God's knowledge of each man's secrets and is accompanied by the recognition that human diversity is necessarily jeopardised if they are counted and totalised: 'for, as their faces do not resemble each other, neither are their minds alike but each and every one has a mind of his own' (MR to Nu.21:2).

28. Nietzsche, *Werke* I, ed. Schlechta, p.566.

29. E. H. Gombrich, *Meditations on a hobby-horse*, London, Phaidon, 1963, p.10.

30. Nelson Goodman (*Languages of art*, Oxford UP, 1969, p.20) argues that imitation is no test of realism and takes the case of the bronze bust that is to portray 'a mobile, many-faceted and fluctuating person . . . Duplicating the form of the head at a given instant is unlikely to yield a notably faithful representation. The very fixation of such a momentary phase embalms the person much as a photograph taken at too short an exposure freezes a fountain or stops a racehorse'. But, however long the exposure, can the fountain not but be frozen, the racehorse stopped and the person *embalmed*?

31. H. Bergson, *Le Rire*, Geneva, 1945, pp.41 ff.

32. G. W. F. Hegel, *Aesthetik I*, Engl. trans., Oxford UP, 1975, pp. 528–9.

33. For a discussion of the resulting paradox, See Luc Ferry, *Homo Aestheticus*, Paris, Grasset, 1990, pp.186 ff.

34. This would be *a fortiori* the case where the statue purportedly depicts

an aspect of the Godhead. This is the reason why the neo-Kantians, Ludwig Steinheim and Hermann Cohen, looked on Christianity as a religion of pantheism; see L. Kochan, 'Steinheim und der Bilderdienst im Judentum', in J. H. Schoeps (ed.), *Studien zu S. L. Steinheim*, Zurich/New York, Olms, 1993, pp.135–141; and H. Cohen, Religion der Vernunft, pp.63 ff.

35. M. Mendelssohn, Morgenstunden, in *Schriften zur Metaphysik und Ethik, I,* ed. M. Brasch, Leipzig, Voss, 1880, pp.324–5; see also H. v. Heimberger, 'Die Rolle der Illusion in der Kunst nach Moses Mendelssohn', *Mendelssohn Studien* II, 1975; and L. Goldstein, *Moses Mendelssohn und die deutsche Ästhetik,* n.p., 1904, pp.124–148.

36. Paperna, op. cit., p. 53.

37. E. Lévinas, 'Reality and its shadow', in S. Hand (ed.), *The Lévinas Reader,* Engl. trans., Oxford, Blackwells, 1989, pp.129–143, here, p.138; see also L. Flam, 'L'esthétique et le sacré', in H. Dethier and E. Willems (eds), *The cultural hermeneutics of modern art,* Amsterdam/ Atlanta, Editions Rodopi, 1981, pp.151–2.

38. See H. Bergson, *Creative evolution,* Engl. trans., London, Macmillan, 1911, chap.4, esp. pp.351 ff.

39. M. Proust, *A la Recherche du Temps Perdu, III,* Paris, Gallimard, 1919, p.79.

40. R. Wollheim (ed.), *The image in form: selected writings of Adrian Stokes,* Harmondsworth, Penguin, 1972, p.73.

41. Ibid.

42. *Phaedrus,* 275. The oral-inscriptional relationship is further discussed in Chapter 8.

43. A very similar particular concern with the three-dimensional marks the writings and actions of Byzantine iconoclasts, Lollards and Reformation image-breakers; see E. Kitzinger, 'The cult of images before iconoclasm', *Dumbarton Oaks Papers,* 8, 1954, p.131; M. Aston, *England's iconoclasts,* Oxford UP, 1988, pp.109, 401, 405; and D. Freedberg, 'The structure of Byzantine and European iconoclasm', in Bryer/ Herrin, op. cit., pp.165–177, here, p.170.

44. For examples of lachrymatory and lactating statues of the Madonna, see D. Freedberg, *The power of images,* University Press of Chicago, 1989, pp.301, 305–6, 319.

45. A. Schopenhauer, *Die Welt als Wille und Vorstellung,* Leipzig, n.d., I, para. 58, p.192.

46. Ibid., II, chap.34, pp.222–223.

47. Only in recent years is modern French thought beginning to catch up with this *rapprochement,* see A. Benjamin (ed.), *The Lyotard reader,* Oxford, Blackwells, 1989, pp.203–4, and J. Dérrida, *La Vérité en peinture,* Paris, Flammarion, 1978, p.153.

48. I. Kant, *Critique of Judgement,* Engl. trans., Oxford, repr.1988, p.127.

49. Ibid., pp.72–73.

50. Ibid., pp.90, 92.

51. See above, page 97, and H.-G. Gadamer, *The relevance of the beautiful,* Engl. trans., Cambridge UP, 1986, p.161.

52. M. Foss, *The idea of perfection in the western world,* Princeton UP, 1946.

53. See for example J. Wohlgemuth, 'Grundgedanken der Religions-philosophie Max Schelers in jüdischer Beleuchtung', in *Festschrift für J. Rosenheim*, Frankfurt am Main, J. Kauffmann Verlag, 1931, pp.42–3; also A. Broadie, 'Maimonides and Aquinas on the names of God', *Religious Studies*, 23 (1987), pp.157–170, esp. p.160.

54. See the discussion in TB AZ 41b–42a regarding the fate of the Philistine fish-god Dagon (1 Sam.5:4).

55. D. Freedberg, *Iconoclasts and their motives*, Maarssen (The Netherlands), Schwartz, 1985, p.35.

56. Quoted in J. Halpérin and G. Lévitte (eds.), *Idoles – Données et Débats*, Paris, Denoël, 1985, p.71.

57. TB AZ 43b; cf. the claim by R. Eliezer b. Zadok (c.100 CE): 'all countenances were in Jerusalem except alone the human countenance' (*Tosefta*, ed. M. S. Zuckermandel, Passewalk, 1881, Avodah Zarah, 5:2, p.468).

58. See Caro's commentary to the codification in the Tur of the discussion in TB RH 24a and Yoma 54b (Beth Yosef ad Yoreh Deah, Laws of Idolatry 141:17–18).

59. This is echoed in the somewhat nebulous terminology of Lévinas: 'the other is not the incarnation of God, but precisely through his face, where he is disincarnated, the manifestation of the height where God reveals himself' (E. Lévinas, *Totalité et Infini*, Paris, Kluwer Academic, 1990, p.77; see also C. Chalier, 'En attente du visage', *Les Nouveaux Cahiers*, Spring 1991, No.104, p.76).

60. G. Simmel, *Essays on Sociology, Philosophy and Aesthetics*, ed. K. Wolff, New York, Harper and Row, 1965, p.276; see also idem, *Soziologie*, Munich/Leipzig, Duncker and Humblot, 1923, p.485.

61. Simmel, *Soziologie*, p.278 (italics in original).

62. It may well be that the factor of banalisation and abuse is also relevant: a snatch comes to mind from a ditty current at the time of the Queen's coronation (1953):
The Queen's face is
In the most peculiar places.
Luther T-shirts, biscuits and playing cards are now on sale; a parchment copy of the 95 Theses costs DM16.50 (*Observer*, February 11, 1996).

63. See above, page 118; and R. Draï, *Identité juive, identité humaine*, Paris, Armand Colin, 1995, pp.46–7.

64. Jacob Leveen, op. cit., pp.94–5; see also the grotesque figures reproduced in E. Cohn-Wiener, *Die jüdische Kunst*, Berlin, Wasservogel Verlag, 1929, plate 135, and p.202; and the material cited in Carmilly-Weinberger, op. cit., p.9. One of Schönberg's self-portraits shows the subject in *rear* view (see A. Schönberg, *Schöpferische Konfessionen*, ed. W. Reich, Zürich, Verlag der Arche, 1964, Pl.2). This is consistent with Adorno's argument that the libretto of Schönberg's opera, *Moses und Aron*, revolves round the image ban (see M. Mäckelmann, Arnold Schönberg und das Judentum, Hamburg, K. D. Wagner, 1984, p.153). But portrait-painting remains perfectly legitimate – see p.188, fn. 22.

65. Tos. to TB AZ 43a s.v. *Lo.*
66. *Sefer Mitzvot Hagadol*, Negative Commandment No.23.
67. See his comments to Sh A Yoreh Deah, Laws of Idolatry, 141.
68. Ibid., 141:7 (referring to the comments of Rabbenu Asher to TB AZ 43b).
69. See gloss to TB Yoma 54a–b s.v. *kheruvim.*
70. *Sefer Hatam Sofer*, pt. vi, New York, 1958, no.4.
71. R. Abraham Kuk, *Da'at Cohen*, op. cit., No.65.
72. But at least one noted rabbi of the eighteenth century, Zvi Hirsch Ashkenazi of Hamburg and Amsterdam, refused to allow his portrait to be painted – a subterfuge had to be employed (see R. Jacob Emden, *She'ilot Yavetz*, Altona, 1739, Pt.I, No.170). The article by Y. (R.) Cohen referred to above, p.188, fn. 22 contains innumerable reproductions of portrait paintings of rabbis from the seventeenth to the twentieth century.
73. R. Joseph Mitrani, *She'elot u-T'schuvot*, Bk.II, Fürth, 1768, No.35.
74. TB AZ 43b; and Rashi, ad loc.
75. Tos. ad loc s.v. *Ve-Ha.*
76. T. Reik, *Jewish wit*, New York, Gamut Press, 1962, pp.170–1.
77. *Sefer Hatam Sofer*, pt. vi, New York, 1958, no.6.
78. See F. Landsberger, 'The origin of the decorated *mezuzah*', *Hebrew Union College Annual*, 31, 1960, p.163 and illustration 9.
79. R. Abraham Zvi-Hirsch Eisenstadt, ('Pithei Tshuvah') to Sh A Yoreh Deah, Laws of Idolatry, 141:7, note 10.
80. TB AZ 43a; see also D. Kaufmann, 'Etudes d'archéologie juive', *Revue des Etudes Juives*, XIII, 1868.
81. Rashi on Ex.20:20.
82. W. Benjamin, 'Das Kunstwerk im Zeitalter seiner technischen Reproduzierbarkeit', in *Illuminationen*, Frankfurt a.M., Suhrkamp, 1961, pp.148–184.
83. See W. Munninghaus, Walter Benjamin's Variations of Imagelessness, in T. Bahti and M. S. Fries (eds.), *Jewish Writers, German Literature*, Michigan UP, 1995, ch. 9.
84. Perhaps also from certain sculptors, such as Michelangelo and Rodin, who left large numbers of their works in a fragmentary state: see the articles by H. von Einem and J. A. Schmoll gen. Eisenwerth in the symposium, *Das Unvollendete als künstlerische Form*, Bern/Munich, Francke, 1959, pp.69–82, 117–139; also the critical discussion of these articles in E. Wind, *Kunst und Anarchie*, Frankfurt am Main, Suhrkamp, 1979, pp.158 ff.
85. The analogy with certain notions in Zen Buddhism is also striking and makes Kant's reference to the English garden as one model of irregularity all the more apposite, for in garden design can be embedded, deliberately and with philosophic emphasis, the Zen notion of 'the teasing charm of incompleteness – the suggestion that the onlooker finish his own idea according to his own imagination' (L. Warner, 'Gardens', in N. W. Ross (ed.), *The world of Zen*, London, Collins, 1962, p.103). As a means to meditation 'the aniconic principle' becomes indispensable 'in order to indicate the

unrepresentable and ungraspable in such a way that no intellectual fettering by images is the consequence . . . The mandala is then most serviceable when it no longer displays the innumerable figures of the Buddhist "pantheon" but more or less symbolic signs which essentially facilitate the reductive dismantling of obstructive imagery into imagelessness, "emptiness" ' (D. Seckel, *Jenseits des Bildes*, Heidelberger Akademie der Wissenschaften I, 1976, pp.38–9). Obviously there are basic differences, for meditation is hardly a Jewish practice, and certainly not meditation inspired by an image, however abstract and symbolic; the closest comparison is probably the message conveyed by a teacher's portrait to his erstwhile pupil. But in a mutual welcome for the partial and incomplete as opposed to the mimetic whole, with its inhibiting and obfuscating effect on the intellect, there is clear convergence (See also I. Murdoch, *The fire and the sun*, Clarendon Press, Oxford, 1977, p.71).

86. Halpérin and Lévitte (eds), *Idoles*, p.130; see also S. Kern, *The culture of time and space, 1880–1918*, Harvard UP, 1983, pp.142 ff.
86a See G. Smith, *Annonce auf ein Lebenswerk*, in P. Schäfer and G. Smith (eds), *Gerschom Scholem zwischen den Disziplinen*, Frankfurt am Main, Suhrkamp Verlag, 1995, pp.282 ff.
87. See Hegel, *Asthetik*, I, op. cit., p.81.
88. E. H. Gombrich, *Meditations on a hobby-horse*, London, Plaidon, 1963, p.10.
89. M. Mendelssohn, *Gesammelte Schriften*, I, ed. F. Bamberger, Berlin, 1929, pp.439–441.
90. D. Frey, 'Das Fragmentarische und das Wandelbare bei Rembrandt', in J. A. Schmoll gen. Eisenwerth (ed.), op. cit., pp.91–116, here p.91.
91. J. Sabil, 'Les juifs dans la peinture française moderne', in E.-J. Finbert, *Aspects du génie d'Israel*, Paris, Cahiers du Sud, 1950, pp.274–286, here pp.284–5.
92. H. Bergmann, 'Die Heiligung des Namens', in *Vom Judentum*, Leipzig, Kurt Wolff Verlag, 1913, pp.32–43, here p.37; see also E. Fromm, *You shall be as gods*, New York, Fawcett Publication, 1966, p.27.
93. Midrash Tehillim, ed. S. Baber, repr. Jerusalem, 1966, p.201 (Hebrew pagination); see also E. Bloch, *Das Prinzip Hoffnung*, Frankfurt am Main, Suhrkamp, 1959, pp.1458–9; and L. Strauss, 'Jerusalem and Athens', in *Studies in Platonic Political Philosophy*, Chicago/London, 1983, p.162.

CHAPTER 7

1. See J. Barr, *Biblical words for time*, 2nd revised ed., London, SCM Press, 1969, pp.122 ff.
2. E. Bloch, op. cit., p. 1454.
3. Cf. E. Lévinas, 'Dagam shel mahshava hayehudit modernit', *Da'at*, No.6, winter 1981, pp.59–69, esp. p.63.
4. C. Lévi-Strauss, *The savage mind*, Engl. trans., London, Weidenfeld and Nicolson, 1966, pp.234–5.

5. C. Lévi-Strauss *Myth and meaning*, Engl. trans., London, Routledge, 1978, p.43.
6. Schopenhauer, op. cit. Bk.IV, paras. 54, 57.
7. See also Ecclesiastes 9:4.
8. See R. Hayyim of Volozhin, *Nefesh ha-Hayyim*, repr. Jerusalem, 1973, ch.1, pt.3, p.76.
9. M. Stern (ed.), *Greek and Latin authors on Jews and Judaism, I, From Herodotus to Plutarch*, Jerusalem, Magnes Press 1976, pp.39–40.
10. Cf. Dt.18:10 ff.; also Lev.19:26; Is.44:24.
11. For a medieval example, see R. Judah b. Asher, *Zikhron Yehudah*, Berlin, Daniel Friedländer 1846, No.91.
12. Commentary to Dt.18:9.
13. E. Lévinas, *Autrement que l'être ou au-delà de l'essence*, The Hague, Nijhoff, 1974, p.6.
14. *A Maimonides reader*, ed. and trans. I. Twersky, New York, Behrman, 1972, p.380.
15. 'Epistle to Yemen (1172)', ibid., p.452. At no level, sophisticated or popular, can it be said that these admonitions and arguments had anything but a limited success. Maimonides is very much an isolated figure. The philosophers (especially the neo-Platonists), astronomers, mathematicians, Biblical commentators, figures of the stature of Abraham ibn Ezra, R. Abraham b. Hiyya, R. Levi b. Gerson (Gersonides) were no more immune to the pull of astrology than their untutored fellow-Jews. In his commentary on Deuteronomy 18:9 ff. – a passage which explicitly manifests an 'abhorrence' for augury, soothsaying, and so on. – Nahmanides writes as a self-proclaimed believer in the power of 'the expert in necromancy', to exploit in the appropriate manner and for his own benefits a particular constellation of the stars and planets: 'and therefore it is proper that the *Torah* prohibit these activities in order to let the world remain in its customary way and in its simple nature which is the desire of its creator'. In short, in the view of Nahmanides, the necromancer practises a nefarious but effective art, with the power to disturb the divinely ordained order of the world. In some cases the élite succumbed with a degree of sophistication. R. Levi b. Gerson maintained that human affairs were indeed subject to the influence of the heavenly bodies; but it was 'impossible to have the repeated observations required for these empirical principles of astrology, since the zodiacal position of a heavenly body at any given time is only repeated once in many thousand years'; also, God had endowed man with the intellect to counteract any such effect once it had been predicted (See R. Levi b. Gershom, *Wars of the Lord*, ed. and trans. S. Feldman, Philadelphia/New York, Jewish Publication Society of America, 1987, II, 2; also C. Touati, *La pensée philosophique et théologique de Gersonide*, Paris, Editions de Minuit, 1977, pp.138 ff.). In seventeenth-century Venice, R. Judah Leon of Modena had his horoscope read by four astrologers – two Jews and two Christians (*The life of Judah*, ed. and trans. Mark Cohen, Princeton UP, 1988, p.111). Generally, see C. Sirat, *La Philosophie juive au moyen âge*, Paris, Editions

du CNRS, 1983, pp.109 ff.; J. Trachtenberg, *Jewish magic and superstition*, New York, Harper and Row, 1939; J. Wochenmark, *Die Schicksalsidee im Judentum*, Stuttgart, 1933, pp.48 ff. (For the role taken by astrology in messianic calculations, see page 152)

16. H.-P. Stähli, *Antike Synagogenkunst*, Stuttgart, Calwer Verlag, 1988, pp.55 ff.; see also E. L. Ehrlich, op. cit., p.87.

17. D. Davidowitz, *Omanut ve-umanim be-vatei knesset shel Polin*, Jerusalem, Ha-Kibbut ha-Meuchad, 1982, pp.20–1.

18. Yargina, op. cit., p.43.

19. F. Landsberger, 'Illuminated marriage contracts', *Hebrew Union College Annual*, vol. 36, (1955), pp.502–42.

20. Quoted Y.-Z. Kahana, *Meḥkarim be-sifrut ha-tshuvot*, Jerusalem, 1973, p.362.

21. See also J. Muilenburg, 'The Biblical view of time', *Harvard Theological Review*, LIV (Oct.1961), No.4, pp.225–252.

22. A. J. Heschel *The Sabbath*, New York, Harper and Row, 1966, pp. 7–8 (italics in original).

23. MT Book of Seasons: Laws for sanctification of the new moon, II:10.

24. ShA Orekh Ḥayyim, Laws of Blessings, 55:10. (The Jewish calendar is a combination of lunar and solar. In order to align the length of the lunar year – 354 days – with that of the solar year – 365 $\frac{1}{4}$ days – a second month of Adar is periodically intercalated.)

25. M. Fishbane, *The garments of Torah*, Indiana UP, 1989, pp.54–5.

26. See M. Shabbat 2:7; also J. Elbogen, 'Eingang und Ausgang des Sabbats' in M. Brann and J. Elbogen, *Festschrift Israel Lewy*, Breslau, M. and H. Marcus Verlag, 1911, pp.173–187.

27. J. Katz, 'Ma'ariv bi-zmano u-shelo bi-zmano', *Zion*, Vol.35 (1970), Nos.1–4, pp.35–60.

28. TB San. 11a-b; see also the comprehensive description in M. D. Heer, 'The calendar', in S. Safrai and M. Stern (eds.), *The Jewish people in the first century*, II, Amsterdam, n.d., pp.834–864.

29. J. Neusner, 'Beyond myth, after apocalypse', *Response*, Vol.14, No.2, 1984, pp.17–35, here p.26.

30. See R. Wischnitzer, 'Jewish pictorial art in the late classical period', in C. Roth (ed.), *Jewish art*, Jerusalem, Vallentine Mitchell, 1971, p.86; and P. Prigent, *Le Judaïsme et l'image*, Tübingen, Mohr, 1990, pp. 224–5.

31. For the following, I am deeply indebted to Nissan Rubin, 'Zman, historiyah u-zman liminali', *Historiyah Yehudit*, II, pt.2, 1984, pp. 5–22; V. Turner, *Dramas, fields and metaphors* (Cornell UP, 1974, pp. 231–71) discusses liminality in a variety of contexts.

32. Rubin, op. cit., p.18.

33. TB Nazir 7a; see the discussion of this point in M. Grossberg (ed.), *Tsfunot Ha'Rogatschever*, Jerusalem, 1958, p.4, and in idem, *Mishnat Ha'Rogatschever*, Jerusalem, 1976, pp.37–8; also in R. Avigdor Amiel, 'Musag Ha-Zman ba-halakha', *Sinai* yr.4, Vol.7, 1940-1, pp.292– 302, here pp.297–8.

34. This case is discussed in R. Joseph Henkin, *Hemshekh Ha-Zman ba-Mitzvot*, St.Louis, Missouri, 1955, pp.75 ff.

35. See the discussion in R. Avigdor Amiel, *Ha-Midot le-Ḥeker ha-Halakha*, Tel Aviv, 1942, p.326.
36. Boman, op. cit., p.120; see also L. A. Hoffman, *Beyond the text*, Indiana UP, 1987, pp.82 ff.; Lévinas, op. cit. . . . pp.63 ff.; Samson Raphael Hirsch makes an analogy between *Ohel Mo'ed* ('tent of meeting' – cf. Ex.29:30) which, 'in the spatial sense refers to the locality' of an appointed place of assembly, and a temporal *Mo'ed* which 'summons us communally to an appointed . . . inner activity' (S. R. Hirsch, *Horeb*, Engl. trans., London, Soncino Press, 1962, I, p.84).
37. *Mishnat Rabbenu Yosef Ha-Rogatschever*, ed. M. S. Kasher, Jerusalem, 1976, pp.38–9.
38. Ibid., pp.38–40; see also the Rogatschever's *Mefaneaḥ Tsfunot*, ed. Rabbi M. S. Kasher, Jerusalem, 1976, pp.87–8.
39. Ibid., p.87.
40. See also S. Talmon, *King, cult and calendar in ancient Israel*, Jerusalem, Magnes, 1986, pp.205 ff.
41. Ibid., pp.140–164.
42. A. Funkenstein, *Tadmit ve-Toda'ah historit be-Yahadut*, Tel Aviv, Am Oved, 1991, p.105.
43. Commentary to M San. Chap.X (Perek Ḥelek). There is perhaps a reference here to the Talmudic discussion (TB San. 99a) where it is maintained that the days of the messiah will last (a) for three generations (R. Judah Ha-Nasi); (b) for seven thousand years (Abimi).
44. Berman, op. cit., p.112; see also A. Funkenstein, 'Maimonides: Political theory and realistic messianism', *Miscelleanea Medievalia*, XI, 1977, p.101.
45. *Religion der Vernunft*, p.340.
46. Ibid., p.323.
47. Boman, op. cit., pp.131–133.
48. See H. Atlan, in J. Halpérin and G. Lévitte (eds), *Mémoire et Histoire*, Paris, Denoël 1986, pp.33 ff.; and A. Néher, *L'essence du prophétisme*, Paris, Calmann-Lévy, 1972, pp.231 ff.
49. *The 18th Brumaire of Louis Bonaparte*, Marx-Engels Werke, Berlin, 1960, VIII, p.115.
50. *Stern*, p.244.
51. For examples of such messianic constructions, see L. Kochan, *Jews, idols and messiahs*, Oxford, Blackwells, 1990, pp.160–191.
52. W. Benjamin, *Illuminationen*, Frankfurt am Main, Suhrkamp, 1961, p.279.
53. B. Z. Wacholder, 'Chronomessianism', *Hebrew Union College Annual*, Vol.46, 1975, pp.201–218.
54. Cf. also Kimche on Habakkuk 3:13; and on Amos 9:7; Micah 7:8. I owe these references and translation to F. Talmage, *David Kimche – The man and his commentaries*, Harvard UP, 1975, pp.139–140.
55. Mekhilta to Ex.31:13; see also TB Ber. 57b; AZ 3a.
56. J. Neusner, *Judaism and its social metaphors*, Cambridge UP, 1989, p.17.
57. H. Vaihinger, *Die Philosophie des Als Ob*, 7–8 edn., Leipzig, Felix Meiner, 1922, pp.39 ff., 147 ff.

58. S. Atlas, *Netivim ba-mishpat ha-ivri*, New York, American Academy for Jewish Research, 1978, pp.267–8, fn.4; see idem, *From critical to speculative idealism*, The Hague, Nijhoff, 1964, p.36.
59. From Leibniz's Third Letter to Clarke, *Philosophische Schriften*, ed. C. Gerhardt, VII, Hildesheim, Olms, repr. 1965, p.363.
60. See A. Benjamin, *The plural event*, London, Routledge 1993, pp. 117–118.
61. As described, for example, in J.-F. Lyotard, *L'Inhumain*, Paris, Galilée, 1988, pp.76 ff.
62. R. Judah Loewe b. Bezalel, *Netzah Yisrael*, repr., Jerusalem, 1971, ch.28.
63. It is no doubt the emphasis on purposive action that averts the schizophrenia otherwise characteristic of those who 'treat concrete things as though they were abstract' (S. Freud, *The Unconscious*, Engl. trans., in Standard Edition of the Complete Psychological Works, London, Hogarth Press, 1953–1974, XIV, p.204).
64. *Republic* 592.
65. Kant, op. cit., p. 59.
66. *Religion der Vernunft*, p.365.
67. H. Cohen, *Asthetik des reinen Gefühls*, I, Berlin, Cassirer, 1912, p.158 (italics in the original).
68. H. Cohen, *Jüdische Schriften*, I, Berlin, 1924, p.328.
69. H. Cohen, *Ethik des reinen Willens*, 2nd rev.ed., Berlin, Cassirer, 1907, p.406.
70. H. Cohen, *Jüdische Schriften*, I, p.325.
71. H. Cohen, *Ethik des reinen Willens*, p.408.
72. Ibid., pp.408 ff.
73. See *Religion der Vernunft*, pp.297 ff.; also Cohen's open letter to Martin Buber in his *Jüdische Schriften*, II, Berlin, 1924, pp.328–40; the 'anomaly' referred to in the text is amply illustrated in E. I. J. Rosenthal, 'Hermann Cohen and Heinrich Graetz', in *S. W. Baron Jubilee volume*, Engl. Sec., II, Jerusalem, American Academy for Jewish Research, 1974, pp.725–744.
74. *Stern*, p.337.
75. F. Rosenzweig, *Kleinere Schriften*, Berlin, Schocken, 1937, p.19.

CHAPTER 7

1. E. Lévinas, *L'Au-delà du verset*, Paris, Editions de Minuit, 1982, p.174.
2. Thus Olivier Revault d'Allones errs in finding that Abraham 'quitte l'espace pour le temps' (*Musique – variations sur la pensée juive*, Paris, Christian Bourgois, 1979, p.58). For further discussion of this point, see B.-D. Hercenberg, *La Parole et la représentation*, Brussels, Louis Musin, 1985, pp.41 ff.
3. *Stern*, pp.331 ff.
4. *Religion der Vernunft*, p.363.
5. Wagner's reason: 'their vision having been always too steadily fixed upon things far more practical than beauty and the spiritual con-

tents of a world of imagination' (R. Wagner, *Judaism in music*, Engl. trans., London, William Reeves, 1910, p.17).

6. M. Buber (ed.), *Jüdische Künstler*, Berlin, 1903, introduction. In its sociologically orientated awareness of the relationship between culture and material existence, Abraham Paperna's analysis is not basically different from Buber's (see his *Kankan Hadash Maleh Yashan*, Vilna, 1867, pp.28–29). It is also relevant to the Hebrew-Greek confrontation (see pages 162–3).

7. See the lengthy extract from Kuk's letter (1908) welcoming the newly formed Bezalel association for the promotion of the fine arts in Palestine, quoted in G. Hansel, *Esthétique et Idolâtrie, Tradition et Modernité dans la pensée juive*, Paris, Festival International de la Culture Juive 1983, pp.71–72.

8. R. Jakobson, *Selected writings II*, The Hague/Paris, Mouton, 1971, p.340.

9. Cf. the material cited in D. Hartman, *Conflicting visions*, New York, Schocken, 1990, pp.126 ff.

10. This is largely the theme of Bruno Zevi's article 'Judaïsme et conception spatio-temporelle en art', *Dispersion et unité*, No.14, 1975, pp.128–140; see also N. Viallaneix, 'Kierkegaard: La voix et l'ouïe', *Les Etudes Philosophiques*, 1969, pp.211–224; and Kierkegaard's remarks on the static nature of perceived beauty (*Either/Or*, Penguin ed., p.561).

11. I. Unna, 'Asthetische Gesichtspunkte im Religionsgesetz', *Jeschurun*, I, No.1 (1914), pp.13–19, here, p.13. This is not the only comparison: to Jaroslav Pelikan, the Byzantinologist, 'the coming of the Word made flesh, carried the clear implication that in addition to hearing the voice of the spoken word of God, as faithful believers have done throughout the Old Testament, New Testament believers were in a position to see the flesh of the incarnate Word of God. The ancient priority of hearing in biblical thought, therefore, had now been forced to yield to the priority of seeing, as a consequence of the Incarnation' (*Imago Dei*, Yale UP, 1990, p.99); see also R. Debray, *Vie et mort de l'image*, Paris, Gallimard, 1992, p.107.

12. *Studies in Platonic political philosophy*, Chicago/London, 1983, p.165..

13. J. Derrida, *Writing and difference*, ed. and trans. A. Bass, London, Routledge, 1978, p.153; see also S. Wolosky, 'Derrida, Jabès, Lévinas: Sign theory as ethical discourse', *Prooftexts*, II, 1982, pp.283–302; and S. Handelman, 'Derrida and the heretic hermeneutic', in M. Krupnick (ed.), *Displacement*, Indiana UP, 1983, pp.98–129.

14. A. Momigliano, 'Juifs et Grecs', in L. Poliakov (ed.), *Ni juif ni grec*, Paris, Mouton, 1978, pp.47–63, here p. 59.

15. *She'elot u-Tshuvot Ha-Rama*, ed. Asher Ziv, Jerusalem, 1971, No.7.

16. H. Kohn, *The idea of nationalism*, New York, Macmillan, 1945, pp.30–3. A very similar argument is presented by I. Eldad in his *Hegyonut Yehudah*, Tel Aviv, 1981, pp.150–7; see also Y. Shavit, *Ha-Yahadut be-Rai ha-Yavnut*, Tel Aviv, Am Oved, 1992, pp.193 ff.; M. Landmann, *Ursprungsbild und Schöpfertat*, Munich, Nymphenburger Verlag, 1966, p.298; and the *Lyotard Reader*, ed. Andrew Benjamin, Oxford, Blackwells 1989, pp.82 ff. There are cases where the co-presence in one individual of being and time, 'Greek' and 'Jew', creates an irreconcilable

tension: in his celebrated essay on Heine (1863), Matthew Arnold
writes: 'by his perfection of literary form, by his love of clearness,
by his love of beauty, Heine is Greek; by his intensity, by his
untameableness, by his "longing which cannot be uttered", he is
Hebrew'. (For an extended treatment of this theme, see also Arnold's
essay, 'Hebraism and Hellenism', in his *Culture and anarchy*, repr.
London, Smith Elder, 1905, pp.89–103. In Walter Benjamin's analysis of two poems by Hölderlin, where the defined Greek element
yields to the 'oriental' undefined (that is, Jewish), the juxtaposition
is similar (W. Benjamin *Gesammelte Schriften*, 2:1, Frankfurt am Main,
Suhrkamp, 1977, p.126).

17. It could also be applied to Aristotle, in whose work it is maintained
that the threat offered by matter to perfection is mastered by the
concept of entelechy: 'the process of becoming, this unstable stream
of change – always in danger of vanishing into the unlimited, the
infinite – is caught again in boundaries: in the concept of an end,
of "telos". Becoming is the realisation of this its end which was also
its beginning. All becoming turns out to be a limited and static cir-
cular movement of "first cause"' (M. Foss, *The idea of perfection in the
Western world*, Princeton UP, 1946, p.18).

18. K. Joel, *Seele und Welt*, Jena, 1912, pp.260–298, esp. pp.266 ff.; see
also, R. David Hacohen, *Kol ha-Nevuah*, Jerusalem, Mossad ha-Rav
Kuk, 1970, pp.24 ff.; and H.-G. Gadamer, *The relevance of the beautiful*, Engl. trans., Cambridge UP, 1986, pp.158–160. A. Melberg (*Theories
of mimesis*, Cambridge UP, 1995, p.23), discusses the 'visual orienta-
tion' of Plato's thinking, with further references. Schopenhauer understands the relationship of the artifact to the idea in terms of
ascribing to art the purpose of facilitating the cognition of the Platonic ideas, as a 'medium' for the transmission of the intuitive (*Welt
als Wille und Vorstellung*, II, chap.34).

19. H. Bergson, *La Pensée et le Mouvant*, Paris, ed. 1946, p.221. For a
complementary statement of this comparison, see also Bergson's *Creative
evolution*, Engl. trans., London, Macmillan, 1911, pp.334 ff.; also V.
Jankélévich, *Henri Bergson*, Paris, Presses Universitaires de France, 1959,
p.268, for the anti-Hellenic cast of Bergson's thinking in relation to
becoming as against being.

20. See A. Altmann, 'Zum Wesen der jüdischen Ästhetik', *Jeschurun*, XIV,
Nos.5–6 (1927), pp.209–226; Altmann notes: 'the path to the Acropolis
is marked by the statues of Praxiteles' (p.216).

21. See H. Jonas, *Philosophical Essays*, Englewood Cliffs, 1974, p.227.

22. G. Simmel, *Soziologie*, Munich, Duncker und Humblot, 1923, p.486.

23. Simmel, ibid., p.487.

24. See also Hans Jonas, *The phenomenon of life*, New York, Harper and
Row, 1966, pp.137–139; Landmann, op. cit., p.300; and José Faur,
Golden doves with silver dots, Indiana UP, 1986, pp.29 ff.

25. M. Merleau-Ponty, *Signes*, Paris, Gallimard, 1960, p.232.

26. *The Essential Philo*, (ed.) N. N. Glatzer, New York, Schocken, 1971,
pp.112 ff.; see also A. Kamesar, 'Philo and the literary quality of the
Bible', *Journal of Jewish Studies*, Vol.XLVI, Nos.1–2 (1995), pp.55–68.

27. The above is based on David Kaufmann, *Die Sinne – Beiträge zur Geschichte der Physiologie und Psychologie im Mittelalter,* Gregg repr.1972, pp.139–43 (first published Budapest, 1884).
28. Tos. s.v. *kadur* to TB San. 26a; cf. also the comment of Rabbi Joseph Soloveitchik: that the study of the *Torah* 'should be a dialogue not a monologue. If I look at the *Gemara* as simply paper and print, as merely a text, I would never be creative' (*Shiurei HaRav,* ed. J. Epstein, New York, Ktav, 1994, p.182.)
29. See the comment of R. Abraham ibn Daud to MT Book of Knowledge: Laws of Idolatry, I:3; also C. Chalier, 'L'Idolâtrie de l'être à travers la pensée d'Emmanuel Lévinas', in *Idoles,* op. cit., pp.89–102.
30. See also Caro's commentary (Bet Yosef) to this passage and his elucidation in the same terms of a passage from Chapters of the Fathers, 5:23.
31. S. Langer, *Philosophy in a new key,* 3rd ed., Harvard UP, 1963, p.96.
32. J. Derrida, *Writing and difference,* ed. and trans. A. Bass, London, Routledge, 1978, p.12.
33. J. Derrida, *De la Grammatologie,* Paris, Editions de Minuit, 1967, p.57.
34. See above, Chapter 3 and M. Mendelssohn *Jerusalem,* Engl. trans., p.103.
35. Ibid., pp.127–128. (Italics in original.)
36. But Maimonides held the innovation responsible for 'the multiplicity of opinions, the variety of schools, the confusions occurring in the expression of what is put down in writing, the negligence that accompanies what is written down, the divisions of the people, who are separated into sects, and the production of confusion with regard to actions' (Guide, I:71). His own Mishneh Torah (see the Introduction) was designed to put an end to this 'multiplicity', 'variety', and so on, and to that extent may be regarded as an attempt to mediate between freedom of interpretation and an authoritative text.
37. R. Judah Loew b. Bezalel, *Be'er Ha-Golah,* repr. London, 1960, p.18.
38. For all the above see ibn Zimra's exposition of commandments 117, 473 and 572, in his *Metzudat David,* Zolkiev, 1862.
39. B.-D. Hercenberg, 'Deux Modèles d'écriture', *Revue Philosophique,* No.3, 1982, pp.465–486, here p.470.
40. Derrida, *Writing and difference,* p.25.

Glossary

Amora name given to the rabbinic authorities in Palestine and especially Babylon in third to sixth centuries; their work is recorded in the Talmud.

Baalim heathen gods.

etrog citron, one of four species (willow, myrtle, lulav q.v.) used in synagogue services during the Feast of Tabernacles.

Haggadah narrative recited prior to partaking of the evening meal of the first and second nights of the Passover festival.

halakhah (adj. halakhic) from Hebrew *halakh* ('go', 'walk') used of legal portions of the Talmud and later rabbinic literature.

Hallel (lit. 'praise') Pss.113–118 recited in the synagogue as part of the service on festivals.

lulav palm branch (see also etrog above).

matzah see Seder Plate below.

menorah candelabrum with seven arms, a prominent feature of Tabernacle and Temple.

mezuzah rectangular piece of parchment inscribed with certain paragraphs from the *Torah* (see Dt.6–9) and affixed to a doorpost.

Midrash elaborations of new meanings to Scripture, often of legendary and ethical character.

Seder Plate large plate, usually decorated and with separate compartments to contain the essential ingredients of the Passover domestic ritual: bitter herbs, unleavened bread (matzah), shank bone, parsley, burnt egg, and so on).

tallit prayer shawl.

tefillin phylacteries, small boxes containing Biblical passages, and wound round forehead and arm at morning prayers (see Dt.6:8).

tsitsit fringes attached to tallit (q.v.) and outer garments (see Nu.15:37 and Dt.22:12).

Yeshivah institute for advanced study of the Talmud and cognate literature.

Abbreviations

1. BIBLICAL

Dt.	Deuteronomy
Ex.	Exodus
Ezek.	Ezekiel
Gen.	Genesis
Is.	Isaiah
Jer.	Jeremiah
Josh.	Joshua
Ju.	Judges
K.	Kings
Lam.	Lamentations
Lev.	Leviticus
Nu.	Numbers
Prov.	Proverbs
Ps.	Psalms
Sam.	Samuel
Zech.	Zechariah
Zeph.	Zephaniah

2. TALMUDIC TRACTATES

(The Babylonian Talmud is referred to throughout as TB, followed by an abbreviated reference to the relevant Tractate.)

AZ	Avodah Zarah
BB	Baba Batrah
Ber.	Berakhot
Git.	Gittin
Ket.	Ketubot
Kid.	Kiddushin
Meg.	Megilah
Men.	Menahot
Pes.	Pesahim
RH	Rosh Ha-Shanah
San.	Sanhedrin
Shab.	Shabbat
Tem.	Temurot
Yeb.	Yebamot
Zev.	Zevahim

3. GENERAL

LBYB   Leo Baeck Year Book.
M   Mishnah.
MR   Midrash Rabbah.
MT   Mishneh Torah; code of Jewish law compiled by Maimonides (1135–1204).
Sh A   Shulhan Arukh (lit. 'The Prepared Table'); legal code compiled by R. Joseph Caro (1488–1575).
Tos.   Tosafot (lit. 'addenda'); critical and explanatory glosses to the Talmud by French and German rabbinical scholars (the Tosafists, 12th–14th centuries).
R.   Rabbi.
Rashi   acronym for R.Solomon Yitzhaki (1040–1105), French rabbinic scholar and author of standard commentaries to Bible and Talmud.
Tur   abbreviation for Arba'ah Turim ('Four Rows' – ref. to Ex.39:10), a legal code compiled by R. Jacob ben Asher (c.1270–c.1343).

Index

Aaron 6, 10, 33, 130
Abbahu, Rabbi 135
Aboab, Samuel 103
Abrabanel, Isaac 85, 107, 188
Abraham 48, 64, 82, 98, 147, 159, 165
Abrahams, I. 193
Adar, intercalation of additional month 143, 145
Adler, E. N. 190
Adler, I. 193, 194
Adler, N. M. 114
Adorno, T. 24, 26, 78, 175, 186
adultery, synonymous with idolatry 6, 7
Akiva, Rabbi 47
Alexander, King 138
Allemanno, Johanan 85
altar 9, 82–3, 84
Altmann, A. 185, 191, 193, 195, 206
Altschul, David 22
Amalek
    attack from 77
    God's promise to exterminate memory of 85
Améry, J. 187
Amiel, Avigdor 202
Amos 39
Anatoli, Jacob 53, 65, 182
angels 32, 53, 55, 84, 107, 113
aniconic cult/aniconism 23, 74–5, 84
Anielewicz, Mordecai 81
anonymity of images to permit variety of messages 80
Apple, R. 194
Arama, Isaac 16, 103, 107, 171, 174
Archivolti, Samuel 99, 107, 194
Aristotle 162, 165, 206
Ark of the covenant 39–40, 42, 61, 82–3, 99, 102

Arnold, M. 205–6
art/adornment/decoration
    beauty a danger 9
    danger of completeness 125
    place of 93–111, 112–13, 115, 133–5
artisans see craftsmen
'as if' mode of thought 153–4, 170
Ashkelon 50, 51
Aston, M. 197
astrology see occult practices
Atlan, H. 91, 189, 203
Atlas, S. 154, 203
Atonement, Day of 67, 69, 103, 143
Avot (Pirkei Avot) 66
Azaryahu, M. 187, 195

baalim 8
Babylon 14, 51
Babylonian exile 12, 50
Bahya b. Asher 165
Bahya ibn Pakuda 16
Balaam 96–7
Bar-Kochba revolt 146, 153
Baron, S. W. 176
Barr, J. 195, 200
Baruch b. Isaac 50
beauty
    danger of idolatry 9, 97–100, 110–11
    Kant's view of 124–5
Belgiojoso 80
Belting, H. 175
Ben Gurion 81, 114
Benjamin, A. 197, 204
Benjamin, W. 131, 152, 199, 203, 206
Berger, P. 175
Bergmann, H. 134–5, 200
Bergson, H. 86, 119, 121, 163, 196, 197, 206

Berkowitz, E. 185
Berkowitz, M. 185
Berl, H. 192
Berman, L. 176
Berner, U. 183
Beth-El 3, 20, 80
betrothal of a minor 148
Bezalel 99–100, 161
Bible
books of: Amos 8, 39;
Daniel 14, 16;
Deuteronomy 3, 6–11, 14,
16, 18, 19, 27, 32, 33, 48,
52–5, 62, 69, 76–7, 80,
86–7, 91–2, 116–17, 151,
166; Ecclesiastes 137–8,
167; Esther 85;
Exodus 3, 5–10, 13–19,
23, 32, 38, 40, 53, 56, 64,
76–7, 84, 86–8, 91, 94, 97,
99, 114, 135, 137, 144, 159,
166; Ezekiel 5, 27, 35, 48,
77, 137–8, 165; Genesis 4,
6, 15, 24, 25, 46, 80, 98,
135, 141–2, 150, 159, 162,
170; Habakkuk 121;
Hosea 20, 21; Isaiah 5,
8, 16, 19–22, 28, 69, 82,
86, 113, 139, 140, 151, 158,
165; Jeremiah 3, 5, 7–9,
12, 20–2, 28, 51, 58, 138,
139, 151, 153, 165;
Job 16; Joshua 80, 82,
86, 166; Judges 7, 8;
1 Kings 19, 37, 150, 163;
2 Kings 5, 7, 34, 139, 166;
Lamentations 152;
Leviticus 9, 11, 14, 18, 27,
38–40, 47, 49, 56, 70, 116,
148, 154, 160; Micah 29,
38, 150; Nehemiah 166;
Numbers 4, 7, 8, 18, 40,
53, 77, 82, 97, 140, 147;
Obadiah 153;
Proverbs 8, 98, 117, 149,
159; Psalms 12, 18, 20,
21, 28, 46, 53, 66–7, 110,
118, 125, 135, 142, 152,
165, 167; 1 Samuel 4, 5,

18, 38, 73, 108, 139;
2 Samuel 19, 118; Song
of Songs 105, 114–15;
Tobit 53; Zechariah 2,
165: N.T.; Acts 21; 1
Timothy 53
challenge to idolatry 3–29
illustrations in 103
read as literature 104–6
Bickerman, E. 179
Biur 94
blasphemy of idolatry 19, 22, 30,
34
Bloch, E. 136
Bloch, J. 181
Blumenberg, H. 31, 52, 114, 177
Bohlman, P. V. 192–3
Boman, T. 189
Bos, G. 188
Boyarin, D. 17, 174
Breuer, M. 193
Brion, M. 93, 189
Brockington, L. H. 182
Brown, P. 177
Brueggemann, W. 174
Brunkhorst, H. 189
Buber, Martin 106, 160–1, 178,
204–5
bull statue 18, 20, 22
Byzantine art 21, 134

calendar 142
calf
golden:
Aaron blamed 6; God's
anger at 77; Israelites'
invocation to 14; Moses'
reactions to 7, 34, 53; sin
of remembered 94; used
as intermediary 56, 58
of Samaria 20
symbols warning of sin of 62
Canaanites 10, 13, 14, 49
candlesticks *see menorah*
cantor, virtues of 108–9
Carmichael, C. 172
Carmilly-Weinberger, M. 189,
194
Caro, Joseph 126, 128, 186, 207

Carroll, R. P. 12, 23, 173
Cascardi, A. J. 176
Cassirer, E. 12, 23, 64–5, 173, 184
Chagall, M. 134, 193
Chalier, C. 172, 198, 207
Charlesworth, J. H. 172
Childs, B. S. 171, 186, 189
Christianity
  see also Jesus Christ
  art of 21, 134
  holiness of graves of saints 33
circumcision 67, 82, 98, 146–8
cohen see priests
Cohen, Hermann
  aesthetic/religious love 104
  messianic era 151, 156–8
  Michelangelo's statue of Moses 96
  on music 106
  no feeling located in matter 60–1
  references 174, 183, 189, 190, 192, 197, 204
  theory of symbolism 65, 68–70, 74
  tribal fathers 160
Cohen, S. 71, 185
Cohen, Y. 188
Cohn-Wiener, E. 198
commandments 6–7, 47, 51, 64, 68–9, 73–4
completeness/
  incompleteness 126–35
Connerton, P. 88, 189
consecration of images 14–15, 23, 25
Constantine V 112
Covenant
  at Sinai 3, 18, 25, 48, 54, 77, 86–7
  circumcision reminder of 82
  destruction of man's self-created religion ·55
  fulfilment of 13
  Land and 52, 159
  warnings against disloyalty to 7, 48, 76
Cox, H. 25, 26, 175

craftsmen, creators of idols 21, 23
creation story 6, 25, 148–9, 150
crowns of *Torah*, priesthood and monarchy 71

D'Allones, O. R. 204
Danto, A. 104, 187, 192
Daube, D. 191
David, King 18, 19, 45, 71, 102, 108–10, 118, 165–6
Davidovitz, D. 191, 202
Davidson, H. 174
Davies, E. W. 180
de Vaux, R 188
dead, worship of 33
death
  cessation of 151
  cycle of birth and death 137–8
  depiction of 84
  penalty of 5
Debray, R. 205
Decalogue 71
Deitsch, Eliezer 141
Delphi oracle 49
demons, worship of 33
Derrida, J. 162, 167, 168, 197, 205, 207
desacralisation 36, 126
Deuteronomy, redaction of 19–20
Deuteronomy Rabbah 116
Deutsch, Émile 126
devekut (cleaving) 64
Dilthey, Wilhelm 60
divination *see* occult practices
divine word
  elevation of 23
  only words can be vehicle of the Word 81
Dohmen, C. 172, 173
Don Yehiya, E. and C. Liebman 185
Draï, R. 172, 198
Dreyer, M. 185
Duran, Shimon ben Zemaḥ 149, 165
Durkheim, E. 31, 45–6, 72–3, 177, 186

ear as means of enlightenment 7–8, 166
ear/eye interface 7–10, 15–16, 28, 159–70
Egyptians 10, 11–12, 14
Ehrlich, E. L. 178
Eibeschütz, Jonathan 34, 177
Eisenstadt, Abraham Zvi-Hirsch 130, 132
El Lissitzky 99
Elbogen, J. 202
Eldad, I. 205
Eliach, Y. 177
Eliade, M. 31, 177
Eliezer, Rabbi 47
Eliezer b. Samuel of Metz 177
Elijah 37, 163
Elior, R. 182
Eliot, T. S. 137
Elisha b. Abuyah 162
Elster, J. 186
Elyakim b. Joseph 34
Emden, Jacob 128–9, 199
Enosh 57, 59
Ephraim of Regensburg 102
Epstein, J. 189
eroticism and idolatry 4, 7, 8, 26
eternity (time without limits) 151, 157
etrog 61
exile
 see also Babylonian exile
 following Roman occupation 50
Exodus, the 3, 15, 25, 37, 76–7, 87–91, 144, 166
eye as medium of deception 7–8, 9
Ezekiel 35, 100, 117
Ezra 50

face 127–9
Falaquera 107
Farmer, H. G. 192
fate, idolator's submission to 136
Faur, J. 173, 174, 183, 206
Ferry, L. 196

festivals, celebration of 88, 143
fetishism
 confusion with holiness 31
 examples in Judaism 34
 reduction of paganism to 13
 symbols equated with fetishes 54, 57
 warning against 11
Fine, L. 177
Finesinger, S. B. 184
Finkelstein, L. 73, 173, 186
Firmage, E. 178
Fishbane, M. 202
flag of state of Israel 71–3
Flam, L. 197
'flask' 61
folklore 59–60
Foss, M. 125, 197, 206
Fossoli 'monument-museum' 80
France, statues and monuments 78–9
Frank, M. 176
Frankel, Z. 114
Frankfort, H. 24, 175
Freedberg, D. 187, 197, 198
Freud, S. 23, 96, 190, 204
Frey, D. 200
Frey, J.-B. 171, 173
Friedländer, M. 172
Friedmann, M. 171, 188
fringes (*tsitsit*) 82, 97
Fromm, E. 175, 200
Fulchignoni, E. 187
funerary monuments 61, 79–80
Funkenstein, A. 184, 186, 203

Gabirol, Solomon ibn 103
Gadamer, H. -G. 118, 196, 206
Gamaliel, Rabban 15, 95
Gamaliel, Rabban II 162
Gammie, J. G. 178
Gans, David 190
Gehinnom (hell) 84
Geiger, A. 102–3, 191
gentiles
 appeal to abandon idolatry 20–1
 freedom from obligations 51
Gerhardsson, B. 184

Geshuri, M. S. 193
Gideon 7
Ginsberg, L. 177
God
 see also Covenant
 active involvement with his
  people 18
 agent of disenchantment of
  idols 28
 anonymity of 15–16
 anthropomorphised 16–17, 56,
  62, 113–14, 117, 125, 163
 attributes of 3
 in the consuming fire 84
 direct access available for
  individuals 9, 23, 30, 53ff
 hand of 17, 54, 113
 idolatrous acts against worse
  than defiance of 34
 Jacob's encounters with 3, 80
 jealous 3, 10, 12–14
 likeness of 83–4, 112–35
 man as icon of 65, 70, 116–19,
  125–7, 131
 'model' for morality of man
  (*Urbild*) 68–70
 name of 15, 135
 negative attributes 125–6,
  134–5
 no identification with matter *see*
  matter
 possession of Land 45–6
 promises of *see* messianic hope
 source of laws 68
 sovereignty of 4, 7, 16, 48,
  142
 transcendental 19–20
 verbal descriptions 15–18
 visibility of 18
 voice of 8, 11, 23, 53–4, 159,
  163, 165
golden calf *see* calf
Goldman, S. L. 184
Gombrich, E. H. 133, 190, 196,
 200
Goodenough, E. R. 61, 183
Goodman, N. 63, 184, 196
Gotthold, Z. 181
Govrin, M. 189

Graetz, Heinrich 9–10, 24–6,
 172, 175
gravestones *see* funerary
 monuments
Greece, classical *see* Hellenistic
 world
Greenberg, M. 173, 176, 180,
 181
Grether, O. 174
Grotte, A. 194
Guttmann, J. 184

Habermas, J. 176
Hacohen, David 206
Haggadah 88, 113, 127
Halbertal, M. and Margalit,
 A. 13, 171
Halevi, Joel 177
Halevi, Salomo 165
Hallo, W. 11, 171
Halpérin, J. 186, 198, 200
Hama, Rabbi 116
Hamburg Sephardi cemetery 54
Hana b. Bizna 114
hand
 see also God, hand of
 depicted on headstones 54
 idols not made by 21
Handelman, S. 205
Handel's *Messiah* 109
Hanina, Rabbi 74
Hansel, G. 178, 205
Hanukkah 43, 44
Hartman, D. 205
Hayman, P. 182
Hayyim of Volozhin 201
Hebraic-Hellenic encounter 17,
 162–3, 169, 205–6
Hebrew text, diversity of readings
 of 6
Hecataeus of Abdera 138–9
Heer, M. D. 202
Hegel, G. W. F. 119–20, 123,
 125, 131, 132, 196, 200
Heine, H. 106, 205–6
Heinemann, J. 182
Hellenistic world 21, 25, 47, 54,
 120
Heller-Wilensky, S. 192

Hempel, J. 174
Henkin, Joseph 202
Hercenberg, B. -D. 168, 177, 204, 207
Herzl, T. 71, 185
Heschel, A. J. 87, 143, 183, 189, 195, 202
Hezekiah, King 34
hieroglyphs, possible occasion for regression to fetishisation 65–6
hierophany 31
Hildesheimer, E. 110, 194
Hillel 116
Hinukh 115
Hirsch, S. R. 65, 66–8, 74, 114, 185, 203
history *see* time
Hizkiyah b. Manoah 92
Hoffman, L. A. 180, 203
hol (literal meaning sand) 35–6, 38, 41, 45
Holocaust 34, 80–1, 88
holy
    see also kedushah; sanctification
    days 162
    limitations/transience of 30–52, 60, 170
    places 33, 37, 45–9
    relationship with idols 32
Honor, L. L. 186
Horkheimer, M. and Adorno, T. 24, 26, 175
Horovitz, H. S. and I. Rabin 180, 195
Horvitz, R. 178
Hosea 20, 22
household gods of patriarchs 3, 5
Hultgard, A. 195
human representation question 112–31, 141, 170
Hume, David 14, 173

Ibn Daud, Abraham 50, 114, 148, 207
Ibn Ezra, Abraham 5, 9, 21, 23, 171
Ibn Zimra, David 168

iconoclasm 24–5, 93
Idel, M. 117, 195
idols
    domination of visual 159
    images or 7, 93–111
    mimetic rupture/breakage 126, 128, 130, 132–5, 169–70
    prohibition: dependent on intention 15, 94–7, 161; secondary to requirement to vanquish other gods 93
    rabbinic struggle against 138
    risk of idolisation for tablets of stone 166–7
    Torah challenge to 3–29, 30
illuminated prayerbooks and texts 55, 101, 103, 113, 127
imagination, creations of 59–60
Isaac 64, 84
Isaiah 12, 19, 21, 28, 86
Ishmael, Rabbi 97
Islam *see* Moslems
Israel
    historical destiny of 144, 153–4
    Land of 44–52
    state of 71–2
Israeli, Isaac 16
Israelites
    holy/chosen people 12, 38–9, 47–8
    relationship to Land 46, 49, 52
Isserles, Moses 55, 95, 108, 162, 182

Jackson, B. S. 187
Jacob 3, 15, 79–80
Jacob, Rabbi 66, 67
Jacobsen, T. 174
Jakobson, R. 164, 205
Jay, M. 159
Jeremiah 7, 9, 12, 20, 28, 58, 139, 151
Jeroboam, King 20, 22
Jerusalem
    see also Temple
    counter to Athens 169

pilgrimage to 145
tomb of David 45
Yad Va'Shem memorial 80
Jesus Christ
  iconography of 112
  incarnation of 31, 120, 205
  mediator 53
Jew-Greek encounter *see* Hebraic-
  Hellenic encounter
Joel Halevy 102
Joel, K. 163, 206
Johanan, Rabbi 50, 95, 97, 98
Jonas, H. 25, 175
José b. Halafta 50
Joseph 79–80
Joshua 37, 50, 80, 86
Joshua b. Levi 116
Josiah, King 5
Jospé, A. 175, 182
Joyce, J. 162
jubilee year 69, 143, 153
Judah, Rabbi 51, 98, 130
Judah Halevi 16, 23, 47, 107, 175
Judah Ha'Nasi 51
Judah Loew b. Bezalel 5, 55,
  155, 167, 171, 182, 204
Judah of Modena 83–4, 188, 201
Judah the Pious 102
Judgement, Day of 64

Kabbalists 32
kadosh (setting apart) 36–9
Kadushin, M. 188
Kahana, Y. Z. 92
Kalir, Eleazar 53
Kant, I. 74, 123–5, 131–3, 136,
  154, 156–8, 197
Kaplan, Mordecai 45
Katz, J. 145, 202
Katzenellenbogen, Ezekiel 42,
  102, 179, 191
Kaufman, W. 180
Kaufmann, D. 206
Kaufmann, Y. 12–13, 173
kedushah
  see also kadosh
  forfeiture debated following
    political change 50
  meaning of 36–43

not to be confused with
  pantheism 52
process of 45
Kierkegaard, S. 104, 106, 172,
  192, 205
Kimche, David 2, 5, 18, 28, 139,
  153, 157, 174, 203
Kitzinger, E. 197
Klein, S. 128
Knohl, I. 178
Kochan, L. 174, 197, 203
Kohn, H. 163, 205
Kotlar, D. 173
Krauss, S. 172
Kuk, Abraham Isaac 47, 96,
  128–9, 161, 191, 205
Künzl, H. 182

Labuschagne, C. J. 172
Laffranque, M. 172
Lamm, N. 177
land
  contamination by idols 3
  cultivation of 160
  holiness of 44–52, 154, 160
  Promised Land 146
Landmann, M. 205
Landsberger, F. 177, 199, 202
Langer, S. 207
laws
  see also commandments; Scroll
    of the Law
  abuses of 48–9
  denial of Law by believers in
    fate 140
  governing sanctification 45
Lazarus, M. 171, 194
Lederer, C. 177
Leibniz, G. W. 154
Leibowitz, Isaiah 47, 72, 180, 186
Leibowitz, Nehama 171
Leoni, G. 187
Leveen, J. 195, 198
Levi b. Gershom 201
Levi, P. 187
Lévi-Strauss, C. 136, 200
Lévinas, E. 25, 36, 121, 162,
  175, 177, 182, 197, 198, 200,
  201, 204

Leviticus Rabbah 154
Levy, Z. 171, 194
Lévy-Bruhl, I. 15, 174, 183
Lewandowski, Louis 109
Lieberman, S. 54, 182
Liebeschütz, H. 176
light
    creation of 96
    indication of God's
        presence 113
liturgy
    music in 106–10
    New Year 63–4
Loewenstamm, S. E. 172
Löwith, K. 176
Lukes, S. 177
lulav 42, 46, 48, 61, 97
Luria, Solomon 162
Lyotard, J.-F. 204

Mackler, A. L. 183
Maharal of Prague *see* Judah
    Loew b. Bezalel
Maimonides
    adornment of synagogues
        unacceptable 99
    astrology refuted 140, 201
    on circumcision 147–8
    Code (Mishneh Torah) 85,
        89, 115
    creation *ex nihilo* 149
    dangers of communicating with
        matter 60
    distinction between
        metaphorical and
        literal 16–17, 61, 62
    Guide 27, 57, 59, 125, 149,
        169, 171, 178–9, 207
    health of the soul 103
    on idolatry 161, 169
    Land and soil 47, 50
    man to become as far as
        possible like God 70
    mediator not required 54–9
    messiah 151
    Moslems not idolators 95
    on music 107–9
    theology of negative
        attributes 125

Torah's aim to defeat
    idolatry 3, 23–4
man
    actions which bring him closer
        to God 65
    created in the image of
        God 112
    as icon of God *see* God
Manasseh, King 139
marriage relationship between
    God and Israel 5
Marvell, A. 236
Marx, K. 152
Mashash of Tlemsin 101, 191
matter (mere 'wood and stone')
    incapable of pointing beyond
        itself 19, 30–3, 48–9, 52,
        55–6, 60–1, 68, 77, 119–20
    sustaining power 27
Matzah (unleavened bread) 90
Mecca 49
mediator
    Jesus Christ as 53
    not required by God 9, 23,
        30, 53ff
    spirit as mediating concept 70
Meir, Rabbi 117, 162
Meir b. Baruch 92, 103
Meir-Simha Cohen of Dvinsk 34,
    177, 181
Melberg, A. 206
Memorial Books (*Yizkorbikher*) 81
memory 76–92, 168
Menasseh, King 5
Mendelssohn, Moses
    on decoration and fine art 98,
        133–4
    references 184, 191, 200
    theory of symbolism 65–6, 68,
        70, 74, 120–1, 167
menorah 61, 71, 82–3, 129, 131
Merleau-Ponty, M. 164, 206
Mesopotamia 12, 14
Messer Leon, Judah 82–3, 107,
    184, 188
messianic hope 64, 69, 150–7
metaphorical/literal
    distinction 16–17, 57, 62
Mettinger, T. 172

Metzger, M. 194
Meyerhof, M. 193
mezuzot 42
Micah 29
Michelangelo 96, 112
midrash 53–4, 98, 107, 116
Miller, J. M. 194
mimetic rupture/breakage/
 incompleteness of
 images 126, 128, 130, 132–5
miracle
 fallacy of miracle-working
 icons 78
 of saving life 37
Mishnah
 catalogues of catastrophe
 145–6
 chanting of 85
 map of sanctity based on
 Temple 49
 time 149
Mitrani, Joseph 129, 195, 199
mockery of idols 20–1, 139
Modena *see* Judah of Modena
Modigliani 134
Mölln, Jacob 103
Momigliano, A. 162, 176, 205
Mommsen, W. J. 176
monarchy, power of 71
monumental architecture 71–2,
 78–81
Moore, Henry 130, 132
'Mordecai' 128
Moriah, Mount 64
Moscato 107
Moses
 breaking of his staff 34
 burial 80
 communications with God 17,
 53, 77, 114, 166
 confrontation with Aaron 10
 criticised by Miriam 77
 destruction of golden calf 7
 destruction of Tablets of Law 34
 performance of signs and
 wonders 10
 representations in art and
 music 96, 102–3, 130
Moses of Coucy 127, 128

Moslems 95, 113
Mosollamus 138–9, 158
Mosse, G. L. 185
Muilenburg, J. 172, 201
Müller, H. -P. 171
Munninghaus, W. 199
Murdoch, I. 200
music 106–10, 124
mysticism 32–3, 64, 117, 150
myth, synonymous with
 idolatry 31

Nahman b. Isaac 40
Nahman of Braslav 56, 81–2,
 181, 182, 188
Nahmanides 23, 32, 43, 94, 140,
 172, 179, 201
name of God *see* God
Nathan 19
Nathanson, Joseph Saul 38, 178
nature
 see also matter
 fulfilment of *Torah* 27
 holiness of 30–1, 33
 man's mastery over 141–2
 repository of legal norms 28
 struggle against 4, 24, 27, 150
nazirite status 147–8
Nebuchadnezzar 14, 50
necromancy *see* occult practices
negative attributes
 theology 125–6, 131
Nehemiah 50
Néher, A. 203
Neusner, J. 146, 153–4, 202, 203
New Moon, sanctification of 67
New Year 63–4, 67, 69–70
Nietzsche, F. 16, 24, 76, 78, 104,
 119, 125, 131, 137, 175, 186,
 192
Nobel, Nehemiah 35, 177
Nora, P. 187

occult practices 5, 27, 29, 32–3,
 35, 138–44, 201–2
Oppenheimer, A. 182
Otto, R. 31, 177
Ouellette, J. 93, 172, 190
Ozymandias 79

pagan gods 10, 13
pantheism *see* symbolism
Paperna, Abraham 121, 192,
205
Passover 62, 88, 90, 145
past, attitude towards 76–92
Peel, J. 173
Pelikan, J. 205
Philo 164, 183, 206
photographs 82, 91, 121, 129
phylacteries 34, 42, 62, 82, 97,
114
Picasso 132
pilgrimage 55, 79, 145
Pissarro 134
Plato 16, 81, 101, 136, 163, 206
Polen, N. 178
Polinker, D. 187
political idolatry 4–5, 10, 32–3,
78–9
polytheism, identity with
idolatry 12–13
Poussin 132
Prague ghetto 61
prayerbooks, illuminated *see*
illuminated prayerbooks
Preuss, H. D. 174
priests 38, 40, 41, 50, 118
Prigent, P. 191, 202
prophets
challenge through words and
speech 8, 164–5
future often referred to in
terms of the past 153
kingdom bound up with this
earth 157
polemic against idols 12,
17–29, 122–3
political involvement 5
symbolical understanding of
the messiah 69
Proust, M. 121, 197
Psalmist 12, 20, 21–2, 122–3,
152
punishment 48–9

Quintilian 83

Raba 42, 85

Rabbenu Asher 128, 130
Rabbenu Jacob b. Asher b.
Yehiel 99, 165
Rachel's tomb 45
ram's horn, *see* shofar
Ramus, Peter (Pierre de la
Ramée) 82, 83
Raphaël, F. 176
Rapoport, Nathan 80–1, 187
Rashi (Solomon Yitzhaki)
abhorrence of idols 6, 20
diminishing of image 130
first commandment 22
Genesis 1:1 46
Greek language 162
insight into self-worship 22
Leviticus 11, 39, 56
references 171, 182
reproduction of Temple
decorations banned 131
Temple procedures 118
rationality 23–6
Rava 117
Ravitsky, A. 180, 185
re-enactment 89–91
recitation by heart
see also repetition
prohibition on 168
Reik, T. 130, 199
Reiner, E. 177
Rembrandt 96, 133, 134
remember
see also memory
call to 85
Renan, E. 76, 186
repetition
see also recitation by heart
Covenant at Sinai a repetitive
event 87
favoured way of training
memory 84–5
Ricoeur, P. 87, 189
Ringgren, H. 178
ritual 61–2, 65–7, 143
Rosen, Joseph ('Rogatchever')
84, 149, 188
Rosenberg, Shalom 47, 180
Rosenfeld, A. 191
Rosenthal, M. 189

Rosenzweig, F.
  absence of epochs for the
    Jews 158
  Genesis 24
  God's own anti-religion to
    destroy human religion
    3, 28, 55
  no screen/intermediary
    between God and man 64
  references 171, 175, 182, 204
  spirit of exile 160
Roskies, D. G. 187
Rousseau, J. J. 167
Rubin, N. 202
Ruskin, J. 78

Saadya Gaon 168
Sabbath 35, 62–74, 77, 91–2,
  142, 144, 153, 162
sabbatical year 143, 153
Sabil, J. 200
sacrifice of animals 9, 41, 44
Salmen, W. 193
Saltman, E. 194
Samson 8
Samuel 4–5, 139
Samuel b. Meir 172
Samuel of Babylon 130, 151
Samuels, S. J. 192
sanctification
  see also holy
  risk of leading to idolatry 45–6
Sarason, R. 180
Satan 84
Saul 5, 108, 139
Saussure, F. de 167
Schneidau, H. 32, 175
Scholastics 125
Scholem, G. 132, 200
Schönberg, A. 96, 198
Schopenhauer, A. 107, 123, 125,
  131, 197, 206
Schpira, Zvi Hirsch 100, 191
Schreckenburg, H. and
  K. Schubert 190
Schreiber, A. 195
Schreiber, Moses ('Hatam Sofer')
  128, 130
Schubert, W. 195

Schwarzschild, S. 113, 194
Scroll of the Law 41, 44, 98,
  100–2, 130
Seckel, D. 200
secularisation 26, 27
Sefer Ha-Hinukh (Book of
  Training) 73–4
Sefer Hassidim 103, 107
Segal, B. -Z. 172
Segal, Jacob 103
self-worship in idol worship 21–3
sexual desire see eroticism
sexual prohibitions on Israelites
  39
Sforno, Obadiah 23, 94, 171
Shabtai Ha-Cohen (the 'Shakh')
  128
Shachrit 145
Shavit, Y. 205
Shavuot/Pentecost 67
Sherwin, B. L. 195
Shohat, E. 172
shofar 42, 62–4, 70
Shulḥan Arukh 108, 128
sick, prescription to visit 144
Simmel, G. 127, 164, 198
Simon, Ernst 114
Simon, M. 190
Simon, U. 181
Sinai
  Covenant at see Covenant
  God's presence makes holy 40
  memory of events at 88
  nothing to see at 18
  sounding of ram's horn 64
  unmediated presence of
    God 53–4
  voice heard at 8, 159
Sirat, C. 201
Sistine Chapel 112–13
Socrates 156, 158
Sofer, Hayyim 179
Solomon, King 18, 19, 20, 71
Soloveitchik, Joseph 28, 87, 176,
  207
soothsaying see occult practices
Soutine 134
space, malleability of 35, 142,
  158, 161

Spero, M. H.   187
Spinoza   125
spirit as mediator   70
Stähli, H. -P.   202
Stein, Menahem   181
Steinheim, A. L.   194, 197
Steinsalz, A.   63, 70, 184
Stern, M.   201
Stern, S.   62–3, 183, 184
Stokes, A.   197
Strauss, Leo   162
Sulzer, Salomon   109, 193
sun/moon/stars   11, 23–4, 33,
    35, 37–8, 57–8, 95, 138–42
symbolism
   acceptable in Judaism   62–75
   action in response to
       command   74–5
   dematerialisation of
       symbols   62–5
   'efficient' symbol   73
   flag of nation-state   71–3
   identification of action with
       symbol   68–70
   manifestations of   61
   motive of intention   73
   pantheism as symbolism   68
   in ritual   61–2
   symbols identified as
       fetishes   54, 57
synagogues
   adornment of   99–103, 105,
       141, 146
   indications of God's presence
       depicted   113
   music in   108–10
   symbols in   61
   transient sanctity   42–4, 46, 48
Szold, Henrietta   114

tabernacle   42–3, 44, 46, 82, 97
Tablets of the Law   34, 61, 166
Tal, U.   177
Talmon, S.   203
Talmud
   acronyms and mnemonics used
       as an aid to recall   85
   fears concerning writing down
       of Oral Law   122

idolatry question   4, 34–7, 126
Sinai source of wisdom   54
Tractates: Avodah Zarah   27,
    34, 36, 95, 96, 114; Baba
    Batrah   132; Berakhot   8,
    84, 99, 114; Gittin   122,
    167; Kiddushin   74;
    Megilah   77, 82, 85, 162;
    Menahot   82; Pesahim   89;
    Sanhedrin   4, 5, 95, 105,
    117, 151, 155; Shabbat   56,
    92, 98, 141, 144; Sotah   8,
    110, 162; Ta'anit   146;
    Temurot   122, 167;
    Yebamot   50; Yoma   4,
    118, 149; Zevahim   84
Tannenbaum, Shraga Zvi   179
tefillin   34, 42
Temple
   appurtenances   82–4, 131
   built at Jerusalem   18–19,
       48–51
   destruction of   50, 146
   Herod's   132
   loss of   140
   prohibition on replication of
       Temple and its
       appurtenances   131
   role in justification of state   72
   sanctity of objects dedicated
       to   44, 48, 50–1
   sanctity of Temple Mount   49–51
   worship in   61, 67, 118
Tent of Meeting   18, 40
teraphim see household gods
Tillich, P.   60, 183
time, Jewish concept of   136–58,
    170
tithing   50
Titian   78, 132
Torah
   acceptance essential before
       world can be disenchanted
       28
   cantillation of   108–9
   ceremonial law   65–6
   different readings possible   168
   frees Jews from temporality and
       historicity of life   158

ground of the commandments
167–8
Hirsch's commentary on 67–8
memory of 81–2, 84–5, 167
method of counting votes in an
assembly 118
music and 108–10
nature as means of fulfilment
of 27
not 'just a story-book' 105
not yet accepted in liminal
time 146
past ever-present 87–8
prescriptions of 147
on statues and carvings 128–9
teaching on idolatory 3–29,
150
unmediated teaching 75
Tosafists 127–8, 130, 165, 168
Touati, C. 201
tourist trade, and holy places 45
Touro, Judah 114
Trachtenberg, J. 201
Trinity, doctrine of 117
Tsarfati, G. 183
Tur (law code) 99, 165

Unna, I. 162, 173, 205
Uz 39–40

Vaihinger, H. 154, 203
Viallaneix, N. 172, 205
Von Rad, G. 19, 172

Wacholder, B. Z. 203
Wagner, R. 161, 204
Walzer, M. 189
war memorials 71
Warsaw Ghetto memorial 80–1
Weber, M. 25–6, 28, 176

Weinfeld, M. 172, 174, 179–80
Weitman, S. 186
Wellmer, A. 176
Whitelam, K. W. 174, 185
Winckelmann, J. 176
Wischnitzer, R. 202
witchcraft *see* occult practices
Wochenmark, J. 201
Wohlgemuth, J. 198
Wolff, Edgar 46
Wollheim, R. 197
Wolosky, S. 205
women
idols to be cast away like a
menstruous woman 165
Maimonides' fears concerning
women singers 109
right of inheritance 53
word *see* divine word
Wörner, K. H. 190
writing/printing 65–6, 166–9

Yargina, Z. 191
Yates, F. 83, 188
Yishmael, Rabbi 107
Yizkorbikher 81
Young, J. E. 81, 187

Zafrani, H. 189
Zalman, Schneur 33, 177
Zeitlin, I. M. 175
Zen Buddhism 199
Zeno 158
Zevi, B. 205
Zimmerli, W. 172, 174
Zinger, Z. 180
Zionism 71
zodiac, signs of 136, 140–1
Zohar 105
Zunz, L. 182